PRAISE FOR

"*God's Problem* is a wonderful book, powerful in its questions and bold in its answers. A hard look at the difficult morality of theism in a world that includes so much pain. Believers will be met on their own terms and drawn into important questions; Doubters will enjoy a smart and friendly tour of some key ideas, from the enlightening perspective of an author who long believed."

— Jennifer Michael Hecht, author of *Doubt: A History* and *The Happiness Myth*

"No one has so eloquently told the history of the biblical God's absences and traditional excuses as Ehrman."

— Willis Barnstone, author of *The Other Bible*

"Though I have come to a different conclusion, I believe this riveting book should be read by all people of faith. More than anything it shows why our understanding of God must either change or die."

— John Shelby Spong, author of *Jesus for the Non-Religious*

"Ehrman has done it again. He addresses one of the most compelling issues in all of human experience, and he has done so with clarity and insight. You may be surprised, you may be troubled, but you will certainly be challenged and moved by this book."

— Marvin Meyer, author of *Judas*

"Ehrman, a prolific and popular author, has put his journey into words in a new book. *God's Problem* shares his change of heart while also exploring the common biblical explanations for why bad things happen . . . Ehrman actually ends *God's Problem* on an upbeat note, a kind of call to arms for people to be good—to themselves and to others . . ."

— *San Diego Tribune*

# God's Problem

*How the Bible Fails to Answer*

*Our Most Important Question—*

*Why We Suffer*

**Bart D. Ehrman**

HarperOne
*An Imprint of* HarperCollins*Publishers*

HarperOne

GOD'S PROBLEM: *How the Bible Fails to Answer Our Most Important Question—Why We Suffer.* Copyright © 2008 by Bart D. Ehrman. All rights reserved. Printed in the United States of America. No part of this book may be used or reproduced in any manner whatsoever without written permission except in the case of brief quotations embodied in critical articles and reviews. For information, address HarperCollins Publishers, 195 Broadway, New York, NY 10007.

HarperCollins books may be purchased for educational, business, or sales promotional use. For information, please e-mail the Special Markets Department at SPsales@harpercollins.com.

HarperCollins Web site: http://www.harpercollins.com
HarperCollins®, 📖®, and HarperOne™ are
trademarks of HarperCollins Publishers.

FIRST HARPERCOLLINS PAPERBACK EDITION PUBLISHED IN 2009

*Designed by Joseph Rutt*

Library of Congress Cataloging-in-Publication Data
is available.
ISBN 978–0–06–117392–9

18 19 20 LSC 22 21 20 19 18 17

To Jeff Siker and Judy Siker—Fuzzy and Judes—who have had their share, but remain as beacons.

# Contents

# Preface

This book deals with a matter that is very important to me, not just professionally but also personally. I have written it for a broad audience of regular readers, not for a narrow audience of specialists (who might, I suppose, be considered irregular readers). In view of the intended audience, I have kept endnotes and references to a sparse minimum. Anyone interested in further, in-depth scholarship can easily find it by looking around a bit. Two excellent places to start are James L. Crenshaw's *Defending God: Biblical Responses to the Problem of Evil* (New York: Oxford University Press, 2005), and Antti Laato and Johannes C. de Moor's *Theodicy in the World of the Bible* (Leiden: E. J. Brill, 2003). Both books are fully documented, and the former provides an extensive bibliography.

I have focused on the biblical "solutions" to the problem of suffering that strike me as the most important. Since the so-called classical view dominates the Hebrew Bible and the apocalyptic view dominates the New Testament, I have devoted two chapters to each. A single chapter is devoted to each of the other views I discuss.

Translations of the Hebrew Bible are from the New Revised Standard Version; translations of the New Testament are my own.

Special thanks go to my wife, Sarah Beckwith, Professor of Medieval English at Duke and dialogue partner *sans pareille;* to Roger Freet, Senior Editor at HarperOne, who is tops in his field, and who gave the manuscript a thorough and helpful review; and to my daughter Kelly, who worked over every line with a keen eye.

I would like to thank three gracious, generous, and very smart people who have read the manuscript for me, asking me to make changes, and laughing at my folly for occasionally refusing: Greg Goering, my temporary colleague in Hebrew Bible at UNC–Chapel Hill; my longtime friend and confidant Julia O'Brien, Hebrew Bible scholar at Lancaster Theological Seminary; and one of my oldest friends in the field, the Neutestamentler Jeff Siker, at Loyola Marymount.

I have dedicated the book to Jeff and his wife, Judy Siker. I introduced them to each other more than eleven years ago; they fell madly in love and have lived happily ever after. I take all the credit. They continue to be two of my closest and dearest friends who, knowing the most intimate details of my life, still deign to spend long evenings with me drinking fine scotch, smoking fine cigars, and talking about life, family, friends, work, love, virtues, vices, and desires. Does it get any better than that?

# one

# Suffering and a Crisis of Faith

If there is an all-powerful and loving God in this world, why is there so much excruciating pain and unspeakable suffering? The problem of suffering has haunted me for a very long time. It was what made me begin to think about religion when I was young, and it was what led me to question my faith when I was older. Ultimately, it was the reason I lost my faith. This book tries to explore some aspects of the problem, especially as they are reflected in the Bible, whose authors too grappled with the pain and misery in the world.

To explain why the problem matters so much to me, I need to give a bit of personal background. For most of my life I was a devout and committed Christian. I was baptized in a Congregational church and reared as an Episcopalian, becoming an altar boy when I was twelve and continuing all the way through high school. Early in my high school days I started attending a Youth for Christ club and had a "born-again" experience—which, looking back, seems a bit strange: I had been involved in church, believing in Christ, praying to God, confessing my sins, and so on for years. What exactly did I need to convert from? I think I was converting from hell—I didn't want to experience eternal torment with the poor souls who had not been "saved"; I much preferred the option of heaven. In any event, when I became born again it was like ratcheting my religion up a notch. I became very serious about my faith and chose to go off to a fundamentalist Bible college—Moody Bible Institute in Chicago—where I began training for ministry.

I worked hard at learning the Bible—some of it by heart. I could quote entire books of the New Testament, verse by verse, from memory. When I graduated from Moody with a diploma in Bible and Theology (at the time Moody did not offer a B.A. degree), I went off to finish my college work at Wheaton, an evangelical Christian college in Illinois (also Billy Graham's alma mater). There I learned Greek so that I could read the New Testament in its original language. From there I decided that I wanted to commit my life to studying the Greek manuscripts of the New Testament, and chose to go to Princeton Theological Seminary, a Presbyterian school whose brilliant faculty included Bruce Metzger, the greatest textual scholar in the country. At Princeton I did both a master of divinity degree—training to be a minister—and, eventually, a Ph.D. in New Testament studies.

I'm giving this brief synopsis to show that I had solid Christian credentials and knew about the Christian faith from the inside out—in the years before I lost my faith.

During my time in college and seminary I was actively involved in a number of churches. At home, in Kansas, I had left the Episcopal church because, strange as this might sound, I didn't think it was serious enough about religion (I was pretty hard-core in my evangelical phase); instead I went a couple of times a week to a Plymouth Brethren Bible Chapel (among those who *really* believed!). When I was away from home, living in Chicago, I served as the youth pastor of an Evangelical Covenant church. During my seminary years in New Jersey I attended a conservative Presbyterian church and then an American Baptist church. When I graduated from seminary I was asked to fill the pulpit in the Baptist church while they looked for a full-time minister. And so for a year I was pastor of the Princeton Baptist Church, preaching every Sunday morning, holding prayer groups and Bible studies, visiting the sick in the hospital, and performing the regular pastoral duties for the community.

But then, for a variety of reasons that I'll mention in a moment, I started to lose my faith. I now have lost it altogether. I no longer go to church, no longer believe, no longer consider myself a Christian. The subject of this book is the reason why.

In an earlier book, *Misquoting Jesus: The Story Behind Who Changed the Bible and Why*, I have indicated that my strong commitment to the Bible began to wane the more I studied it. I began to realize that rather than being an inerrant revelation from God, inspired in its very words (the view I had at Moody Bible Institute), the Bible was a very human book with all the marks of having come from human hands: discrepancies, contradictions, errors, and different perspectives of different authors living at different times in different countries and writing for different reasons to different audiences with different needs. But the problems of the Bible are not what led me to leave the faith. These problems simply showed me that my evangelical beliefs about the Bible could not hold up, in my opinion, to critical scrutiny. I continued to be a Christian—a completely committed Christian—for many years after I left the evangelical fold.

Eventually, though, I felt compelled to leave Christianity altogether. I did not go easily. On the contrary, I left kicking and screaming, wanting desperately to hold on to the faith I had known since childhood and had come to know intimately from my teenaged years onward. But I came to a point where I could no longer believe. It's a very long story, but the short version is this: I realized that I could no longer reconcile the claims of faith with the facts of life. In particular, I could no longer explain how there can be a good and all-powerful God actively involved with this world, given the state of things. For many people who inhabit this planet, life is a cesspool of misery and suffering. I came to a point where I simply could not believe that there is a good and kindly disposed Ruler who is in charge of it.

The problem of suffering became for me the problem of faith. After many years of grappling with the problem, trying to explain it, thinking through the explanations that others have offered— some of them pat answers charming for their simplicity, others highly sophisticated and nuanced reflections of serious philosophers and theologians—after thinking about the alleged answers and continuing to wrestle with the problem, about nine or ten years ago I finally admitted defeat, came to realize that I could no longer believe in the God of my tradition, and acknowledged that I was an agnostic: I don't "know" if there is a God; but I think that if there is one, he certainly isn't the one proclaimed by the Judeo-Christian tradition, the one who is actively and powerfully involved in this world. And so I stopped going to church.

Only on rare occasions do I go to church now, usually when my wife, Sarah, very much wants me to go. Sarah is a brilliant intellectual—a distinguished professor of medieval English literature at Duke University—and a committed Christian, actively involved in the Episcopal church. For her the problems of suffering that I wrestle with are not problems. It's funny how smart and well-meaning people can see things so differently, even on the most basic and important questions in life.

In any event, the last time I was in church was with Sarah, this past Christmas Eve, while visiting her brother Simon (another agnostic) in Saffron Walden, a market town near Cambridge, England. Sarah had wanted to attend the midnight service at the local Anglican church, and Simon and I—who both respect her religious views—agreed to go with her.

When I was young I always found the Christmas Eve service to be the most meaningful worship experience of the year. The sacred hymns and carols, the prayers and praises, the solemn readings from Scripture, the silent reflections on this most powerful of nights, when the divine Christ came into the world as a human infant—I still have a strong emotional attachment to the moment. Deep down I am profoundly stirred by the story of God coming into the world for the salvation of sinners. And so I was prepared, even as one who no longer believes, to find the service on this Christmas Eve to be moving and emotional.

It was emotional, but not in the way I had expected. Hymns were sung, the liturgy recited, the sermon delivered. What moved me most, however, was the congregational prayer, which did not come from the Book of Common Prayer but was written for the occasion, spoken loudly and clearly by a layperson standing in the aisle, his voice filling the vast space of the cavernous church around us. "You came into the darkness and made a difference," he said. "Come into the darkness again." This was the refrain of the prayer, repeated several times, in a deep and sonorous voice. And it brought tears to my eyes as I sat with bowed head, listening and thinking. But these were not tears of joy. They were tears of frustration. If God had come into the darkness with the advent of the Christ child, bringing salvation to the world, why is the world in such a state? Why *doesn't* he enter into the darkness again? Where is the presence of God in this world of pain and misery? Why is the darkness so overwhelming?

I knew that the very essence of the message of the Bible lay beneath this heartfelt and well-meaning prayer. For the authors of the Bible, the God who created this world is a God of love and power who intervenes for his faithful to deliver them from their pain and sorrow and bring them salvation—not just in the world to come but in the world we live in now. This is the God of the patriarchs who answered prayer and worked miracles for his people; this is the God of the exodus who saved his suffering people from the misery of slavery in Egypt; this is the God of Jesus who healed the sick, gave sight to the blind, made the lame walk, and fed those who were hungry. Where is this God now? If he came into the darkness and made a difference, why is there still no difference? Why are the sick still wracked with unspeakable pain? Why are babies still born with birth defects? Why are young children kidnapped, raped, and murdered? Why are there droughts that leave millions starving, suffering horrible and excruciating lives that lead to horrible and excruciating deaths? If God intervened to deliver the armies of Israel from its enemies, why doesn't he intervene now when the armies of sadistic tyrants savagely attack and destroy entire villages, towns, and even countries? If God is at work in the darkness, feeding the hungry with the miraculous multiplication of loaves, why is it that one child—a mere child!—dies every five seconds of hunger? Every five seconds.

"You came into the darkness and you made a difference. Come into the darkness again." Yes, I wanted to affirm this prayer, believe this prayer, commit myself to this prayer. But I couldn't. The darkness is too deep, the suffering too intense, the divine absence too palpable. During the time that it took for this Christmas Eve service to conclude, more than 700 children in the world would have died of hunger; 250 others from drinking unsafe water; and nearly 300 other people from malaria. Not to mention the ones who had been raped, mutilated, tortured, dismembered, and murdered. Nor the innocent victims caught up in the human trade industry, nor those suffering throughout the world from grinding poverty, the destitute migrant farmworkers in our own country, those who were homeless and inflicted with mental disease. Nor to mention the silent suffering that so many millions of the well-fed and well-tended have to experience daily: the pain of children with birth defects, children killed in car accidents, children senselessly taken by leukemia; the pain of divorce and broken families; the pain of lost jobs, lost income, failed prospects. And where is God?

Some people think that they know the answers. Or they aren't bothered by the questions. I'm not one of those people. I have been thinking intensely about these questions for many, many years. I have heard the answers, and even though I once "knew" and was satisfied with these answers, I am no longer satisfied.

I think I know when suffering started to become a "problem" for me. It was while I was still a believing Christian—in fact, it was when I was pastoring the Princeton Baptist Church in New Jersey. It was not the suffering that I observed and tried to deal with in the congregation—failed marriages, economic hardship, the suicide of a teenage boy—that prompted my questioning, but something that took place outside the church, in the academy. At the time, in addition to working in the church, I was writing my Ph.D. dissertation and also teaching part time at Rutgers University. (It was a busy

time. On top of it all, I was also married with two young children.)
One of the classes I taught that year was a new one for me. Until
then, I had mainly taught courses on the Hebrew Bible, the New
Testament, and the writings of Paul. But I had been asked to teach
a course called "The Problem of Suffering in the Biblical Traditions." I welcomed the opportunity because it seemed like an interesting way to approach the Bible: examining the responses given by
various biblical authors to the question of why there is suffering in
the world, in particular among the people of God. It was my belief
then, and continues to be my belief now, that different biblical authors had different solutions to the question of why God's people
suffer: some (such as the prophets) thought that suffering came
from God as a punishment for sin; some thought that suffering
came from God's cosmic enemies, who inflicted suffering precisely
because people tried to do what was right before God; others
thought that suffering came as a test to see if people would remain
faithful despite suffering; others said that suffering was a mystery
and that it was wrong even to question why God allowed it; still
others thought that this world is just an inexplicable mess and that
we should "eat, drink, and be merry" while we can. And so on. It
seemed to me at the time, and seems so now, that one of the ways to
see the rich diversity of the scriptural heritage of Jews and Christians was to see how different authors responded to this fundamental question of suffering.

For the class I had students do a lot of reading throughout the
Bible and also assigned several popular books that discuss suffering
in the modern world—for example, Elie Wiesel's classic *Night,*[1]
which describes his horrifying experiences in Auschwitz as a teenager, Rabbi Harold Kushner's best-selling *When Bad Things Happen
to Good People,*[2] and the much less read but thoroughly moving
story of Job as rewritten by Archibald MacLeish in his play *J.B.*[3] In
the class students wrote a number of papers, and each week we discussed the biblical passages and the extra reading that had been
assigned.

I began the semester by laying out for the students the classical "problem" of suffering and explaining what is meant by the technical term *theodicy*. Theodicy is a word invented by one of the great intellectuals and polymaths of the seventeenth century, Gottfried Wilhelm Leibniz, who wrote a lengthy treatise in which he tried to explain how and why there can be suffering in the world if God is all powerful and wants the absolute best for people.[4] The term is made up of two Greek words: *theos,* which means "God," and *dikē,* which means "justice." Theodicy, in other words, refers to the problem of how God can be "just" or "righteous" given the fact there is so much suffering in the world that he allegedly created and is sovereign over.

As philosophers and theologians have discussed theodicy over the years, they have devised a kind of logical problem that needs to be solved to explain the suffering in the world. This problem involves three assertions that all appear to be true, but if true appear to contradict one another. The assertions are these:

God is all powerful.

God is all loving.

There is suffering.

How can all three be true at once? If God is all powerful, then he is able to do whatever he wants (and can therefore remove suffering). If he is all loving, then he obviously wants the best for people (and therefore does not want them to suffer). And yet people suffer. How can that be explained?

Some thinkers have tried to deny one or the other of the assertions. Some, for example, have argued that God is not really all powerful—this is ultimately the answer given by Rabbi Kushner in *When Bad Things Happen to Good People.* For Kushner, God wishes he could intervene to bring your suffering to an end, but his hands are tied. And so he is the one who stands beside you to give you the strength you need to deal with the pain in your life, but he cannot do anything to stop the pain. For other thinkers this is to put a limit on the power of God and is, in effect, a way of saying that God is not really God.

Others have argued that God is not all loving, at least in any conventional sense. This is more or less the view of those who think God is at fault for the terrible suffering that people endure—a view that seems close to what Elie Wiesel asserts when he expresses his anger at God and declares him guilty for how he has treated his people. Others, again, object and claim that if God is not love, again he is not God.

There are some people who want to deny the third assertion; they claim that there is not really any suffering in the world. But these people are in the extreme minority and have never been very convincing to most of us, who prefer looking at the world as it is to hiding our heads in the sand like ostriches.

Most people who wrestle with the problem want to say that all three assertions are true, but that there is some kind of extenuating circumstance that can explain it all. For example, in the classical view of the prophets of the Hebrew Bible, as we will see at length in the next couple of chapters, God is certainly all powerful and all loving; one of the reasons there is suffering is that his people have violated his law or gone against his will, and he is bringing suffering upon them to force them to return to him and lead righteous lives. This kind of explanation works well so long as it is the wicked who suffer. But what about the wicked who prosper while the ones who try to do what is right before God are wracked with interminable pain and unbearable misery? How does one explain the suffering of the righteous? For that, another explanation needs to be used (for example, that all will be made right in the afterlife—a view not found in the prophets but in other biblical authors). And so it goes.

Even though it was a scholar of the Enlightenment—Leibniz—who came up with the term *theodicy,* and even though the deep

philosophical problem has been with us only since the Enlightenment, the basic "problem" has been around since time immemorial.
This was recognized by the intellectuals of the Enlightenment
themselves. One of them, the English philosopher David Hume,
pointed out that the problem was stated some twenty-five hundred years ago by one of the great philosophers of ancient Greece,
Epicurus:

> Epicurus's old questions are yet unanswered:
>     Is God willing to prevent evil but not able? Then he is
>         impotent.
>     Is he able but not willing? Then he is malevolent.
>     Is he both able and willing? Whence, then, evil?[5]

As I was teaching my course on biblical views of suffering at
Rutgers, more than twenty years ago, I began to realize that the
students seemed remarkably, and somewhat inexplicably, detached
from the problem. It was a good group of students: smart and at-
tentive. But they were for the most part white, middle-class kids
who had yet to experience very much pain in their lives, and I had
to do some work to help them realize that suffering was in fact a
problem.

As it turned out, that was the time of one of the great Ethiopian
famines. In order to drive home for my students just how disturbing suffering could be, I spent some time with them dealing with
the problem of the famine. It was an enormous problem. In part
because of the political situation, but even more because of a massive drought, eight million Ethiopians were confronting severe
shortages and, as a result, starving. Every day there were pictures in
the papers of poor souls, famished, desperate, with no relief in sight.
Eventually one out of every eight died the horrific death of starvation. That's one million people, starved to death, in a world that has
far more than enough food to feed all its inhabitants, a world in
which American farmers are paid to destroy their crops and most

Americans ingest far more calories than our bodies need or want. To make my point, I would show pictures of the famine to the students, pictures of emaciated Ethiopian women with famished children on their breasts, desperate for nourishment that would never come, both mother and children eventually destroyed by the ravages of hunger.

Before the semester was over, I think my students got the point. Most of them did learn to grapple with the problem. At the beginning of the course, many of them had thought that whatever problem there was with suffering could be fairly easily solved. The most popular solution they had was one that, I suspect, most people in our (Western) world today still hold on to. It has to do with free will. According to this view, the reason there is so much suffering in the world is that God has given human beings free will. Without the free will to love and obey God, we would simply be robots doing what we were programmed to do. But since we have the free will to love and obey, we also have the free will to hate and disobey, and this is where suffering comes from. Hitler, the Holocaust, Idi Amin, corrupt governments throughout the world, corrupt human beings inside government and out—all of these are explained on the grounds of free will.

As it turns out, this was more or less the answer given by some of the great intellectuals of the Enlightenment, including Leibniz, who argued that human beings have to be free in order for this world to be the best world that could come into existence. For Leibniz, God is all powerful and so was able to create any kind of world he wanted; and since he was all loving he obviously wanted to create the best of all possible worlds. This world—with freedom of choice given to its creatures—is therefore the best of all possible worlds.

Other philosophers rejected this view and none so famously, vitriolically, and even hilariously as the French philosopher Voltaire, whose classic novel *Candide* tells the story of a man (Candide) who experiences such senseless and random suffering and misery, in this allegedly "best of all worlds," that he abandons his Leibnizian upbringing and adopts a more sensible view, that we can't know the whys and wherefores of what happens in this world but should simply do our very best to enjoy it while we can.[6] *Candide* is still a novel very much worth reading—witty, clever, and damning. If this is the *best* world possible, just imagine what a worse one would be.

In any event, as it turns out—much to the surprise of my students—this standard explanation that God had to give human beings free will and that suffering is the result of people badly exercising it plays only a very minor role in the biblical tradition. The biblical authors did not think about the possibilities of *not* having free will—they certainly didn't know about robots, or indeed any machines that more or less did what they were programmed to do. But they had many explanations, other than free will, for why people suffer. The goal of the class was to discuss these other views, evaluate them, and try to see if any resolution of the problem was even possible.

It was, in fact, fairly easy to show some of the problems with this standard modern explanation that suffering comes from free will. Yes, you can explain the political machinations of the competing political forces in Ethiopia (or in Nazi Germany or in Stalin's Soviet Union or in the ancient worlds of Israel and Mesopotamia) by claiming that human beings had badly handled the freedom given to them. But how can you explain drought? When it hits, it is not because someone chose not to make it rain. Or how do you explain a hurricane that destroys New Orleans? Or a tsunami that kills hundreds of thousands overnight? Or earthquakes, or mudslides, or malaria, or dysentery? The list goes on. Moreover, the claim that free will stands behind all suffering has always been a bit problematic, at least from a thinking perspective. Most people who believe in God-given free will also believe in an afterlife. Presumably people in the afterlife will still have free will (they won't be robots then either, will they?). And yet there won't be suffering (allegedly) then. Why will people know how to exercise free will in heaven if they can't know how to exercise it on earth? In fact, if God gave people free will as a great gift, why didn't he give them the intelligence they need to exercise it so that we can all live happily and peaceably together? You can't argue that he wasn't *able* to do so, if you want to argue that he is all powerful. Moreover, if God sometimes intervenes in history to counteract the free will decisions of others—for example, when he destroyed the Egyptian armies at the exodus (they freely had decided to oppress the Israelites), or when he fed the multitudes in the wilderness in the days of Jesus (people who had chosen to go off to hear him without packing a lunch), or when he counteracted the wicked decision of the Roman governor Pilate to destroy Jesus by raising the crucified Jesus from the dead—if he intervenes *sometimes* to counteract free will, why does he not do so more of the time? Or indeed, all of the time?

At the end of the day, one would have to say that the answer is a mystery. We don't know why free will works so well in heaven but not on earth. We don't know why God doesn't provide the intelligence we need to exercise free will. We don't know why he sometimes contravenes the free exercise of the will and sometimes not. And this presents a problem, because if in the end the question is resolved by saying that the answer is a mystery, then it is no longer an answer. It is an admission that there is no answer. The "solution" of free will, in the end, ultimately leads to the conclusion that it is all a mystery.

As it turns out, that *is* one of the common answers asserted by the Bible. We just don't know why there is suffering. But other answers in the Bible are just as common—in fact, even more common. In my class at Rutgers I wanted to explore all these answers, to see what the biblical authors thought about such matters, and to evaluate what they had to say.

Based on my experience with the class, I decided at the end of the term that I wanted to write a book about it, a study of suffering and biblical responses to it. But the more I thought about it, the more I realized that I wasn't ready to write the book. I was just thirty years old at the time, and although I had seen a lot of the world, I recognized that I had not seen nearly enough of it. A book like this requires years of thought and reflection, and a broader sense of the world and fuller understanding of life.

I'm now twenty years older, and I still may not be ready to write the book. It's true, I've seen a lot more of the world over these years. I've experienced a lot more pain myself, and have seen the pain and misery of others, sometimes close up: broken marriages, failed health, cancer taking away loved ones in the prime of life, suicide, birth defects, children killed in car accidents, homelessness, mental disease—you can make your own list from your experiences of the last twenty years. And I've read a lot: genocides and "ethnic cleansings" not only in Nazi Germany but also in Cambodia, Rwanda, Bosnia, and now Darfur; terrorist attacks, massive starvation, epidemics ancient and modern, mudslides that kill thirty thousand Colombians in one fell swoop, droughts, earthquakes, hurricanes, tsunamis.

Still, even with twenty years' additional experience and reflection, I may not be ready to write the book. But I suppose in another twenty years, with the horrible suffering in store for this world, I may feel the same way then. So I've decided to write it now.

As I've already intimated, my basic goal in writing the book is to explore the biblical answers to the problem of suffering. I think this is an important task for a number of reasons:

1. Many people turn to the Bible as a source of comfort, hope, and inspiration. Even for those people who do not, the Bible lies at the foundation of Western culture and civilization, providing the background for the ways we think about the world and our place in it (in my opinion this is true for all of us, believers and unbelievers alike; the Bible informs our thinking in more ways than we are inclined to allow).

2. The Bible contains many and varied answers to the problem of why there is suffering in the world.

3. Many of these answers are at odds with one another, and at odds with what most people seem to think today.

4. The majority of people—even "Bible believers," as well as regular people on the street who might have some kind of vague respect for the Bible but no particular commitment to it—have no idea what these various biblical answers to the problem of suffering are.

Over the years I've talked with a lot of people about issues pertaining to suffering, and I am struck by the kinds of reactions I get. A lot of people, frankly, just don't want to talk about it. For them, talking about suffering is kind of like talking about toilet habits. They're there and can't be avoided, but it's not really something you want to bring up at a cocktail party. There are other people—again, a lot of people—who have simple and pat answers for the problem and really don't see why there's such a problem. I imagine a lot of people reading this first chapter are like that. When I go on about all the suffering in the world, they're tempted to write me an e-mail to explain it all to me (it's because of free will; suffering is meant to make us stronger; God sometimes puts us to the test; and so on). Other people—including some of my brilliant friends—realize why it's a religious problem for me but don't see it as a problem for themselves. In its most nuanced form (and for these friends everything is extremely nuanced), this view is that religious faith is not an intellectualizing system for explaining everything. Faith is a mystery and an experience of the divine in the world, not a solution to a set of problems.

I respect this view deeply and some days I wish I shared it. But I don't. The God that I once believed in was a God who was active in this world. He saved the Israelites from slavery; he sent Jesus for the salvation of the world; he answered prayer; he intervened on behalf of his people when they were in desperate need; he was actively involved in my life. But I can't believe in that God anymore, because from what I now see around the world, he doesn't intervene. One answer to *that* objection is that he intervenes in the hearts of the suffering, bringing them solace and hope in the time of their darkest need. It's a nice thought, but I'm afraid that from where I sit, it simply isn't true. The vast majority of people dying of starvation, or malaria, or AIDS feel no solace or hope at all—only sheer physical agony, personal abandonment, and mental anguish. The pat answer to *that* is that it doesn't need to be that way, if they have faith. I, on the other hand, simply don't think that's true. Look around!

In any event, my ultimate goal in this book is to examine the biblical responses to suffering, to see what they are, to assess how they might be useful for thinking people trying to get a handle on the reality of suffering either in their own lives or in the lives of others, and to evaluate their adequacy in light of the realities of our world. As I've already intimated, what comes as a surprise to many readers of the Bible is that some of these answers are not what they would expect, and that some of the answers stand at odds with one another. I will try to show, for example, that the book of Job has two sets of answers to the problem of suffering (one is in the story of Job found at the beginning and end of the book, the other is in the dialogues between Job and his friends that take up most of the chapters). These two views are at odds with each other. Moreover, both views differ from the views of the prophets. And the prophetic answer—found throughout much of the Hebrew Bible—is at odds with the views of Jewish "apocalypticists" such as Daniel, Paul, and even Jesus.

It is important, I think, to realize that the Bible has a wide range of answers to the problem of suffering because this realization reveals the problem of thinking that the Bible has one simple answer to every issue. Many people in our world take a smorgasbord approach to the Bible, picking and choosing what suits them and their views without acknowledging that the Bible is an extremely complex and intricate concatenation of views, perspectives, and ideas. There are millions of people in our world, for example, who suffer social estrangement because of their sexual orientation. Some of this social alienation originates among simpleminded Bible believers who insist that gay relationships are condemned in Scripture. As it turns out, that is a debated issue, one on which serious scholars disagree.[7] But apart from that, this condemnation of gay relations "because the Bible condemns it" is a case of people choosing to accept the parts of the Bible they want to accept and ignoring everything else. The same books that condemn same-sex relations, for example, also require people to stone their children to death if they are disobedient, to execute anyone who does any work on Saturday or who eats pork chops, and to condemn anyone who wears a shirt made of two kinds of fabric. No special emphasis is placed on one of these laws over the others—they are all part of the biblical law. Yet, in parts of society, gay relations are condemned, while eating a ham sandwich during a lunch break on a Saturday workday is perfectly acceptable.

It is important, then, to see what the Bible actually says, and not to pretend it doesn't say something that happens to contradict one's own particular point of view. But whatever the Bible says needs to be evaluated. This is not a matter of setting oneself up as God, dictating what is and is not divine truth. It is a matter of using our intelligence to assess the merit of what the biblical authors say—whether this involves questions of suffering, sexual preferences, working on weekends, or culinary and sartorial choices.

Having said this, I should stress that it is not the goal of this book to convince you, my reader, to share my point of view about suffering, God, or religion. I am not interested in destroying anyone's faith or deconverting people from their religion. I am not about to urge anyone to become an agnostic. Unlike other recent agnostic or atheist authors, I do not think that every reasonable and reasonably intelligent person will in the end come to see things my way when it comes to the important issues of life. But I do know that many thinking people think about suffering. This is in no small measure because all of us suffer, and many of us suffer a lot. Even those of us who are well off, who are well educated, who are well cared for— even we can experience professional disappointment, unexpected unemployment and loss of income, the death of a child, failed health; we can get cancer, or heart disease, or AIDS; all of us will eventually suffer and die. It is worth thinking about these things, and in doing so it is worth seeing how others have thought about them before us—in this case, those others who produced the books that became the Bible, the best-selling book of all time and the book that lies at the core of our civilization and culture.

And so my goal is to help people think about suffering. There are, of course, numerous books about suffering already. In my opinion, though, many of these books are either intellectually unsatisfying, morally bankrupt, or practically useless. Some of them attempt to give an easy or easy-to-digest answer to the question of why people suffer. For people who prefer easy answers, those can be useful books. But for people who struggle deeply with life's questions and do not find easy answers at all satisfying, such books merely irritate the mind and grate on the nerves—they are not helpful. Still, there is a good deal of simplistic schlock written about suffering. Pious-sounding or pat (and very old, unimaginative) answers sell well, after all these years.[8]

Other books are morally dubious, in my opinion—especially those written by intellectual theologians or philosophers who wrestle with the question of evil in the abstract, trying to provide an intellectually satisfying answer to the question of theodicy.[9] What I find morally repugnant about many such books is that they are so far removed from the actual pain and suffering that takes place in our world, dealing with evil as an "idea" rather than as an experienced reality that rips apart people's lives.

This book will neither provide an easy solution nor attack the question philosophically by applying difficult intellectual concepts and making hard-to-understand claims with sophisticated and eso- teric vocabulary. My interest for this book is instead with some of the age-old and traditional reflections on evil found in the founda- tional documents of the Judeo-Christian tradition.

The questions I will be asking are these:

What do the biblical authors say about suffering?

Do they give one answer or many answers?

Which of their answers contradict one another, and why does it matter?

How can we as twenty-first-century thinkers evaluate these an- swers, which were written in different contexts so many centu- ries ago?

My hope is that, by looking at these ancient writings that eventu- ally came to form the Bible, we will be empowered to wrestle more responsibly and thoughtfully with the issues they raise, as we ponder one of the most pressing and wrenching questions of our human existence: why we suffer.

# two

# Sinners in the Hands of an Angry God: The Classical View of Suffering

## Suffering and the Holocaust

How can we discuss the problem of suffering without beginning with the Holocaust, the most heinous crime against humanity in the known history of the human race? It is relatively easy to cite the standard numbers of those murdered by the Nazi killing machine but almost impossible to imagine the intensity and extent of the misery produced. Six million Jews, murdered in cold blood, simply for being Jews. One out of every three Jews on the face of the planet, obliterated. Five million non-Jews—Poles, Czechs, gypsies, homosexuals, religious "deviants," and others. A total of eleven million people killed, not in battle as enemy combatants but as human beings unacceptable to those in power and brutally murdered. Knowing the numbers somehow masks the horror. It is important to remember that each and every one of those killed was an individual with a personal story, a flesh-and-blood human being with hopes, fears, loves, hates, families, friends, possessions, longings, desires. Each of them had a story to tell—or would have had, if they had lived to tell it.

The firsthand accounts of those who survived will haunt you and give you nightmares, accounts of being systematically starved, beaten, abused, experimented upon, worked almost to death in foul and inhumane conditions. We treat animals better.

It is the killings, of course, that are most remembered: some three million Jews from Poland; one and a half million from Russia; entire Jewish populations of some smaller places. From Budapest: 440,000 Jews were deported in May 1944; 400,000 of them were killed in Auschwitz. In Romania, the city of Odessa had some 90,000 Jews when the city fell to the Germans in October 1941. Most of them were shot to death that month.[1] So too in nearby villages, as recounted in a later report:

> In the fall of 1941 an SS detachment appeared in one of the villages and arrested all the Jews. They were arrayed in front of a ditch by the road and told to undress. Then the leader of the SS group declared that the Jews had released the war and that the assembled people had to pay for that. After this speech the grown-ups were shot and the children slain with rifle butts. The bodies were covered with gasoline and set on fire. Children who were still alive were tossed into the flames.[2]

Children burned alive. This is a theme repeated throughout the sources.

Most of the Jews, and others, were killed in the camps. One of the best-known and most widely read survivors of Auschwitz, Primo Levi, provided one of the earliest firsthand accounts in his *Auschwitz Report*.[3] Levi was one of 650 people crammed into cattle cars for transport to Auschwitz from his hometown of Fossoli, Italy. In the end, only twenty-four survived. Upon arrival some 525 were chosen for the gas chambers. Within a couple of hours they were dead and loaded in elevators to the furnaces. Another hundred were worked to death in the camps. The brutal conditions are thoroughly documented. Levi himself provides one account, just under two years after the events:

Before that period [February 1944] there were no medical services and the sick had no possibility of getting treatment, but were forced to labour as usual every day until they collapsed from exhaustion at their work. Naturally, such cases occurred with great frequency. Confirmation of death would then be carried out in a singular fashion; the task was entrusted to two individuals, not doctors, who were armed with ox sinews and had to beat the fallen man for several minutes on end. After they had finished, if he failed to react with some movement, he was considered to be dead, and his body was immediately taken to the crematorium. If, on the contrary, he moved, it signified that he was not dead after all, so he would be forced to resume his interrupted work.[4]

The cold efficiency of the Nazi killing machine is nowhere described with more dispassion than in the autobiography of the Auschwitz camp's commandant, Rudolph Höss, written during his free time while standing trial at Nuremberg.[5] With some pride he describes how he himself came up with the idea of using Zyclon B—a pesticide for rats—to gas hundreds of people at a time and then of using specially built crematoria to dispose of the bodies. With some fondness he recalls having built the two large crematoria in 1942–43, each with "five ovens with three doors per oven, [which] could cremate about two thousand bodies in twenty-four hours."[6] There were two smaller crematoria as well. This was a killing machine unlike anything the world had ever seen. As Höss recalls, "The highest total figure of people gassed and cremated in twenty-four hours was slightly more than nine thousand."[7] It reads like a contest.

As horrible as it was, the gas chamber was in some ways preferable to the other options. The right-hand man of the mad doctor Mengele, Miklos Nyiszli, a Hungarian Jewish prisoner with advanced medical training, who did most of the requisite autopsies (for example, on twins, as Mengele "experimented" to determine how to make Aryan women doubly productive), tells of what happened when the gas chambers were overcrowded with victims. The "surplus" were taken out, kicking and screaming, to be shot in the back of the neck in front of a huge pyre built inside a deep ditch. They were then tossed into the flames. The fortunate ones were dead first: "Even the ace shot of the number one crematorium, Oberschaarführer Mussfeld, fired a second shot into anyone whom the first shot had not killed outright. Oberschaarführer Molle wasted no time over such trifles. Here the majority of the men were thrown alive into the flames."[8]

On other occasions, with the children, the rush to murder meant that there was no bullet anesthesia at all. A particularly haunting image was given at the Nuremberg trials by a Polish woman named Severina Shmaglevskaya, an Auschwitz detainee who managed to survive the camp for over two years, from October 7, 1942, until its liberation in January 1945. At the trial she described the "selection" process by which some Jews were sent to the labor camp, whereas most—including all women with their children—were taken off to an immediate death. In this excerpt from her testimony, she is being questioned by the prosecuting counsel, named Smirnov:

MR. COUNSELLOR SMIRNOV: Tell me, Witness, did you yourself see the children being taken to gas chambers?

SHMAGLEVSKAYA: I worked very close to the railway which led to the crematory. Sometimes in the morning I passed near the building the Germans used as a latrine, and from there I could secretly watch the transport. I saw many children among the Jews brought to the concentration camp. Sometimes a family had several children. The Tribunal is probably aware of the fact that in front of the crematory they were all sorted out.... Women carrying children in their arms or in carriages, or those who had larger children, were sent into the crematory together with their children. The children were separated from their parents in front of the crematory and were led separately into gas chambers.

At that time when the great number of Jews were exterminated in the gas chambers, an order was issued that the children were to be thrown into the crematory ovens or the crematory ditches without previous asphyxiation with gas.

MR. COUNSELLOR SMIRNOV: How should we understand that? Were they thrown into the ovens alive or were they killed by other means before they were burned?

SHMAGLEVSKAYA: The children were thrown in alive. Their cries could be heard all over the camp.[9]

The cries of children, screaming from the midst of the blazing ovens.

Those who were not killed but "selected" for the labor camp were scarcely treated any better. They were systematically starved, abused, beaten, and—in most cases—literally worked to death. Mengele's assistant Nyiszli estimated that the vast majority died from such treatment within three or four months. And this was not simply at Auschwitz: other camps were as bad or worse. Belzek, for example, had hundreds of thousands of inmates. Only one is known to have survived.[10]

Once one gets beyond the statistics, beyond the numbers, beyond even the mind-numbing experiences of these millions of people inhumanly treated and brutally murdered—once we try to understand it all, how can we make sense of the Holocaust? Putting aside for a moment the five million non-Jews who were killed, how can we fathom the heartless extermination of six million Jews? The Jews were to be God's chosen people, elected by God to enjoy his special favor in exchange for their devotion to him. Were the Jews chosen for *this*?

As hard as it is to believe, there are Christians in the world who have argued that they were. This is one of the many ways in which anti-Semitism continues to thrive as much in our day as it did during the pogroms of eastern Europe, during the Inquisition, all the way back through the Middle Ages into the early period of the church. Right after the Second World War, the German Evangelical Conference at Darmstadt—in the country that was responsible for the genocide—claimed that Jewish suffering in the Holocaust had been a divine visitation and called upon Jews to stop rejecting and crucifying Christ.[11] This was not German Christianity's finest moment. Any way you look at it, the vast majority of those who died in the Holocaust were innocent sufferers, people like you and me, uprooted from their homes, families, and careers and subjected to unspeakable cruelty.

How could God allow it to happen? One innocent death would be hard to explain, one five-year-old boy gassed to death, one teenager starved to death, one mother of three frozen to death, one upright banker, chemist, doctor, or teacher beaten to a bloody pulp and shot when he refused to rise to his feet. But we're not talking about one, two, or three deaths like this. We're talking about six million Jews, and five million others. It would take many volumes to detail the pain, misery, and suffering; the world itself could hardly hold the books. How could God allow this to happen to anyone, let alone his "chosen people"?

The modern philosophical problem of theodicy, which has been with us since the Enlightenment, is how we can imagine that God exists given such senseless pain and suffering. For ancient peoples, however, there was never, or almost never, a question of whether God (or the gods) actually existed. The question was how to explain God's (or the gods') relationship to people given the state of the world. Given the fact—which almost every ancient person took as a fact—that God is both above the world and involved with it, how can one explain the corollary fact that people suffer?

Many of the biblical authors were concerned with this question—even obsessed with it. From Genesis to Revelation, biblical writers grapple with this issue, discuss it, agonize over it. A very large portion of the Bible is devoted to dealing with it. If God has chosen the Jews—or (also? alternatively?) the Christians—to be his people, why do they experience such horrible suffering? It is true that there was nothing in the ancient world quite like the Holocaust. That required the technological "advances" of modernity: the ability to transport millions by rail and kill thousands by gas and incinerate hundreds in specially built crematoria. But there were slaughters aplenty in the ancient world and wretched suffering of all kinds caused by all manner of circumstances: military defeat, cruelty to POW's, and torture; drought, famine, pestilence, epidemic; birth defects, infant mortality, infanticide; and on and on.

When these things happened, how did ancient authors explain them?

One of their most common explanations—it fills many pages of the Hebrew Bible—may seem simplistic, repugnant, backward, or just dead-wrong to many modern people. It is that people suffer because God wants them to suffer. And why does God want them to suffer? Because they have disobeyed him and he is punishing them. The ancient Israelites had a healthy sense of the power of God, and many of them were convinced that nothing happens in this world unless God has done it. If God's people are suffering, it is because he is angry with them for not behaving in the ways they should. Suffering comes as a punishment for sin.

Where does this view come from, and how can we explain it within a biblical context? To make sense of this "classical" view of suffering as a punishment for sin, we need to consider some historical background information.

## Suffering as Punishment: The Biblical Background

The religion of ancient Israel was rooted in historical traditions that had been passed from one generation to the next for many centuries. The books of the Bible are themselves written products that come at the tail end of this long period of oral (and earlier written) tradition. The first five books of the Hebrew Bible—sometimes called the Pentateuch (meaning the "five scrolls") or the Torah (meaning "instruction," "guidance," or "the law," since they contain

the Law of Moses)—recount many of these important ancient traditions, beginning with the creation of the world in Genesis,
through the times of the Jewish ancestors (Abraham, the father of
the Jews, his son Isaac, Isaac's son Jacob, and Jacob's twelve sons
who became the founders of the "twelve tribes" of Israel; all in
Genesis), through the enslavement of the Jewish people in Egypt
(the book of Exodus), to their salvation from slavery under the great
leader Moses, who led the people out of Egypt and then received
the Law of God (the Torah) from God himself on Mount Sinai
(Exodus, Leviticus, and Numbers). The Pentateuch continues by
describing the wanderings of the Israelites through the wilderness
(Numbers) until they were on the verge of entering Canaan, the
land that God had promised to given them (Deuteronomy). Traditionally these books were thought to have been written by none
other than Moses himself (he would have lived about 1300 BCE),
but the books do not claim to be written by him, and scholars are
now convinced, as they have been for more than 150 years, that they
were written much later based on sources that had been in oral circulation for centuries. Today scholars maintain that there were
various written sources behind the Pentateuch; typically they date
its final production, in the form we now know it, to some eight
hundred years after the death of Moses.[12]

Whenever they were actually written, the books of the Pentateuch contain very ancient understandings of Israel's relationship to
God, the only true God, the one who created the heavens and the
earth. Many ancient Israelites took these traditions to be not only
historically accurate but theologically significant. According to
these traditions, as eventually found in the Pentateuch, God chose
Israel to be his special people—even before they had become a
people. After the world was created, destroyed by a flood, and re-
inhabited (Gen. 1–11), God chose one man, Abraham, to be the
father of a great nation that would be uniquely tied to the Lord of
all. Abraham's descendants would be specially favored by God
and so were thought to be his people. But two generations after

Abraham, his family was forced to enter Egypt to escape famine in the land of Israel. There they multiplied and became a great nation. Out of fear of their size and strength, the Egyptians enslaved the people of Israel, and they suffered miserably as a result.

But God remembered his promise to Abraham that he would be the father of this people, and he raised up a powerful savior, Moses, to deliver them from the hands of the Egyptians. Moses performed many miracles in Egypt to compel the Egyptian Pharaoh to release the people; eventually he was forced to do so and they escaped into the wilderness. Pharaoh then had second thoughts and pursued the children of Israel, but suffered an irreversible defeat at the hands of God, who destroyed Pharaoh and his armies when the Israelites crossed the "Red Sea" (or the "sea of reeds"). God then led the people of Israel to his sacred mountain, Sinai, where he gave Moses the Ten Commandments and the rest of the Jewish law and established his covenant (or "peace treaty") with them. They would be his covenant people—meaning that he and they had entered into a kind of political agreement, a peace accord, with each other. They would be his chosen people whom he would protect and defend in perpetuity, just as he had done when they were enslaved in Egypt. In exchange, they were to keep his Law, which dictated how they were to worship him (much of the book of Leviticus spells out the details) and how they were to relate to one another as the people of God.

After the Pentateuch comes another set of historical books in the Hebrew Bible: Joshua, Judges, the books of Samuel, and the books of Kings. These take the story yet further, showing how God gave the promised land over to Israel (there were already people living there, so the Israelites had to destroy them in war, as described in the book of Joshua); how he ruled them through local charismatic leaders (Judges); how the monarchy was eventually formed (1 Samuel), and what happened during the time of the united kingdom, when both north and south were ruled by one king (under the reigns of Saul, David, and Solomon), and then in the divided monarchy, when the kingdom split into two parts, Israel (or Ephraim) in the north and Judah in the south. Among other things, these books detail the disasters that struck the people of Israel over the years, culminating in the destruction of the nation of Israel (the northern kingdom) in 722 BCE at the hands of the Assyrians, Mesopotamia's first "world empire," and the destruction of Judah (the southern kingdom) a century and a half later in 586 BCE by the Babylonians, who had overthrown the Assyrians.

It is not my purpose here to discuss the historical question of whether any of this—especially the accounts of the Pentateuch—actually happened. Some scholars think that the accounts of Genesis through Deuteronomy are essentially historical in their descriptions, others think they are much later fabrications, and probably the majority think there are some historical roots for these traditions, which developed significantly over time as the stories were told and retold in the course of centuries of oral tradition.[13] What is certain is that many ancient Israelites believed such traditions about their ancestors. The people of Israel were the chosen people of God. He had entered into a special relationship with their ancestors; he had delivered them from slavery in Egypt; he had given them his Law; and he had bestowed upon them the promised land. This God was the Lord God Almighty, the maker of heaven and earth and sovereign over all that exists. He was powerful and could accomplish his mighty purposes on earth simply by saying the word. And he was on the side of tiny Israel, agreeing to protect and defend his people and to make them prosper in the land he had given them, in exchange for their devotion to him.

Given this theology of election—that God had chosen the people of Israel to be in a special relationship with him—what were ancient Israelite thinkers to suppose when things did not go as planned or expected? What were they to make of the fact that Israel sometimes suffered military defeat or political setbacks or economic hardship? How were they to explain the fact that the people of God suffered from famine, drought, and pestilence? How were they to explain suffering—not only nationally, but also personally, when they were starved or seriously wounded, when their children were stillborn or born with defects, when they faced grinding poverty or personal loss? If God is the powerful creator, and if he has chosen Israel and promised them success and prosperity, how is one to explain the fact that Israel suffers? Eventually the northern kingdom was utterly destroyed by a foreign nation. How could that be, if God had chosen them to be his people? In another 150 years the southern kingdom was destroyed as well. Why did God not protect and defend it as he had promised?

These were questions naturally asked—fervently asked—by many of the people of Israel. The most resounding answer to the question came from a group of thinkers known as the prophets. To a person, the prophets maintained that Israel's national sufferings came because it had disobeyed God, and it was suffering as a punishment. The God of Israel was not only a God of mercy, he was also a God of wrath, and when the nation sinned, it paid the price.

## Introduction to the Prophets

The writings of the prophets are among the most misunderstood parts of the Bible today, in no small measure because they are commonly read out of context.[14] Many people today, especially conservative Christians, read the prophets as if they were crystal-ball gazers predicting events that are yet to transpire in our own time, more than two thousand years removed from when the prophets were actually speaking. This is a completely egocentric approach to the Bible (it's all about *me*!). But the biblical writers had their own contexts and, as a result, their own agendas. And those contexts and agendas are not ours. The prophets were not concerned about us; they were concerned about themselves and the people of God living in their own time. It is no wonder that most people who read the prophets this way (they've predicted the conflict in the Middle East! they foresaw Saddam Hussein! they tell us about Armageddon!)

simply choose to read one or another verse or passage in isolation, and do not read the prophets themselves in their entirety. When the prophets are read from beginning to end, it is clear that they are writing for their own times. They often, in fact, tell us exactly when they were writing—for example, under what king(s)—so that their readers can understand the historical situation they were so intent on addressing.

What makes a prophet? In the Hebrew Bible there are, roughly speaking, two kinds of prophets. Some prophets—probably the majority, historically—delivered "the word of God" orally. That is, they were spokespersons for God, the ones who communicated (their understanding of) God's message to his people, to let them know what God wanted them to do or how God wanted them to act—in particular, how they needed to change their ways in order to stand in God's good favor (see, e.g., 1 Samuel 9; 2 Samuel 12). Other prophets—these are the ones who are more familiar to us today—were writing prophets, spokespersons for God whose (oral) proclamations were also written down, on the ancient equivalent of paper. The writings of some of the ancient Israelite prophets later became part of the Bible. In English translations of the Bible they are divided into the "major" prophets, the well-known figures of Isaiah, Jeremiah, and Ezekiel, and the "minor" prophets. This differentiation is not made to suggest that some prophets are more important than others but rather to indicate which writings are longer ("major") than others ("minor"). The twelve minor prophets are somewhat less well known, but many of them deliver powerful messages: Hosea, Joel, Amos, Obadiah, Jonah, Micah, Nahum, Habbakuk, Zephaniah, Haggai, Zechariah, and Malachi.

What ties all these prophets together is that they were delivering God's message, speaking God's word, as they understood it, to God's people. They saw themselves, and (some) others saw them, as the mouthpieces of God. In particular, they were delivering God's message to people in concrete situations, telling them what, in God's view, they were doing wrong, what they needed to do right, how they needed to change, and what would happen if they refused. This matter of "what would happen if they refused" is the full extent of the "predictions" made by the prophets. They were not speaking about what would happen in the long term, thousands of years after their own day. They were speaking to living people of their own time and telling them what God wanted them to do and what he would do to them if they failed to obey.

As a rule, the prophets believed there were dire consequences for not following their instructions, given by God. For them God was sovereign over his people and was bound and determined to see that they behaved properly. If they did not, he would punish them—as he had punished them before. He would cause drought, famine, economic hardship, political setbacks, and military defeat. Most of all, military defeat. The God who destroyed the Egyptian armies when he delivered his people out of slavery would destroy *them* if they did not behave as his people. For the prophets, then, the setbacks the people experienced, many of the hardships they endured, many of the miseries they suffered, came directly from God, as a punishment for their sins and in an effort to get them to reform. (As we will see later, the prophets also thought that human beings themselves were often to blame for the suffering of others, as the rich and powerful, for example, oppressed the poor and powerless: it was precisely for such sins that God had determined to punish the nation.)

Most of the writing prophets were producing their work around the time of the two great disasters experienced by ancient Israel: the destruction of the northern kingdom by the Assyrians in the eighth century BCE and the destruction of the south by the Babylonians in the sixth. To explore further the specific burdens of these authors, here I will simply highlight the message of several of them. Those I have chosen are representative of the views found in the others, but they present their messages of sin and punishment in particularly graphic and memorable terms.[15]

## Amos of Tekoa

One of the clearest portrayals of the "prophetic view" of the relationship of sin and suffering comes in one of the gems of the
Hebrew Bible, the book of Amos.[16] We learn little about the man
Amos himself from the book, and he is not mentioned in any other
book of the Bible. What he tells us is that he was from the southern
part of the land—that is, from the country of Judah—from the
small village of Tekoa in the hills south of Jerusalem (1:1). He twice
mentions that he was a shepherd (1:1; 7:14) and a farmer—one who
tended sycamore trees (7:14). It has often been thought, based on his
occupation, that he was from the Judean lower class; but given the
fact that he was literate and obviously trained rhetorically, he may
well have been a relatively prosperous landowner with flocks of his
own. He was, in any event, no champion of the rich upper classes;
on the contrary, much of his book is directed against those who had
acquired wealth at the expense of the poor. It was because of the
abuses of the well-to-do, he believed, that judgment was soon to
come to Israel. It was against the north in particular that Amos
spoke his prophecies, traveling up from his southern clime to an-
nounce God's judgment on the kingdom.

The preface to Amos's book (1:1) indicates that his prophetic
ministry was undertaken when Uzziah was king of the northern
kingdom (783–742 BCE) and Jeroboam was king of the south
(786–746 BCE). This was a relatively calm and peaceful time in the
life of the divided kingdom. Neither the large foreign empire to the
south—Egypt—nor the larger empire to the northeast—Assyria—
was an immediate threat to the tranquillity of the peoples living in
the "promised land." But that was soon to change. Amos predicted
that God would raise up a kingdom to oppose his people because
they had violated his will and broken his covenant. In the future, he
contended, lay military defeat and disaster. As it turned out, he was
right.[17] Some twenty years after Uzziah's peaceful reign, Assyria

flexed its muscles and invaded, destroying the northern kingdom and dispersing its people. At the time of Amos's proclamation, however, his dire predictions may well have seemed unnecessarily bleak, as life was relatively good for those living in the land, especially for those who had prospered during the time of peace.

Amos begins his prophecies on a note that will characterize his entire book, uttering fearful predictions of destruction for Israel's neighbors, destruction to be brought by God as a punishment for their sins.[18] Thus, at the outset, comes a prophecy against the capital city of Syria, Damascus, for its destruction of the smaller town of Gilead:

> Thus says the LORD:
> For three transgressions of
>     Damascus,
>     and for four, I will not revoke
>         the punishment;[19]
> because they have threshed Gilead
>     with threshing sledges of iron.
> So I will send a fire on the house
>         of Hazael,...
> I will break the gate bars of
>         Damascus,
>     and cut off the inhabitants from
>         the Valley of Aven. (Amos 1:3–4)

Military defeat (a fire and broken gates) awaits the citizens of Damascus in exchange for their military exploits. So too with the Philistine city-state Gaza:

> Thus says the LORD:
> For three transgressions of Gaza,
>     and for four, I will not revoke
>         the punishment;

because they carried into exile
    entire communities,
  to hand them over to Edom.
So I will send a fire on the wall of
    Gaza,
  fire that shall devour its
    strongholds.
I will cut off the inhabitants from
    Ashdod. (Amos 1:6–8)

And so it goes. In chapters 1–2 Amos predicts military defeat and violence in similar terms against seven of Israel's neighbors. And one can just imagine his readers dwelling in Israel nodding their heads in agreement. *That's right! It's exactly what our wicked neighbors deserve: God will judge them in the end.*

But then Amos turns the pointing finger on the people of Israel themselves, and in a rhetorical climax indicates that they too will be destroyed, with particular vengeance, by the God they thought was on their side:

Thus says the LORD:
For three transgressions of Israel,
  and for four, I will not revoke
    the punishment;
  because they sell the righteous for
    silver,
  and the needy for a pair of
    sandals—
they who trample the head of the
    poor into the dust of the
    earth,
  and push the afflicted out of the
    way;

father and son go in to the same
> girl,
> so that my holy name is
> > profaned....
So, I will press you down in your
> place,
> just as a cart presses down
> when it is full of sheaves.
Flight shall perish from the swift,
> and the strong shall not retain
> > their strength,
> nor shall the mighty save their
> > lives;
those who handle the bow shall
> > not stand,
> and those who are swift of foot
> > shall not save themselves,
> nor shall those who ride horses
> > save their lives;
and those who are stout of heart
> among the mighty
> shall flee away naked in that
> > day,

> > > says the Lord. (Amos 2:6–16)

The sins of God's own people, Israel, will lead to military defeat. These sins are both social and what we might call religious. Socially, the people have oppressed the poor and needy; and they have broken the law God has given in flagrant ways (father and son having sex with the same woman; cf. Leviticus 18:15, 20:12). As Amos goes on to indicate, these sins are particularly acute because Israel was to be God's chosen people; therefore, their punishment will be all the more extreme: "You only have I known of all the families of the earth;

therefore I will punish you for all your iniquities" (3:1). Moreover, the nature of this punishment is spelled out in clear terms: "An adversary shall surround the land and strip you of your defense; and your strongholds shall be plundered" (3:11). For Amos, this future military disaster and political nightmare is not simply an unfortunate outcome of human history: it is the plan of God, as God himself has decreed the future catastrophe. In a particularly memorable passage Amos presses home the point by stringing together a number of rhetorical questions, all of which are to be answered with a resounding "no!"

> Do two walk together
>> unless they have made an
>>> appointment?
> Does a lion roar in the forest,
>> when it has no prey?
> Does a young lion cry out from
>> its den,
>> if it has caught nothing?
> Does a bird fall into a snare on the
>> earth,
>> when there is no trap for it?
> Does a snare spring up from the
>> ground,
>> when it has taken nothing?
> Is a trumpet blown in a city,
>> and the people are not afraid?
> Does disaster befall a city,
>> unless the LORD has done it? (Amos 3:3–6)

The reader is compelled by the rhetoric of the passage to answer no to the final question as well. The only reason disaster comes is that the Lord himself brings it. This may sound severe, but it is consistent, according to Amos, with the way God has historically dealt with his people. In another powerful passage Amos claims that God has sent all sorts of natural disasters on his people in order to compel them to return to him and his ways. But they never heeded his voice and never returned. And so God will subject them to a final judgment. Where did the famine, drought, blight, pestilence, and destruction that have plagued Israel come from? According to Amos, they came from God as a punishment for sin and an incentive for repentance:

> I gave you cleanness of teeth [i.e., famine] in all
>> your cities,
>> and lack of bread in all your
>>> places,
> yet you did not return to me,
>>>> says the LORD.
> And I also withheld the rain from
>> you
>> when there were still three
>>> months to the harvest...
> yet you did not return to me,
>>>> says the LORD.
> I struck you with blight and
>> mildew;
>> I laid waste your gardens and
>>> your vineyards,
> the locust devoured your fig
>> trees and your olive trees;
> yet you did not return to me,
>>>> says the LORD.
> I sent among you a pestilence after
>> the manner of Egypt;
> I killed your young men with
>> the sword...
> yet you did not return to me,
>>>> says the LORD

I overthrew some of you,
    as when God overthrew Sodom
        and Gomorrah…
yet you did not return to me,
                    says the LORD.
Therefore thus I will do to you,
    O Israel;
    because I will do this to you,
    prepare to meet your God,
        O Israel! (Amos 4:6–12)

In this context, obviously "meeting your God" is not a happy prospect. This is the God who starves people, destroys their crops, and kills their children—all in an effort to get them to return. And if they don't, only worse things lie ahead. What could be worse than all that? The total destruction of their nation and their entire way of life.

One of Amos's subsidiary messages is that it is only by proper behavior—not by cultic observation—that the people of Israel can be restored to a right standing before God. And so he speaks a word from the Lord:

I hate, I despise your festivals,
    and I take no delight in your
        solemn assemblies.
Even though you offer to me your
        burnt offerings and grain
        offerings,
    I will not accept them;…
Take away from me the noise of
        your songs;
    I will not listen to the melody
        of your harps.

But let justice roll down like
    waters,
  and righteousness like an
    ever-flowing stream. (Amos 5:21–24)

Those who think they can be right with God by following the proper dictates for worship (God himself had commanded them to observe the festivals and to bring him offerings) without also working for social justice and fairness are deceived. The people of Israel have not followed God's call for right living. Their plights came as a result. Sin brings the wrath of God, which will eventually lead to the destruction of the people: "all the sinners of my people shall die by the sword" (9:10).

In the book of Amos as it has come down to us, the prophet does hold out hope that God will return to his people after they have been sufficiently punished. Most scholars see this as an addendum, appended to the book after the predicted destruction had already taken place. Nonetheless, it fits logically, given Amos's view that massive suffering comes to those who violate God's will. Once those who suffer have paid for their sins, there can be a restoration:

I will restore the fortunes of my
    people Israel,
  and they shall rebuild the ruined
    cities and inhabit them;
they shall plant vineyards and
    drink their wine,
  and they shall make gardens and
    eat their fruit.
I will plant them upon their land,
  and they shall never again be
    plucked up

out of the land that I have given
them,
                  says the LORD your God. (Amos 9:14–15)

This final set of predictions was never fulfilled. The northern kingdom of Israel in fact was not restored, and even what later came to be known as Israel (the southern kingdom of Judah) was destroyed, not just once, but repeatedly over the years. On the other hand, the direr predictions of Amos were fulfilled with a vengeance. Twenty or thirty years after Amos's day, an Assyrian monarch named Tiglath-Pileazer III (745–727) became intent on extending his nation's influence and decided to expand into Syria and Palestine. He was not himself responsible for the horrible events leading to the destruction of Israel, but his successors were. The events are described in the biblical book of 2 Kings. The Assyrian kings Shalmaneser V and Sargon II attacked the northern kingdom, laying siege to the capital city, Samaria, and eventually destroying it and many of its inhabitants. Many of those who were not killed were sent away from the land into exile, and people from other conquered nations were brought into the land, where they intermarried with the remaining local population. This was Assyrian policy: by relocating potentially disruptive people and creating intermarriages, they were able to break down any remnants of nationalism and, in effect, within a couple of generations, force a nation's people out of existence.[20] The nation and peoples of the northern kingdom of Israel disappeared from the face of the earth, never to reappear.

## Hosea Son of Beeri

A younger contemporary of Amos was a prophet from the north who, like his southern counterpart, preached a message of coming destruction to the nation of Israel. In this case, too, we know very little about the man, who calls himself the son of (an otherwise unknown) Beeri, except for what he tells us in his book. Hosea indicates some of what happened in his life, but scholars debate whether it is genuine autobiography or a fictional narrative used to make a point.[21] In chapter 1 he says that the Lord told him to marry a woman of ill-repute (it is not clear if she was already a prostitute when they married or simply a woman of loose morals). This marriage was to symbolize Hosea's entire message. The Lord was, in a sense, the husband of Israel. And Israel was not faithful to the relationship but "committed prostitution" with other gods. How would a man feel whose wife not merely had an affair but committed her entire life to sleeping with other men? That's how God feels about Israel. He is outraged at her behavior and determined to punish her for it.

Hosea's wife, Gomer, bears him several children, and God orders him to give them symbolic names. One is a girl called Lo-ru-hamah, which is Hebrew for "Not Pitied," because, says God, "I will no longer have pity on the house of Israel or forgive them" (1:6). That sounds harsh, but no harsher than what happens next: Gomer then has a son named Lo-ammi, which means "Not My People," so named because God has declared that "you are not my people and I am not your God" (1:9).

God's rejection of his own people is stated in graphic terms throughout the book, in oracles of judgment. As he says of the nation:

> I will strip her naked
>> and expose her as in the day she
>>> was born,
> and make her like a wilderness,
>> and turn her into a parched
>>> land,
>> and kill her with thirst.

Upon her children also I will have
no pity,
because they are children of
whoredom. (Hosea 2:3–4)

And why does God treat his people this way? It is because:

She did not know
that it was I who gave her
the grain, the wine, and the oil,
and who lavished upon her silver
and gold that they used for
Baal [a god of the Canaanites].
Therefore I will take back
my grain in its time,
and my wine in its season…
Now I will uncover her shame
in the sight of her lovers…
I will put an end to all her mirth…
I will lay waste her vines and her
fig trees. (Hosea 2:8–12)

Whereas for Amos the problem with the nation was that the wealthy had oppressed the poor and created enormous social injustice, for Hosea the problem is that the people of Israel have started worshiping other gods, especially Baal, the god of the other peoples in the land. Going after other gods, for Hosea, is like a woman going after other lovers, leaving her husband behind. The anger God feels toward this act of betrayal is palpable throughout Hosea's prophecies. Because the Israelites have committed prostitution with the pagan gods, God will starve them and send them into exile:

Do not rejoice, O Israel!
Do not exult as other nations
do;

for you have played the whore,
    departing from your God.
  You have loved a prostitute's
    pay
on all threshing floors.
Threshing floor and wine vat shall
    not feed them,
and the new wine shall fail
    them.
They shall not remain in the land
    of the LORD;
  but Ephraim [another name for Israel] shall return to
    Egypt,
and in Assyria they shall eat
    unclean food. (Hosea 9:1–3)

At the same time, the idolatrous ways of Israel also involved acts of "wickedness" and "injustice," which would lead to final destruction: "Therefore the tumult of war shall rise against your people and all your fortresses shall be destroyed, as Shalman destroyed Beth-arbel on the day of battle, when mothers were dashed in pieces with their children. Thus it will be done to you ... because of your great wickedness" (10:14–15). Mothers dashed with their children? Yes, that's the punishment Israel can expect for departing from the ways and worship of their God.

Nowhere is Hosea's message stated more graphically than near the end of his book, where he indicates that because Israel had been the chosen people, its disobedience will turn God from the faithful shepherd who unerringly guided them on their way to a wild animal that tears them to shreds:

Yet I have been the LORD your
    God
    ever since the land of Egypt;
you know no God but me,

and besides me there is no
      savior.
It was I who fed you in the
      wilderness,
   in the land of drought.
When I fed them, they were
      satisfied;
   they were satisfied, and their
      heart was proud;
   therefore they forgot me.
So I will become like a lion to
      them,
   like a leopard I will lurk beside
      the way.
I will fall upon them like a bear
      robbed of her cubs,
   and will tear open the covering
      of their heart;
there I will devour them like a
      lion,
   as a wild animal would mangle
      them.
I will destroy you, O Israel;
   who can help you? (Hosea 13:4–9)

This is not the kind, loving, caring, forgiving God of nursery
rhymes and Sunday school booklets. God is a fierce animal who
will rip his people to shreds for failing to worship him. Or as Hosea
states in his most disturbing image of all:

Samaria [i.e., the capital of the northern kingdom] shall bear her
      guilt,
because she has rebelled against
      her God;

they shall fall by the sword,
  their little ones shall be dashed
    in pieces,
  and their pregnant women
      ripped open. (Hosea 13:16)

The predicted fall of Israel came to pass soon after Hosea's day (or possibly during the final years of his prophetic activity). Assyria was on the march and wanted very much to control the entire area that later became known as the Fertile Crescent. Israel had the geographical misfortune of lying just east of the Mediterranean in the land mass that led from Mesopotamia south to Egypt. Any world empire wanting to control the region needed control of Israel. Assyria's armies marched against tiny Israel and overcame it, destroying the capital city of Samaria, killing the opposition, and, as indicated earlier, sending many of the people into exile.

This kind of military defeat might be read by a secular historian as a natural event that took place because of political currents and national ambition. Not so for a religious prophet like Hosea. For him, the reason the nation Israel had suffered so mightily was that it had displaced its faith in the God who had delivered it from Egypt and gone after other gods. The true God could not abide this false behavior, and so sent out the powerful troops from the north. The army was destroyed, the land decimated, and the people violently killed or exiled as a punishment for their sin.

## Other Prophets, Same Refrain

The prophets Amos and Hosea were not alone in seeing the sufferings of the people of Israel as a punishment from God. In fact, this is a constant refrain of *all* the writing prophets, whether they were prophesying against the northern kingdom Israel or the southern kingdom Judah, and whether they were prophesying at the time of the Assyrian ascendancy in the eighth century or at the time of the

Babylonians in the sixth—or at any other time or place. Page after page of the prophets' writings are filled with dire warnings about how God will inflict pain and suffering on his people for disobedience, whether through famine, drought, pestilence, economic hardship, and political upheavals, or, most commonly, through resounding military defeat. God brings disasters of all kinds, both to punish his people for their sin and to urge them to return to him. If they return, the pain will cease; if they don't, it will get worse.

Rather than rehearse all the writings of all the prophets, here I shall briefly discuss the words of two of the most famous, Isaiah and Jeremiah, both of Jerusalem, so-called major prophets whose powerful rhetoric continues to make them moving reading two and a half millennia later.[22] It is important to remember, however, that they, and all the prophets, were speaking to the people of their own day, instructing them in the word of the Lord, urging them to return to God, and reciting the dire fate awaiting them should they fail to do so. Both of these prophets had long ministries of about forty years; both of them prophesied not against the northern kingdom but against the south. But their essential message did not differ significantly from that of their colleagues to the north.[23] God's people had departed from his ways and fearful suffering was in store for them as a result. God, for them, was a God who punishes.

Consider the powerful lament of Isaiah's opening chapter:

Ah, sinful nation,
    people laden with iniquity,
offspring who do evil,
    children who deal corruptly,
who have forsaken the LORD,
    who have despised the Holy
        One of Israel,
    who are utterly estranged!
Why do you seek further beatings,
    Why do you continue to rebel? ...

Your country lies desolate,
　　your cities are burned with fire;
in your very presence
　　aliens devour your land;
　　it is desolate, as overthrown by
　　　　foreigners...
If the LORD of hosts
　　had not left us a few survivors,
we would have been like Sodom,
　　and become like Gomorrah. (Isa. 1:4–9)

One can hardly read this without thinking of that fierce cartoon with the caption "Beatings will continue until morale improves." That indeed is Isaiah's message, in words reminiscent of Hosea:

How the faithful city [i.e., Jerusalem]
　　has become a whore!
　　She that was full of justice,
righteousness lodged in her—
　　but now murderers!...
Your princes are rebels
　　and companions of thieves.
Everyone loves a bribe
　　and runs after gifts.
They do not defend the orphan,
　　and the widow's cause does not
　　　　come before them.
Therefore says the Sovereign, the
　　　　LORD of hosts, the Mighty
　　　　One of Israel:
Ah, I will pour out my wrath on
　　　　my enemies,
　　and avenge myself on my foes!
I will turn my hand against you. (Isa. 1:21–25)

The people of God have now become the enemy of God. And he will act accordingly:

> Instead of perfume there will be a
>     stench;
>   and instead of sash, a rope...
>   instead of beauty, shame.
> Your men shall fall by the sword
>   and your warrior in battle.
> And her gates shall lament and
>     mourn;
>   ravaged, she shall sit upon the
>     ground. (Isa. 3:24–26)

In one of the most famous passages of the book, Isaiah recounts a vision he has had of God himself, "sitting on a throne, high and lofty" above the Temple (6:1–2). The prophet is commissioned by God to proclaim his message, a message that the people will reject. When he asks the Lord how long he is to make this proclamation, he receives bad news—it is until the whole land is destroyed: "Until cities lie waste without inhabitant and houses without people, and the land is utterly desolate; until the LORD sends everyone far away and vast is the emptiness in the midst of the land" (6:11–12). And what has Judah done that makes it worthy of such judgment? They have robbed the poor, not cared for the needy, not tended to the widows and the orphans in distress (10:2–3). God will therefore send another great power against them for destruction.

And yet, as we saw with Amos, Isaiah anticipates that God's wrath will not burn forever. On the contrary, he will save a remnant of his people and start again:

> On that day the remnant of Israel and the survivors of the
> house of Jacob will no more lean on the one who struck them,
> but will lean on the LORD, the Holy One of Israel, in truth. A

remnant will return, the remnant of Jacob, to the mighty God.... For in a very little while my indignation will come to an end, and my anger will be directed to their [i.e., the enemy's] destruction.... On that day his burden will be removed from your shoulder, and his yoke will be destroyed from your neck. (Isa. 10:20–27)

More than a century later, a similar message was proclaimed by Jeremiah, another prophet of Judah who anticipated that God would destroy the nation for its misdeeds.[24] A foreign power would march against it and bring terrible destruction:

> I am going to bring upon you
>     a nation from far away,
>         O house of Israel,
>                     says the LORD.
> It is an enduring nation,
>     it is an ancient nation,
> a nation whose language you do
>                     not know,
>     nor can you understand what
>                     they say....
> They shall eat up your harvest and
>                     your food;
>     they shall eat up your sons and
>                     your daughters;
> they shall eat up your flocks
>                     and your herds;
>     they shall eat up your vines and
>                     your fig trees;
> they shall destroy with the sword
>     your fortified cities in which
>                     you trust. (Jeremiah 5:15–17)

Jeremiah was quite explicit: the holy city, Jerusalem, would be destroyed in the coming onslaught. "I will make Jerusalem a heap of ruins, a lair of jackals; and I will make the towns of Judah a desolation without inhabitant" (9:11).[25] The resultant suffering for the inhabitants of the land would not be pleasant: "They shall die of deadly diseases. They shall not be lamented nor shall they be buried; they shall become like dung on the surface of the ground. They shall perish by the sword and by famine, and their dead bodies shall become food for the birds of the air and for the wild animals of the earth" (16:4). The siege of Jerusalem by the foreign armies would lead to unspeakable horrors, as starvation mounted in the city and people resorted to the worst forms of cannibalism simply to survive: "I will make this city a horror, a thing to be hissed at; everyone who passes by it will be horrified and will hiss because of all its disasters. And I will make them eat the flesh of their sons and the flesh of their daughters, and all shall eat the flesh of their neighbors in the siege, and in the distress with which their enemies and those who seek their life afflict them" (19:8–9).

Like his prophetic predecessors, Jeremiah held out hope as well. If the people would simply return to God, their suffering could be averted: "Therefore thus says the LORD: If you turn back, I will take you back and you shall stand before me…. And I will make you to this people a fortified wall of bronze; they will fight against you, but they shall not prevail over you, for I am with you to save you and deliver you, says the LORD. I will deliver you out of the hand of the wicked, and redeem you from the grasp of the ruthless" (15:19–21).

The logic of this hope is clear. Suffering comes from God. If his people will simply return to him, the suffering will end. But if they refuse, it will intensify until there is a final destruction. Suffering in this view is not simply an unfortunate set of circumstances driven by political, economic, social, or military realities. It is what comes to those who disobey God; it comes as a punishment for sin.

## An Initial Assessment

What are we to make of the prophetic view of suffering? It is not simply the view of several lone voices in remote portions of Scripture, but rather the view attested on page after page by all the prophets of the Hebrew Bible, major prophets and minor prophets alike. Moreover, as we will see in the next chapter, the influence of this view extended well beyond the writings of the prophets. It is precisely this view that guides the chronologies of what happened in the nation of Israel in historical books such as Joshua, Judges, 1 and 2 Samuel, and 1 and 2 Kings. It is a view found in many of the Psalms. It is comparable in many ways to the view found in wisdom literature such as the book of Proverbs. This is a view that permeates the Bible, especially the Hebrew Scriptures. Why do people suffer? In part, it is because God makes them suffer. It is not that he merely causes a little discomfort now and then to remind people that they need to pay more attention to him. He brings famine, drought, pestilence, war, and destruction. Why do God's people starve? Why do they incur dreadful and fatal diseases? Why are young men maimed and killed in battle? Why are entire cities laid under siege, enslaved, destroyed? Why are pregnant women ripped open and children dashed against rocks? To some extent, at least, it is God who does it. He is punishing his people when they have gone astray.

I should stress that the prophets themselves never state this as a universal principle, as a way of explaining *every* instance of suffering. The prophets, that is, were speaking *only* to their contemporaries about their specific sufferings. Even so, there is no escaping the gruesome realities of this view. God sometimes visits judgment on his own people—especially since they are his own people—because they have abandoned him and his ways.

What can we say about such a view? On the positive side, this view takes God and his interactions with the world seriously. The laws that his people broke, after all, were laws meant to preserve the welfare of society. They were laws designed to ensure that the poor were not oppressed, that the needy were not overlooked, that the weak were not exploited. These were laws as well that dictated that God be worshiped and served—God alone, not other gods of other peoples. The prophets taught that adherence to God's will would bring divine favor whereas disobedience would lead to hardship—and surely obedience would be better for everyone involved, especially the poor, needy, and weak. The prophets, in short, were concerned about issues of real life—poverty, homelessness, injustice, oppression, the uneven distribution of wealth, the apathetic attitudes of those who have it good toward those who are poor, helpless, and outcast. On all of these points I resonate deeply with the prophets and their concerns.

At the same time, there are obvious problems with their point of view, especially if it is generalized into some kind of universal principle, as some people have tried to do over the ages. Do we really want to say that God brings starvation as a punishment for sin? Is God at fault for the famines in Ethiopia? Does God create military conflict? Is he to blame for what happened in Bosnia? Does God bring disease and epidemics? Was he the one who caused the 1918 influenza epidemic that killed thirty million people worldwide? Is he killing seven thousand people a day with malaria? Has he created the AIDS crisis?

I don't think so. Even if one wants to limit the prophetic view to the "chosen people," the people of Israel, what are we to say? That the political and military problems in the Middle East are God's way of trying to get Israel to return to him? That he is willing to sacrifice the lives of women and children in suicide bombings to get his point across? Even if we limit ourselves to *ancient* Israel, do we really want to say that innocent people starved to death (starvation does not hit just the guilty, after all) as a divine punishment for the sins of the nation? That the brutal oppression of the Assyrians and then the Babylonians was really God's doing, that he urged the soldiers on as they ripped open pregnant women and dashed little children against the rocks?

The problem with this view is not only that it is scandalous and outrageous, but also that it creates both false security and false guilt. If punishment comes because of sin, and I'm not suffering one bit, thank you very much, does that make me righteous? More righteous than my next door neighbor who lost his job, or whose child was killed in an accident, or whose wife was brutally raped and murdered? On the other hand, if I am undergoing intense suffering, is it really because God is punishing me? Am I really to blame when my child is born with a defect? when the economy takes a nosedive and I can no longer afford to put food on the table? when I get cancer?

Surely there must be other explanations for the pain and misery in the world. And as it turns out, there are other explanations—lots of them—even within the Bible itself. Before examining these, however, we should see how the prophetic view of suffering affected writers who were not prophets but whose books also eventually came to be seen as part of Scripture.

# three

# More Sin and More Wrath: The Dominance of the Classical View of Suffering

As horrible and bloodcurdling as the Holocaust was, it was obviously not the only terrible consequence of the Second World War. War affects entire nations, and, of course, the people who live in them, both civilians and soldiers. It is relatively easy to come up with statistics for the major international conflicts of the twentieth century. With respect to casualties, for example, the First World War is usually thought to have caused fifteen million deaths. Many of these deaths were grim and tortuous; trench warfare was an ugly affair. In terms of sheer numbers, the Second World War was far more significant: something like fifty to sixty million deaths, all told. That was 2–3 percent of the entire population of earth at the time. This is not counting, obviously, the severely wounded—soldiers with legs blown off by landmines or wounded with shrapnel they continued to carry in their bodies for the rest of their lives, and so on. What needs to be remembered whenever the raw numbers of those who die or suffer are tossed about is that each of these numbers represents an individual, a man, woman, or child who had physical needs and desires, loves and hates, beliefs and hopes. For more than fifty million individuals in the Second World War, these hopes were savagely disappointed. And even survivors were scarred for life.

One of the peculiar features of personal suffering is that it may not be worn on the face or evident from the externals of one's later life. That's not always true, of course: soldiers fortunate to have survived a war experience—whether a world war, Korea, Vietnam, or any other of the dozens of conflicts of the past century—were often unfortunate for the rest of their lives, permanently wounded or disfigured or so mentally and emotionally shaken that they could never lead a normal life again. Anyone who is inclined to glorify the exploits of war should delve deeply into Wilfred Owen's poems or Dalton Trumbo's 1971 film *Johnny Got His Gun,* one of the most terrifying movies ever made.

Others, though, managed to survive a war, return to civilian life, and go on to lead a happy and prosperous existence—so much so that simply by looking at them, you would never know the deep anguish and suffering they had been through. There are millions of experiences like that, of course; here I'll mention just one, the one I know best—the experience of my own father in the Second World War.

By the time I reached the age of consciousness (I was a bit slow: say, age 13), my dad had the life of someone living out the American dream. We had a nice four-bedroom colonial house on a large lot, two cars, and a boat; we belonged to the country club and enjoyed an active social life. Dad was a highly successful businessman, working in sales for a corrugated box company in Lawrence, Kansas. He was happily married to a woman he considered his best friend, and they had three kids, one of whom, I might say, was particularly striking for looks and intelligence....

Where is the suffering in a life like this? Well, there were of course the typical forms of disappointment, frustration, unrealized hopes, and the rest. And eventually cancer. But well before that, my dad had gone through more than his share of suffering in the world, particularly in the war. In March of 1943, as an eighteen-year-old, he was taken into the army. After a round of training in different branches of the service (a complicated story in itself), he eventually was sent over as a private first class to fight in Germany as part of the 104th Infantry Division (the "Timberwolves"). The ensuing battles marked him for life.

His first day "on the job" he started out as an ammunition bearer, and by the end of the day was the first gunner on a machine gun. The two guys ahead of him had been killed, and he was the most qualified to take over. And so it went. The biggest trauma happened at a battle at the Roer River in Germany, on February 23, 1945. This was after the German surge at the Battle of the Bulge had been repulsed and the Allies were moving into German territory. The 104th was moving toward the Rhine under heavy fire but first had to cross the small Roer River, which was well protected on the other side by German troops armed to the teeth. The plans for the crossing had been laid, and the time was set, only to be frustrated by a counteraction by the Germans: knowing what was to come, they burst the earthen dam at the head of the river, sending down avalanches of water, making an immediate crossing impossible. The Americans had to wait. Finally on February 22 the orders were given: they would head out at 1:00 A.M. the next morning.

My dad's recollections of the next twenty-four hours need to be pieced together from sundry sources: letters that he wrote after the fact and stories that he (reluctantly) told later. He crossed the river in a boat, paddling with a dozen or so others, with German infantry on the other side firing at them, bullets flying everywhere. The fellow in front of my dad was blown away. Those who made it to the other side needed to hunker down in foxholes while more troops crossed. The foxhole my dad found himself in was filled with water from the flooding of the river. And there they had to stay, my dad and two others, unable to move out with crossfire all around. They had to stay, in fact, for nearly an entire day, legs and feet in freezing water, in the dead of winter.

Eventually they decided they couldn't stay: feet frozen and no prospect of help. They made a run for it, with my dad in the lead. Unfortunately, the only way out was through a minefield. His two buddies were blown to bits behind him. He managed to get back to his line but was unable to go any farther. A medic was called in, gave him a quick examination, and determined that his feet were in serious shape. They took him out on a stretcher to the rear of the line; eventually he was evacuated and flown to Salisbury, England.

Doctors there told him it was a miracle he had been able to stand, let alone run, given the state of his feet. They thought they would need to amputate. Luckily, circulation was sufficiently restored and he survived with two feet intact, but damaged for life. Until his dying day he had problems with circulation and could not keep his feet warm.

The end of the story is that an uncle of his learned that he was at Salisbury and managed to visit him in the army hospital there. At first his uncle didn't recognize him. The sheer terror of my dad's experience had made his hair turn completely white. He was twenty years old at the time.

I tell this story not because it's unusual but because it is altogether typical. Fifty million other people were not nearly so lucky: they were flat-out killed. Many millions more were horribly disfigured or dismembered, with wounds to show for the rest of their lives. Millions of others had experiences comparable to those of my dad. Every one of them suffered horribly. My dad's experience was uniquely his, but in other ways it was typical. At the same time, it was not universal.

Back home in Kansas, where he grew up, there were other twenty-year-olds who on the day of the battle had little more to fret about than getting a D on a chemistry exam or being unable to land a date for the fraternity dance or being jilted by their latest girl-friend. I don't want to underestimate the excruciating pain of un-requited love: most of us have experienced it and it can tear a person apart from the inside out. But it is hard to compare with the physical torment and sheer terror of being under enemy fire with colleagues being blown to bits on your right and left.

At the same time, in contrast to the boys back home, there were other twenty-year-olds not far from the front lines who were being slowly and inexorably tortured and murdered in the experiments of crazed Nazi doctors—subjected to freezing experiments, incendiary bomb experiments, amputations and attempted transplants of arms and legs, and so on. Suffering is not only senseless, it is also random, capricious, and unevenly distributed.

How do we explain the suffering of war—or suffering of any kind?

## The Prophetic View Revisited

As we have seen, the prophets of the Hebrew Bible had a ready explanation for why people had to suffer the excruciating agonies of war. For them—at least with regard to Israel and the nations surrounding Israel at the time—war came as a judgment from God for the sins of the people. I should emphasize that the actual suffering in war in antiquity was no less hair-raising than it is in modern times. Hand-to-hand combat with swords, spears, and knives is just as terrifying as sitting in foxholes with bullets whizzing by and destroying your buddies. For the prophets, God sometimes brings war to teach his people a lesson and force them to repent. I suppose that if there are no atheists in foxholes, then on the individual basis the strategy works.

It would be a mistake, however, to see this perspective on suffering as a view of only a few random authors in the Hebrew Bible. In fact, it is the point of view of the majority of authors who produced the biblical texts. In terms of literary genre, on the opposite end of the spectrum from the prophets were the writers of Hebrew "wisdom." Whereas the prophets spoke "the word of God" to a specific crisis situation, indicating what God wanted his people to do when faced with some concrete problem, the speakers of wisdom delivered wise advice that was to be applicable in a wide range of situations. These authors were concerned with universal truths that could help guide one into a happy and prosperous life. They learned the truths they conveyed not by a special revelation from God but by way of human experience that extended over many generations. There are several books of "wisdom" in the Hebrew Bible—including the books of Job and Ecclesiastes, which we will be considering later—but none of them is more typical of the genre than the book of Proverbs, a collection of wise sayings that, if followed, will purportedly lead to a good and happy life.[1]

Consisting almost entirely of pithy sayings of the wise that need to be reflected on and digested, the book of Proverbs is arranged for the most part (there are a few exceptions) in no discernible pattern. It is the kind of book you can just dip into and not worry about the literary context or the narrative flow because, for the most part, there is none. What is striking is that even though Proverbs is very different from the writings of the prophets, it shares with them the basic view that a life lived righteously before God will be rewarded but that suffering comes to the wicked and disobedient. This is not so much because God punishes sinners as it is that the world has been established in a certain way by God, so that right living leads to happiness but wicked behavior leads to suffering. This is a constant refrain throughout the book. Consider the following examples:

The LORD's curse is on the house
    of the wicked,
  but he blesses the abode of the
      righteous. (3:33)

The LORD does not let the
    righteous go hungry,
  but he thwarts the craving of
      the wicked. (10:3)

The righteous are delivered from
    trouble,
  and the wicked get into it
    instead. (11:8)

Whoever is steadfast in
    righteousness will live,
  but whoever pursues evil will
    die. (11:19)

No harm happens to the
    righteous,
  but the wicked are filled with
    trouble. (12:21)

Misfortune pursues sinners,
  but prosperity rewards the
    righteous. (13:21)

This is the classical view of the prophets writ large in Wisdom. Why do people go hungry, experience bodily harm and personal misfortune, come under God's curse, get into trouble, and die? Because they are wicked: they do not obey God. How does one avoid suffering? How does one guarantee the blessing of God, a full stomach, prosperity in life, deliverance from trouble and harm? By obeying God.

Would that it were true. But historical reality is never so neat. All one needs to do is look around to see that the wicked often thrive and the righteous often suffer, sometimes in horrifying and repulsive ways. Nonetheless, it is interesting to see that even the *historical* writers of the Hebrew Bible—precisely the people you would think could see that the classical view of suffering is riddled with problems, when examined historically—even these writers are for the most part convinced that suffering comes from God as a punishment for sin. This can be seen in some of the best-known historical episodes of the Bible—for example, in the stories from the very first book, Genesis—and even more clearly from the large and extended historical narratives that take up the story of Israel from the conquest of the promised land (the book of Joshua) to the fall of the southern kingdom to the Babylonians (2 Kings).

## Illustration: Some Familiar Stories from the Beginning

In some ways the major themes of the Pentateuch are encapsulated in the story of Adam and Eve told at its beginning. The Pentateuch is about God's relation to the human race he created and the people (of Israel) he specifically chose: he made them his people and gave them his laws; they broke his laws and so he punished them. History "works" for the authors of the Pentateuch in relationship to God: the experiences of the people of Israel on earth are determined by their relationship to the God who called them from heaven. Those who obey God are blessed (Abraham); those who disobey him are cursed (the people of Sodom and Gomorrah). Suffering comes not because of the vicissitudes of history but because of the will of God.

The entire account—all five books—is prefaced with the familiar story of Adam and Eve. Adam is created first and told that he can eat the fruit of any tree in the Garden of Eden except the tree "of the knowledge of good and evil"—if he eats from that tree, he "shall die" (Gen. 2:17). Eve is then formed from the rib of Adam, and they start life together in the utopian garden.

But, we're told, the serpent in the garden was "more crafty than any animal" and tempted Eve, telling her that eating the forbidden fruit (it is not said to be an apple) would not lead to death but would allow human beings to "be like God." The woman succumbs to the serpent's temptation. (The serpent is not said to be Satan, by the way: that's a later interpretation. This is a real snake. With legs.) She eats the fruit and gives some to Adam, who eats as well. Big mistake.

When God appears (walking through the garden in the cool evening breeze), he realizes what they have done and calls down punishment on all three of them: serpent, Eve, and Adam (3:14–19). The serpent will from now on slither on the ground (his legs are removed). More significant, Eve will now experience excruciating pain in childbirth as the result of her sin.

By all accounts (I base this on hearsay), childbirth is about the most painful experience a human can have; they tell me that passing a kidney stone is comparable, but frankly, as one who has never had that little pleasure (and who will certainly never have the other), I have to say that I have trouble believing it. In any event, it may be hard for us to imagine how childbirth would be possible *without* pain, but in this story the pain is the result of disobedience, come as punishment from God.

So too Adam is cursed. Instead of simply collecting fruit from trees in the garden, he will have to work the soil with the sweat of his brow. From now on, life will be hard and survival iffy. This is a permanent form of suffering, incurred as the price of disobedience. The tone of the rest of the Bible has now been set.

One way to read Genesis is to see a connection between this first act of disobedience and the rotten results that follow: the entire human race, sprung from disobedient parents, is filled with sin. It gets so bad that God decides to destroy the world and start over. And so we have the account of Noah's ark and the flood: "The Lord saw that the wickedness of humankind was great in the earth, and that the inclination of the thoughts of their hearts was only evil continually" (6:5). And so he decides to judge the lot of them, and to "blot out from the earth the human beings I have created" (6:6), along with all the animals, "for I am sorry that I have made them." It's not clear what the animals have done to deserve death, but human beings at least are being punished for their wickedness. Only Noah and his family are miraculously saved; everyone else was drowned by the divine flood that God sent.

Most of us know someone who has drowned, and we have thought with agony about their final moments. It is not a pleasant way to go. But an entire world drowned? Why? Because God was angry. Disobedience needs to be punished and so God killed off nearly the entire human race. Predictors of Armageddon think he will do it again—not with water (God promised not to do that again; 9:11) but by war. Others, of course, refuse to believe in a God who is determined to exterminate the people he created because he disapproves of how they behave.

One final story, again from Genesis. The world gets repopulated, but again almost everyone is wicked. So God chooses one man, Abraham, to be in a special relationship with him. Abraham has a nephew named Lot who lives in the city of Sodom, which is otherwise filled with truly nasty people. God decides to destroy the place; Abraham argues with him and gets him to agree that if there are just ten righteous people who live there he won't destroy it. In this back-and-forth with his chosen one, God has an ace up his sleeve: he knows full well there aren't ten righteous people in the city: just Lot, his wife, and two daughters. And so God sends his two avenging angels into town. The townsfolk, showing their unrestrained depravity, think that these are human visitors and come to Lot's house at night demanding that he release the strangers to them so that they can gang-rape them. Lot, in a curious move, driven by ancient codes of hospitality, offers his two virgin daughters instead. Luckily, the two angels intervene. The next day the family flees the city and God destroys it with fire and brimstone. Lot's wife does not obey the angels' instruction, though; she looks back to see the destruction and is turned into a pillar of salt (19:24–26). On every level, disobedience brings punishment.

## At the End of the Pentateuch

A similar theme drives the narrative of all five books of the Pentateuch. In some ways it comes to a climax in the final book, Deuteronomy. The title of this book literally means "second law"; in fact, it is not a second law that is given in the book—instead, the book describes the second time the Law was given to the children of Israel by the prophet Moses. The narrative sequence works like this. In the book of Exodus God saved Israel from its slavery in Egypt and miraculously allowed it to escape the pursuing armies of Pharaoh at the Red Sea (or sea of reeds). He then led the people to Mount Sinai, where he gave them his Law (Exodus and Leviticus). The people were to march north and enter the promised land. When they came to the edge of the land and sent out scouts, however, the spies came back warning that the Israelites would not be able to conquer the land because the inhabitants were too fierce (Numbers 13–14). Because the people refused to believe that God would be behind them to do what he commanded—take the land and destroy its inhabitants— God punished the children of Israel by refusing to allow any of them to enter the promised land (sin brings punishment). As he tells Moses: "None of the people who have seen my glory and the signs that I did in Egypt ... and have not obeyed my voice shall see the land that I swore to give to their ancestors" (Num. 14:22–23).

And so God had the people of Israel wander in the wilderness for forty years, until the entire generation (except for the one faithful spy, Caleb, and the new Israelite commander, Joshua, Moses' successor) died off. After forty years, God ordered Moses to deliver to the people—who had not been there the first time around—the Law he had received on Mount Sinai forty years earlier. The book of Deuteronomy narrates Moses' regiving of the Law.

Near the end of the book, after Moses has delivered the commandments and ordinances, he tells the people in clear and forthright terms that if they want to succeed and prosper under God's guiding hand, they will obey the Law. If, however, they disobey, they will be cursed to experience horrible and excruciating suffering. Deuteronomy 28 is key to understanding the entire theology of the book, for here the "blessings and cursings" are set out in graphic terms, as Moses tells the people:

If you will only obey the LORD your God, by diligently observing all his commandments that I am commanding you today, the LORD your God will set you high above all the nations of the earth; all these blessings shall come upon you and overtake you....

Blessed shall you be in the city, and blessed shall you be in the field.

Blessed shall be the fruit of your womb, the fruit of your ground, and the fruit of your livestock....

Blessed shall be your basket and your kneading bowl.

Blessed shall you be when you come in and blessed shall you be when you go out. (Deut. 28:1–6)

Moses goes on to indicate that if the people obey the Law, they will defeat all their enemies in battle, they will have bounteous crops, they will prosper and thrive. On the other hand, if they disobey, they can expect just the opposite:

Cursed shall you be.... The LORD will send upon you disaster, panic, and frustration in everything you attempt to do until you are destroyed.... The LORD will make the pestilence cling to you until it has consumed you.... The LORD will afflict you with consumption, fever, inflammation, with fiery heat and drought, and with blight and mildew.... The LORD will cause you to be defeated before your enemies; ... Your corpses shall be food for every bird of the air and animal of the field.... The LORD will afflict you with the boils of Egypt, with ulcers, scurvy, and itch, of which you cannot be healed. The LORD will afflict you with madness, blindness, and confusion of mind. (Deut. 28:16–28)

And so there it is. Why does disaster strike God's people? Why do they experience epidemics and disease? Why are there droughts and failed crops, and military defeat and mental illness, and all the other woes experienced by the people of God? God is punishing them for disobedience. This is the prophetic view of suffering put into a historical narrative.

## Other Historical Books of Scripture

The prophetic view is not confined to the book of Deuteronomy; it also dominates the great bulk of the other historical narratives of the Old Testament, most of which were highly influenced by the theology of Deuteronomy. Six large narratives following Deuteronomy—Joshua, Judges, 1 Samuel, 2 Samuel, 1 Kings, and 2 Kings—are referred to by scholars as the Deuteronomistic History, because it has long been known (or at least thought) that these books were written by an author or authors who accepted the basic perspectives found in Deuteronomy and allowed these perspectives to guide their accounts of the Israelites' history in the centuries following Moses (roughly 1250 BCE).[2] As previously indicated, these books narrate how the people finally conquered the promised land (Joshua), how the tribes of Israel lived as separate communities before a king was appointed over them all (Judges), how the kings Saul, David, and Solomon came to rule over all of Israel (1 and 2 Samuel; 1 Kings), and then how the kingdom was divided after Solomon's death, up until the destruction of the northern kingdom by the Assyrians in 722 BCE and the destruction of the southern kingdom by the Babylonians in 586 BCE (1 and 2 Kings). These six biblical books, then, cover the history of Israel over a seven-hundred-year period. And in them, one perspective dominates the entire narrative. It is the perspective of sin and punishment: when Israel obeys God, follows his will, and keeps his Law, it prospers and thrives; when it disobeys, it is punished. Finally it pays the ultimate price of disobedience: it is destroyed by foreign armies.

This perspective is found in each of the books of the Deuteronomistic History. The book of Joshua records how the ragtag army of the Israelites was able to conquer and take possession of the

promised land. At the very beginning the tone of the account is set.
God tells Joshua to go into the land and take it over, and he delivers
to him this promise:

> No one shall be able to stand against you all the days of your
> life.... Only be strong and very courageous, being careful to
> act in accordance with all the law that my servant Moses com-
> manded you; do not turn from it to the right hand or to the
> left, so that you may be successful wherever you go. This book
> of the law shall not depart out of your mouth; you shall medi-
> tate on it day and night, so that you may be careful to act in
> accordance with all that is written in it. For then you shall
> make your way prosperous, and then you shall be successful.
> (Josh. 1:5–8)

This is what in fact happens, as seen in the very first battle scene,
the famous battle of Jericho. How are the Israelites to conquer such
a well-fortified city? Simply by following God's instructions. Joshua
is ordered to have the warriors of Israel march around the city's
walls once a day for six days. On the seventh day they are to march
around seven times, and then have the trumpets blown, and "the
walls'll come a'-tumblin' down." They do so and it works. The
walls fall, the warriors enter the city—and they murder every man,
woman, child, and animal in the city (with the exception of the
prostitute Rahab and her family). A complete and resounding victory (Josh. 6).

Anyone interested in the problem of suffering might wonder, of
course, about the inhabitants of Jericho. For the God of Israel, these
were foreigners who worshiped foreign gods, and so were fit for
nothing but destruction. But one might want to think about all the
innocents who were murdered. Is this really what God is like, one
who orders the slaughter of those who are outside his people? It is
not as if the people of Jericho were given the chance to think things
over or turn to him. They were all slaughtered, even the infants, in
a divinely appointed bloodbath.

Throughout the book of Joshua, the armies of Israel succeed whenever they obey the divine directives. When they deviate from these directives in even minor ways, God punishes them with defeat (for example, in the battle of Ai in Joshua 7). It should be understood that I am not discussing what *actually* happened when a group of exiles from Egypt entered the land of Canaan and took up residence there. Historians have long wrangled over the historical realities behind these stories—there is no archaeological evidence, for example, to support the claim of the complete destruction of Jericho in the thirteenth century BCE.[3] What I am interested in here is how the Deuteronomistic historian himself thought about these events. In his view, success came to the people of Israel when they obeyed God; setbacks occurred when they disobeyed. In fact, the setbacks were rather severe. People suffered horribly if they did not do what God instructed them to do.

The same idea drives the book of Judges, which describes how the twelve tribes of Israel lived in the promised land before there was a king who ruled them all. This two-hundred-year period is portrayed as somewhat chaotic, but one theme dominates the account. When Israel was faithful to God, it thrived; when it departed from God, for example, by worshiping the gods of the other inhabitants of the land (the Israelite armies had failed to annihilate everyone), then God punished them. This overarching view can be seen in the summary of the period given at the very beginning of the book, in a description of what generally happened when the children of Israel began worshiping "the Baals"—that is, the local divinities of the Canaanites:

> Then the Israelites did what was evil in the sight of the LORD and worshiped the Baals; and they abandoned the LORD, the God of their ancestors, who had brought them out of the land of Egypt; they followed other gods, from among the gods of the peoples who were around them; ... and they provoked the LORD to anger.... So the anger of the LORD was kindled against Israel, and he gave them over to plunderers who plundered

them, and he sold them into the power of their enemies all around, so that they could no longer withstand their enemies … and they were in great distress. (Judg. 2:6–9)

Whenever this happened—and it happens continually throughout the book of Judges—God raised up a ruler in one part or another of the land, rulers called judges, who would do his will and restore to his people freedom from foreign oppression. And so here we get stories of such figures as Ehud, the prophetess Deborah, Gideon, and the he-man Samson. The history of the time is stated succinctly in the last line of the book: "In those days there was no king in Israel; all the people did what was right in their own eyes" (21:25). Unfortunately, what was right in their eyes was not what was right in God's, and so the book is filled with incidents of foreign oppression and domination.

The final judge was Samuel, and the books of 1 and 2 Samuel are devoted to showing the transition from the period of local (and chaotic) autonomy among the tribes of Israel to the period of the monarchy. Samuel is directed by God to anoint a king who will rule over his people. The Deuteronomistic History gives mixed reports about whether Israel's demand for a king was a good thing, in line with God's will, or an evil thing that he only grudgingly granted. First to be king is Saul, who is alternately portrayed as a good and godly ruler and a bad and ungodly one. Because of Saul's defects, God appoints Samuel to anoint another king, the young David, who after a number of conflicts with Saul (recounted in 1 Samuel), and after Saul's own death in battle, becomes God's chosen king over all the people. This introduces a kind of golden age for ancient Israel, when the territories it ruled were extensive and when foreign powers such as Egypt and Assyria were not yet intent on dominating the region (2 Samuel). The age continued through the reign of Solomon, described in 1 Kings. Once again the Deuteronomistic narrator sets the tone for Solomon's reign, in a word of God that comes to him:

If you will walk before me, as David your father walked, with integrity of heart and uprightness, doing according to all that I have commanded you... then I will establish your royal throne over Israel forever.... If you turn aside from following me, you or your children, and do not keep my commandments ... but go and serve other gods ... then I will cut Israel off from the land that I have given them. (1 Kings 9:4–7)

As it turns out, Solomon proves not to be faithful to God. As was true for many powerful rulers before and after him, his downfall came because of his love life. We are told that Solomon had more than a thousand wives and concubines (11:3). This in itself was not a problem in a period in which polygamy was widely practiced, and it was not condemned by the Law of Moses (to the surprise of many readers today). The problem was that "King Solomon loved many foreign women along with the daughter of Pharaoh: Moabite, Ammonite, Edomite, Sidonian, and Hittite women" (11:1). God had ordered the Israelites to be married and sexually involved only with Israelites. And the reason becomes evident in the case of Solomon. His foreign wives induce him to worship their gods. God becomes angry and vows that "I will surely tear the kingdom from you." And this is what happens. Solomon's son Rehoboam takes the throne after his death, but the tribes in the northern part of the land decide to secede from the union and start a nation of their own under a rival king, Jeroboam.

The rest of 1 and 2 Kings describes the reigns of the various kings in Israel (the north) and in Judah (the south), until both kingdoms are destroyed by Mesopotamian superpowers. The success of each king, in the eyes of the Deuteronomistic historian, depended not on his political savvy or diplomatic skills, but on his faithfulness to God. Those who obey God are blessed; those who disobey are cursed. Finally the disobedience grows so prominent that God decides to destroy the northern kingdom. The author of 2 Kings is explicit about what led to the Assyrian destruction of the capital city of Samaria, and the entire northern kingdom with it:

> Then the king of Assyria invaded all the land and came to Samaria; for three years he besieged it. In the ninth year of Hoshea the king of Assyria captured Samaria; he carried the Israelites away to Assyria.... 
> 
> This occurred because the people of Israel had sinned against the LORD their God, who had brought them up out of the land of Egypt.... They had worshiped other gods ... and secretly did things that were not right against the LORD their God.... They served idols; they would not listen but were stubborn; they despised [God's] statutes and his covenant that he made with their ancestor, and the warnings that he gave them. They rejected all the commandments of the LORD their God. Therefore the LORD was very angry with Israel and removed them out of his sight; none was left but the tribe of Judah alone. (2 Kings 17:5–18)

A century and a half later, the wicked and godless kings of Judah were similarly rejected by God, and that nation too was destroyed, this time by the armies of Babylonia that had in the meantime conquered mighty Assyria. Again, for this author, the crushing military defeat and the massive suffering it produced were not the result of political missteps or poor troop strength; Judah was destroyed by God for disobeying his commandments:

> Thus says the LORD, I will indeed bring disaster on this place and its inhabitants.... Because they have abandoned me and have made offerings to other gods, so that they have provoked me to anger ... therefore my wrath will be kindled against this place, and it will not be quenched. (2 Kings 22:16–17)

## The Jewish Sacrifice System

We have seen just how dominant the so-called classical view of suffering is. The idea that suffering comes to the people of God as a result of disobedience is found not only throughout the prophets, both major and minor, but also in traditional Israelite "Wisdom" literature (the book of Proverbs) and in the historical books of Scripture (e.g., the Pentateuch and the Deuteronomistic History). In fact, it goes even deeper, into the very heart of the religion of ancient Israel.

Today, many people in our Western world (especially where I live, in the American South) think of religion as a matter of belief: to be sure, religion involves rituals of worship and affects how a person lives, but at heart, religion is a matter of what one believes about God, or about Christ, or about salvation, or about the Bible, and so forth. In ancient Israel, however—as in nearly all ancient societies—religion was not principally a matter of correct belief. Religion was about worshiping God properly. And proper worship was a matter of performing sacred rituals in divinely ordained ways (this was true of ancient pagan religions as well). In particular, the religion of Israel was a religion of sacrifice.

In the Torah, God directs the ancient Israelites to make sacrifices of animals and other foodstuffs to him (see Leviticus 1–7). Modern scholars find the laws of sacrifice complex and confusing, and there is considerable debate over what kinds of sacrifices there were ("sin" offerings, "guilt" offerings, "burnt" offerings, "wave" offerings, and so forth—all of these are discussed in the Torah), how they were performed, and how they actually "worked."[4] One thing, however, appears clear. Some of the sacrifices that were to be offered by Israelite priests in the designated holy place (for example, the ancient Tabernacle; or later, after the days of Solomon, in the Jewish Temple) were made as an atonement for sin. That is, when people either collectively or individually had violated God's law, and thereby fallen out of his favor, God had provided a way for them to make restitution: by offering a sacrifice. The basic idea behind this form of sacrifice is that there is a punishment (i.e., divine suffering) appointed for those who violate God's will; when the appropriate sacrifice is offered, this punishment is rescinded.

This appears clearly to be the case for what Leviticus calls "burnt offerings" ("it shall be acceptable on your behalf as atonement for you"; Lev. 1:4; cf. Job 1:5); for "sin" offerings ("thus the priest shall make atonement on your behalf for the sin that you have committed, and you shall be forgiven"; Lev. 4:35); and for the "guilt" offering ("the priest shall make atonement on your behalf with the ram of the guilt offering, and you shall be forgiven"; Lev. 5:16).

Because sin brings horrible judgment in the manifestation of God's wrath, this wrath needs to be averted. It is averted by the proper sacrifice of an animal. It is not clear, as I've said, how the sacrifice actually "works." Does the animal substitute for the human being, who now no longer needs to be slaughtered because the animal has been? (See Gen. 22:1–14.) Or is some other, more complicated logic at work?[5] Whatever the answer to the question of mechanics, the Israelite temple cult was focused on sacrifice as a way of restoring a lost relationship with God, broken by disobedience. Thus, the classical view of suffering—disobedience leads to punishment—lay at the very heart of the ancient Israelite religion.

Eventually within the history of Israel this notion that one being (an animal) could be a sacrifice for another (a human being) took on symbolic proportions. This, as we will see, was to become very important for early Christians, whose understanding of the death of Jesus was sometimes expressed as the "perfect" sacrifice for sins (see Hebrews 9–10 in the New Testament). It is important to realize, however, that Christians did not invent the idea that the suffering of one could lead to the forgiveness of another. This idea was rooted in ancient Israel itself, as seen in particular in the writings of a prophet active in the years after the destruction of Jerusalem in 586 BCE. Because the writings of this prophet were later combined (on the same scroll) with those of Isaiah of Jerusalem, who lived 150 years or so earlier, he is commonly known as Second Isaiah.[6]

## Substitutionary Sacrifice in Second Isaiah

Historians have used several sources in the Hebrew Bible (2 Kings 25; Jer. 52) to reconstruct how the southern kingdom of Judah fell to the Babylonians.[7] Torn between the competing demands of the Egyptian empire to the south and the Babylonian empire to the northeast, the Judean king Zedekiah made a fateful decision to align himself with the former. The Babylonian armies under King Nebuchadrezzar marched against Judah and laid siege to Jerusalem for eighteen months, causing severe hardship and starvation in the city. Eventually the walls were breached, the opposition killed, and the holy Temple (built by Solomon some four hundred years earlier) destroyed. Zedekiah tried to escape but was captured: Nebuchadrezzar had the king's sons slaughtered before his eyes, then gouged out his eyes and led him back as a captive to Babylon. Many of the elite members of Jerusalem's aristocracy were led off to captivity as well (the thinking was that they could not foment a rebellion away from their homeland). It is in that context that Second Isaiah utters his proclamation.

For well over a hundred years now, scholars have realized that chapters 40–55 of the book of Isaiah could not come from the author who wrote (most of) the first thirty-nine chapters. Those earlier chapters presuppose a situation in which Assyria is set to attack Judah—that is, they were written in the eighth century BCE. Chapters 40–55, on the other hand, presuppose a situation in which the southern kingdom had been destroyed and its people taken into exile—that is, the mid-sixth century BCE. Perhaps because the two books have similar prophetic themes, someone at a later date combined them into one scroll, adding as well chapters 56–66 from a yet later prophet (Third Isaiah) writing in still another context.

Second Isaiah agrees with his prophetic forebears in regarding the suffering that has come upon the people of Israel as a punishment for their sins against God. Indeed, Israel has now "received from the LORD's hand double for all her sins" (40:2). This rule of sin and punishment, however, applies not only to Israel the conquered but also to Babylon the conqueror, as God himself informs the conquering nation:

> I was angry with my people,
>     I profaned my heritage;
> I gave them into your hand,
>     you showed them no mercy....
> But evil shall come upon you [as well],
>     which you cannot charm away;
> disaster shall fall upon you,
>     which you will not be able to
>         ward off. (Isa. 47:6, 11)

A key teaching of Second Isaiah, unlike that of prophets before the disaster, is that now that Judah has paid for its sins by being punished, God will relent and forgive his people, restoring them to the promised land and starting over in a new relationship with them. And so in the familiar opening words of the prophet's account:

> Comfort, O comfort my people,
>     says your God.
> Speak tenderly to Jerusalem,
>     and cry to her
> that she has served her term,
>     that her penalty is paid. (Isa. 40:1–2)

Or as he says somewhat later:

> For a brief moment I abandoned
>         you,

> but with great compassion I will
>     gather you.
> In overflowing wrath for a
>     moment
> I hid my face from you,
> but with everlasting love I will
>     have compassion on you,
> says the LORD, your Redeemer. (Isa. 54:7–8)

Just as God saved Israel from slavery in Egypt so many centuries before, leading it through the wilderness into the promised land, so he will act again, making "in the desert a highway for our God." This return will be miraculously delivered: "every valley shall be lifted up and every mountain and hill be made low; the uneven ground shall become level and the rough places a plain. Then the glory of the LORD shall be revealed" (Isa. 40:3–5). This glorious return through the wilderness will come to all who throw their trust on the Lord:

> He gives power to the faint,
>     and strengthens the powerless.
> Even youths will faint and be
>     weary,
>     and the young will fall
>         exhausted;
> but those who wait for the LORD
>     shall renew their strength,
>     they shall mount up with wings
>         like eagles,
> they shall run and not be weary,
>     they shall walk and not faint. (Isa. 40:29–31)

In several notable passages of the book, God speaks of Israel as his chosen servant, who has been sent into exile but will now be restored, while its enemies are dispersed:

But you, Israel, my servant,
   Jacob, whom I have chosen,
     the offspring of Abraham, my
       friend;
you whom I took from the ends
   of the earth,
and called from its farthest
   corners,
saying to you, "You are my
   servant,
I have chosen you and not cast
   you off";
do not fear, for I am with you,
do not be afraid, for I am your
   God;
I will strengthen you, I will help
   you...
Yes, all who are incensed against
   you
     shall be ashamed and disgraced;
those who strive against you
     shall be as nothing and shall
       perish. (Isa. 41:8–10)

It is important for the understanding of Second Isaiah to recognize that it is explicitly the people of Israel, evidently those taken into exile, who are called "my servant" (41:8). As the prophet says later, "You are my servant, Israel, in whom I will be glorified" (49:3). The reason this matters is because some of the passages of Second Isaiah were taken by the early Christians to refer to none other than the messiah, Jesus, who was thought to have suffered for the sake of others, bringing redemption. And indeed, it is hard for Christians familiar with the New Testament to read passages like Isaiah 52:13–53:18 without thinking of Jesus:

See, my servant shall prosper;
   he shall be exalted and lifted up,
   and shall be very high....
He was despised and rejected by
      others;
   a man of suffering and
      acquainted with infirmity;
and as one from whom others
      hide their faces
   he was despised, and we held
      him of no account.
Surely he has borne our infirmities
   and carried our diseases;
yet we accounted him stricken,
      struck down by God, and
      afflicted.
But he was wounded for our
      transgressions,
   crushed for our iniquities;
upon him was the punishment that
      made us whole,
   and by his bruises we are
      healed.
All we like sheep have gone
      astray;
   we have all turned to our own
      way,
and the LORD has laid on him
   the iniquity of us all.
He was oppressed, and he was
      afflicted,
   yet he did not open his mouth;
like a lamb that is led to the
      slaughter,

and like a sheep that before its
    shearers is silent,
  so he did not open his mouth....
For he was cut off from the land
    of the living,
  stricken for the transgression of
    my people.

For interpreting such a powerful passage, several points are important. The first is the one I stated in an earlier chapter: the prophets of Israel were not crystal-ball gazers looking into the distant future (Jesus would not appear for another five centuries); they were speaking a word of God to people living in their own time. Moreover, there is nothing in the passage to suggest that the author is speaking about a *future messiah*. For one thing, the word *messiah* never occurs in this passage (read the entire book for yourself). Furthermore, the sufferings of this "servant" are said to be in the past, not the future. In light of these points, it is easy to see why, prior to Christianity, no Jewish interpreters thought this passage was indicating what the messiah would be like or do. Ancient Judaism (before Christianity) never did have an idea that the messiah would suffer for others—that's why the vast majority of Jews rejected the idea that Jesus could be the messiah. The messiah was to be a figure of grandeur and power—for example, someone like the mighty King David—who would rule over God's people. And who was Jesus? A crucified criminal, just the opposite of what a messiah would be. Finally, it is important to reiterate the key point: the author of Second Isaiah explicitly tells us who the "servant" who has suffered is: it is Israel itself, specifically Israel taken into exile (41:8; 49:3).[8]

Christians eventually, of course, came to think that this passage *was* referring to their messiah, Jesus. I'll say a few words about that in a moment. For now, the question is what Second Isaiah might have meant in its own historical context. If this passage is referring to "my servant, Israel," what does it all mean?

Like the other prophets, Second Isaiah believed that sin requires a punishment. Israel, the servant of God, exiled to Babylon, had suffered horribly at the hands of its oppressors. This suffering brought an atonement. Just as an animal sacrificed in the Temple had brought atonement for sin, so too had exiled Israel. It had suffered for the transgressions of others. Using a metaphor in which Israel is identified as an individual, a "servant of the Lord," Second Isaiah indicates that the exiled people have suffered vicariously for others. The nation can therefore be forgiven, restored to a right relationship with God, and returned to the promised land.[9] The logic of this passage, in other words, is rooted in the classical understanding of suffering, that sin requires a punishment and that suffering comes because of disobedience.

## The Christian Understanding of Atonement

Even though Second Isaiah was speaking to Israel in exile, to show that the punishment they had received from God was sufficient to bring a reconciliation between God and his people, later Christians thought that his words about the suffering servant were to be taken messianically, as a reference to the crucifixion of Jesus. It is important to remember that when Christians told the stories about Jesus' crucifixion, and when later Gospel writers described what transpired at the crucifixion, they were doing so with passages like Isaiah 53 (and Psalm 22, for example) in mind. The descriptions in those passages of one who suffers came to color how the Christians told their stories of Jesus' passion. Thus, the suffering servant, originally thought to be Israel, was silent "like a lamb" during his sufferings (Isa. 53:7), and Jesus was shown as silent throughout his trial. The suffering servant was "numbered with the transgressors" (53:12), and Jesus was crucified between two evildoers. The servant was "despised and rejected by others" (53:3), and Jesus was rejected by his people and mocked by the Roman soldiers. The servant "was wounded for our transgressions" (53:5), and Jesus' death was thought to bring atonement. The servant "made his tomb ... with the rich" (53:9), and Jesus was thought to have been buried by a rich man, Joseph of Arimathea. The servant was thought to be vindicated after his suffering, so that the Lord would "prolong his days" (53:10), and Jesus was said to have been raised from the dead. It is no accident that the crucifixion accounts of the New Testament sound so much like Isaiah 53—the authors of these accounts were thinking of the suffering servant of Isaiah when writing their accounts.

There is one particularly important implication for our study: the classical view of the relationship of sin and suffering is not simply found throughout the pages of the Hebrew Bible. It is central to the understanding of the New Testament as well. Why is it that Jesus has to suffer and die? Because God has to punish sin. Second Isaiah provided the early Christians with a scheme for understanding Jesus' horrible passion and death: this was suffering undertaken for the sake of others. It was through the death of Jesus that others could be made right with God. Jesus was in fact a sacrifice for sin.

I have already mentioned that this is the view expressed in the New Testament book of Hebrews, a book that tries to show that the religion based on Jesus is far superior to the religion of Judaism, in every way. For this author, Jesus is superior to Moses who gave the Law to the Jews (Heb. 3); he is superior to Joshua who conquered the promised land (Heb. 3); he is superior to the priests who offer sacrifices in the temple (Heb. 4–5); and most notably, he is superior to the sacrifices themselves (Heb. 9–10). Jesus' death is seen as the perfect sacrifice, the sacrifice that took away the need for all other (Jewish) sacrifices, in that it brought perfect holiness (or "sanctification") to those who accepted it: "It is by God's will that we have been sanctified through the offering of the body of Jesus Christ once for all" (10:10); for "Christ offered for all time a single sacrifice for sins" (10:12). Implicit here is the idea that the suffering of one substitutes for the suffering of others, an atonement made vicariously for those who deserve to fall under the wrath of God.

The apostle Paul, writing some decades earlier than the anonymous author of Hebrews (whom later Christian readers mistakenly assumed was Paul), had a roughly similar view. As Paul states in his first letter to the Corinthians, "I handed over to you as of first importance what in turn I had received: that Christ died for our sins in accordance with the Scriptures" (1 Cor. 15:3). Paul is somewhat more expansive in his letter to the Romans, where he indicates that the "wrath of God" (Rom. 1:18) has come upon all people because all have sinned, but that Christ himself brought an atonement by shedding his blood for others:

> For all sinned and fell short of God's glory, but they have been made right with God freely by his grace, through the redemption that is in Christ Jesus, whom God set forth as an atoning sacrifice that comes through faith in his blood." (Rom. 3:23–25)

For Paul there is a relatively simple formula for how God provides eternal salvation for his people: sin leads to punishment; Christ took the punishment upon himself; therefore, Christ's death can atone for the sins of others.

This entire view of atonement is rooted in the classical understanding of suffering: sin requires suffering as punishment. Otherwise, God could simply forgive people whenever he wished, and there would be no reason for Christ to die. The Christian doctrine of atonement, and salvation for eternal life, is rooted in the prophetic view that people suffer because God is punishing them for disobedience.

Nowhere is this view of atonement more graphically portrayed than in Mark, the first of the Gospels to be written. There is little to suggest that the anonymous author of Mark's Gospel had actually read the writings of the apostle Paul—who was writing about

twenty years before Mark itself appeared—but in many ways
Mark's view of the importance of Jesus' death reflects a Pauline understanding of atonement. As Jesus himself is recorded as teaching
his disciples in Mark: "The son of man [i.e., Jesus himself] did not
come to be served, but to serve, and to give his life as a ransom for
many" (Mark 10:45). Here is the doctrine of one life being given for
another, right out of Second Isaiah.

Later in Mark, Jesus interprets his death as an atoning sacrifice
for sin. Before he is arrested he has a final meal with his disciples.
This appears to be a Passover meal—that is, the annual meal celebrated by Jews to commemorate the events of the exodus under
Moses, many centuries earlier. Jews annually would (and still do)
have a special meal on Passover with symbolic foods to recall their
deliverance by God: they would eat a lamb to recall the lambs killed
the night that the angel of death "passed over" the houses of the Israelites en route to killing the firstborn children of the Egyptians;
they would eat bitter herbs to recall their bitter slavery in Egypt;
they would eat unleavened bread to recall that they had to escape
from Pharaoh's people quickly, without having time even to make
bread with leaven; they would drink several cups of wine.

At this meal, according to Mark, Jesus took the symbolic foods of
the meal and instilled yet further significance in them. He took the
bread and broke it, saying, "This is my body." Then he took the cup
of wine and said, "This is my blood of the covenant that is poured
out for many" (Mark 14:22–24). In other words, Jesus' body, like
the bread, had to be broken; and his blood had to be shed. This was
not suffering that he himself deserved as a punishment for his own
sin. It was for the sake of others.

## Other Instances of the Classical View in the New Testament

The Christian doctrine of the atonement is thus based on a kind of
transformation of the classical view of why there is suffering in the
world. According to the prophets, suffering here and now, in this

life, comes to those who disobey God. Some later Jews and most later Christians came to think that suffering for sin would come not in this life but in the afterlife. We will be exploring the reasons for this transformation in chapter 8. For now, it is enough to observe that the atonement brought by Christ's death was thought by Christians to remove the need to suffer eternal torment in the afterlife as a punishment for sin. Christ had taken the punishment upon himself.

There are other reflections of the prophetic view of suffering in the New Testament, even in passages that do not speak about atonement. These too, however, are largely about what happens to a person after death. Nowhere is the teaching of future punishment more graphic than in Jesus' account of the judgment of the sheep and the goats in Matthew 25. Some scholars take this passage, which is found only in Matthew, as one of Jesus' parables; others think it is an actual prediction of what will take place at the end of time. In either case, Jesus is speaking about what will happen when the great cosmic judge of the earth, whom he calls the Son of Man, "comes in his glory with his angels" (Matt. 25:31). All the nations of earth will be gathered before him, and he will separate them into two groups, with the "sheep" at his right hand and the "goats" at his left. To the sheep, the mighty king (Son of Man) will say, "Come, you who are blessed of my Father! Inherit the kingdom that has been prepared for you from the foundation of the world." And why will these people come into God's blessed kingdom? The Lord tells them: "For I was hungry and you gave me something to eat; I was thirsty and you gave me something to drink. I was a foreigner and you welcomed me, naked and you gave me something to wear, sick and you visited me, I was in prison and you came to me" (Matt. 25:34–35). But the blessed ones are confused, because they don't remember doing such things for the great king. He tells them, "Truly I say to you, in so far as you did these things for the least of these my brothers, you did them for me." In other words, righteous acts of kindness done for others who are suffering will bring eternal reward.

And failing to act righteously toward others will bring eternal punishment. The king then speaks to the "goats" and tells them: "Get away from me, you who are cursed, to the eternal fire that has been prepared for the devil and his angels. For I was hungry and you gave me nothing to eat, thirsty and you gave me nothing to drink; I was a stranger and you did not welcome me, naked and you did not give me something to wear, sick and in prison and you did not visit me" (Matt. 25:41–43). These people are equally perplexed: they too do not remember seeing the Lord in need. But he tells them, "Truly I say to you, in so far as you did not do these things to the least of these, neither did you do them for me." And so, Jesus indicates, those who have failed to behave righteously toward others in need "will go away to eternal punishment" (Matt. 25:26).

Eternal punishment. This is suffering in extremis. Baking in fire that never ends, forever and ever. Why do people suffer eternal torment? Because they sinned. Here is the prophetic view recast as a doctrine of the afterlife. God causes suffering because people disobey him.

## A Tentative Evaluation

And so, as we have seen, the classical view of suffering permeates much of the Bible. It is found in the prophets, the book of Proverbs, the historical books of the Hebrew Bible, and in parts of the New Testament. In most of the Hebrew Bible, the view is thought to apply in the present life, in the here and now. Those individuals, groups, or nations that obey God and do his will, thrive; those who do not, suffer. They suffer because God is punishing them for their sins. The New Testament authors often portray this punishment as eternal, with no chance of remission. For most of the writers of the Hebrew Bible, especially the prophets, the suffering is meant as an incentive for repentance. If people return to God and do what is right, he will relinquish the punishment, relieve the pain and suffering, and restore people to health and prosperity. The good times will roll.

Still, there are the unfortunate historical realities. These predictions of future success and happiness never did come to fulfillment. Many people in ancient Israel did return to God, did abandon their worship of idols, did strive to follow God's laws, did keep their part of the covenant. But suffering never ceased and the utopian kingdom never arrived.

The English word *utopia* is interesting. It comes from two Greek words that mean "good place." But if a different etymology is used, it can also mean "no place." The creators of the English term had this irony in mind: utopia is that perfect place that, in fact, does not exist. The utopian kingdom in which there is no more pain, misery, and suffering is nowhere to be found. That was certainly true of ancient Israel. Despite returns to God, despite godly rulers, despite attempts to be the people of God, Israel continued to experience famine, drought, pestilence, war, and destruction. Just on the military front, after the nation was overrun by the Assyrians, there came the Babylonians. After them came the Persians. And then the Greeks. Then the Egyptians. Then the Syrians. And then the Romans. One after another, the great empires of the world overwhelmed and absorbed tiny Israel, leading to one political setback, one military defeat, one social nightmare after another.

In no small measure, that is why the classical prophetic answer to the problem of suffering came to seem empty and dissatisfying to so many later authors of ancient Israel, who took implicitly or explicitly contrary views (Job, Ecclesiastes, Daniel, and so on, as we will see). In another sense, the question raised by the ancient prophets is the question raised by millions of religious people over the ages. The question was rooted in a firmly held belief that God had called Israel and intervened on its behalf by delivering it from its dire suffering under slavery in Egypt. But if God intervened before to help us, why doesn't he help us now? Could it be that he himself is the reason we are suffering? Could it be that we have offended him?

How can we return to his good favor, so that our misery will end? The prophets and other biblical writers, of course, were not stating a general religious principle that was to be accepted as true for all times and places. They were speaking to a specific time and place. But readers over the years have sometimes extracted a universal principle from these writings and insisted that suffering comes because God is punishing us for our sin.

People who take this point of view, as I have pointed out, often suffer unnecessarily from self-imposed guilt. Is suffering really our fault? Is it not the case that this very explanation—as prevalent as it was in antiquity and as it is today—simply doesn't work in view of the realities of our world? Do we really want to say that suffering always (or typically) comes from God as punishment? that children who die in tsunamis are being punished? that God forces millions of innocent people to starve to death? to die of cancer or AIDS? to be the victims of genocide? Is it true that twenty-year-olds stuck in frozen foxholes under enemy fire are being punished for their sins, or that their buddies killed by land mines are even worse sinners? Is it true that those of us who have it good are pleasing to God and those of us who suffer are being punished? Who has the arrogance to make such a claim, or the self-loathing?

There must be other answers. Indeed, the Bible provides us with some—even in the writings of the prophets—as we will see in the chapters that follow.

# four

# The Consequences of Sin

With so many people suffering in so many ways, how does one begin to tabulate the misery? A thirty-year-old neighbor is diagnosed with an inoperable brain tumor. A single mother of three loses her job and with it her health insurance and any way of keeping the house or feeding the children. A car accident kills five teenagers from the local high school. A fire across town destroys a nursing home and three of its elderly occupants.

Much of the time we simply throw up our hands and admit defeat. We can't understand it and never will. But there are times when we feel like we ought to be able to do something. Especially when the suffering comes at the hands of others, when crime is on the rise, when we read of burglaries, car thefts, rape, or murder.

The most horrific—and some people think, the most preventable—forms of human abuse of others come at the national level. We tend to understand wars: sometimes they are fought for just causes (the Allies against Germany), sometimes for questionable causes (Vietnam), and sometimes for downright insidious causes (Iraq's invasion of Kuwait). But for most of us, other forms of large-scale force defy the imagination.

I spoke of the Holocaust, modern history's most notorious example, in chapter 2. Many people who visit the Holocaust Memorial Museum in Washington, or its counterpart in Berlin, or the actual site of a camp like Auschwitz, come away saying "Never again." It's a noble thought, and thinking it makes us feel determined or strong. But do we really mean it? Do we really mean that we will do whatever it takes to stop a massive purge of innocent people on the grounds of their race or nationality? If we are really that determined, how do we explain our recent reactions to events in Rwanda and Bosnia? How do we explain our current reactions to Darfur? Do we really mean *never* again?

These situations are not easy. The political situations are notoriously complex and intricate, and it is rarely possible to deal with national abuses simply by sending in the bombers and then the ground troops to restore a sense of human decency to a region controlled by forces determined to assert their will over the masses, even when that will involves killing millions of innocents. Witness Iraq.

Of the genocides since the Holocaust, none was more notorious than the purge sponsored by the Khmer Rouge in Cambodia. I have a very distant connection to the events, in that I came to know one of the lucky survivors, who went through hell on earth before showing up in Trenton, New Jersey, where I met him.

The history of Cambodia in the late 1960s and early 1970s was not at all pretty. Toward the end of the war in Vietnam, U.S. troops moved into Cambodia as part of their strategy to root out the Vietcong. There was a good deal of what we now euphemistically call collateral damage to the innocents who happened to make Cambodia their home. The B-52 bombers, napalm, and dart cluster bombs used by the Americans to destroy suspected North Vietnamese supply lines also killed an estimated 750,000 Cambodians.

After the war, in 1975, civil unrest broke out. Eventually, the U.S.-backed government of Lon Nol was overthrown by the communists, the Khmer Rouge, headed by the notorious Pol Pot. During the conflict, another 150,000 Cambodians were killed. And then the real purge began. Driven by their communist ideology, the Khmer Rouge emptied out the urban areas, including the capital, Phnom Penh, taking the populations into rural areas to specially constructed camps where they worked, under duress, for the party.

All the opposition was killed. All protesters were killed. Anyone who was thought to be a potential problem was killed. Anyone known to be well educated—doctors, lawyers, teachers—was killed. Anyone known to wear glasses (and thought, therefore, to be educated and a potential problem) was killed. Many others died from disease and starvation. By the time Pol Pot's regime was finished, it had killed off some two million people.

When Pol Pot's toll is added to the total of those killed during the U.S. bombings and the subsequent civil war, we find that nearly half the population of Cambodia had been killed, most of them in very ugly ways.

The survivor I came to know was named Marcei Noun, and I met him almost purely by accident. When I had finished serving as the pastor of the Princeton Baptist Church in Princeton, New Jersey (they eventually found a permanent pastor), I moved off to worship in a nearby church, which happened to be Lutheran. I knew some of the people there and appreciated the rich liturgical emphasis of the church, which stood in sharp contrast with the rather bare liturgy of the Baptist church. But after having been actively involved in churches for many years before that—as a youth pastor, a director of Christian education, and then a pastor—I felt somewhat at a loss and had a burning desire to *do* something that could make a difference, rather than simply attend church once a week.

I was at a point in my life where I was starting to have serious doubts about my faith, both because of my historical research into the origins of Christianity and, perhaps more so, because of my sense of the unfairness and injustice in the world—the problem of suffering. In any event, these various motivations led me to look into doing something more in the line of social work, not as a career (I was already teaching a full load in the Department of Religion at Rutgers University) but as something to do on the side. I learned through my new church of the existence of the Lutheran Social Services, which among other things had a program that involved teaching English as a second language to recent immigrants to the United States. That struck me as just the sort of thing I was looking for: an activity through which I might make a difference to the world, if only in a very small way, and without a lot of religious entanglements. So I signed up.

I was given Marcei Noun's name and told where he lived, in a rundown part of Trenton a half-hour's distance from my house. I called him on the phone and managed through his very broken English to set up a time to come see him. We met, he introduced me to his wife, Sufi, also Cambodian, and their two teenaged children. Marcei was eager to improve his English, and so we started that very day.

From then on I went to Marcei's house once a week for several hours. It was not really enough to make the kind of major impact on his spoken English that either of us wanted, but neither of us had much more time to devote to it—I was teaching full time and he had a job as well, working at the Duke Gardens in nearby Somerville, New Jersey. Over time we did make some progress, and I began working with Sufi as well.

This was one of the most gratifying experiences I had had in a very long time, as our relationship developed and our work progressed. At first Marcei was completely deferential toward me—a university professor from the powerful United States of America. But as we got to know each other, he saw me more and more as just another human being, and I became more and more interested in how he had managed to arrive in Trenton as an immigrant from Cambodia.

Eventually he told me his story, and it sounded like something straight out of *The Killing Fields* (a movie that came out just as we were doing our work together). In the mid-1970s Marcei and his family (Sufi and two young children) had been living in Phnom Penh. He was reasonably well educated, was a part-time poet (with a couple of pieces published), and a full-time gardener. When the Khmer Rouge came to drive out the population, he destroyed his glasses and hid all evidence of learning, wisely pretending to be illiterate. The family was forced from its home and driven into the countryside, with millions of others. The worst of it was that they were separated, Marcei to work on a slave farm, Sufi (with the kids) at a tree nursery. Sufi's experience was probably the hardest: she was forced to work outside all day long, no matter what the weather conditions, and compelled to sleep outside as well, often in standing water.

The details of what happened next are both sketchy and complex, but the short of it is that Marcei managed to escape from his forced labor camp in the dark of night; he somehow had a sense of where Sufi and the children were, and he went off to find them. Together they managed to get away and saw as their only chance of survival a treacherous hike over the mountains into Thailand where, they had heard, refugee camps had been set up. Nearly starved and totally exhausted, they made it to a camp and stayed there under international care for a couple of years. Eventually they were chosen for immigration to the United States, helped by the Lutheran Social Services, which located them in Trenton, found them an apartment (cockroach-infested and dirty, but for them it was like heaven on earth), helped Marcei get a job, got the kids into school, and checked in on them regularly to make sure they were adjusting to their new life.

They were adjusting extremely well. When I got to know them a year or two later, they had met other Cambodians in Trenton and had a solid social network. Marcei made enough money working at the gardens (he put in as much overtime as they would allow) for them to live cheaply but, for them, reasonably well. Sufi had herself gotten a part-time job. The kids were learning English at a fantastic rate (they were virtually fluent when I met them as young teenagers; they certainly had the American slang down). They were even able to save money to send to relatives back in Cambodia.

Later, when I moved away from New Jersey in 1988, they cooked me a final Cambodian meal and went out of their way to express their gratitude for my help. But I had done almost nothing—I'd simply shown up on their doorstep once a week to help them with

English and to help them understand, and operate better in, the American system. What they had given me was beyond calculation. And yet, at the end of our relationship, I was still in awe of what they had been through and how they had managed. Their suffering could be seen in their faces; they still had nightmares about their experiences; they still were reluctant to say much about them and never, apparently, talked about them among themselves.

How can human beings—in this case, the ruthless devotees of the Khmer Rouge (many of them mere children, but children with assault weapons)—treat other human beings in this way? It would have been absurd for me to think that Marcei and his family had gone through this as a punishment for their sin. While they were working in slave labor camps and sleeping in standing water, I was getting an education, driving a car, living in a nice apartment, drinking beer and watching baseball on the weekends. Marcei wasn't any more of a sinner than I was. The classical view of suffering just didn't work, for me, as an explanation for what actually happens in this world.

There are, of course, other explanations for why people suffer, and the Bible itself provides some of them. Somewhat ironically, one of the other answers to the question of why people suffer is found in the writings of the very prophets who think that suffering (sometimes? often?) comes as a penalty from God for disobedience. These writers also indicate that suffering comes from disobedience in another sense. Often "sin" leads to suffering, not because God is punishing the sinner but because other sinners are causing affliction. Suffering is often portrayed in the Bible simply as a consequence of sin.

## The Consequences of Sin According to the Prophets

Even from our earlier discussion of the prophetic understanding of suffering, you will have noticed that the prophets often describe suffering that comes *not* from God as a manifestation of God's wrath, but as the infliction of pain by some human beings on others. The reason for God's wrath in the first place is that people have broken God's law. Sometimes this involves what we might think of as purely religious transgressions—for example, when the people of Israel commit idolatry by worshiping gods such as the Baal of the Canaanite pantheon. At other times, though, sin involves social transgressions, in which people abuse, oppress, and otherwise harm other people, causing *them* (the victims) to suffer. The classical understanding of suffering is that God makes people suffer (by punishment) when they cause others to suffer (through oppression).

This is the biblical analogy to what happens when an adult today spanks a child (doing him violence) for hitting another child (doing him violence). The punished child suffers, of course, from the parent's blows. But the innocent child who was first hit suffers as well, not from the parent as punishment but from the child who decided to strike out in the first place. So too in the biblical traditions: people who sin afflict their innocent victims.

We have already seen instances of this in the prophetic writings we have examined. The eighth-century prophet Amos, in particular, was incensed by the social injustices he observed in his world. You'll recall that his world was one of relative peace and tranquillity. Amos wrote in the middle of the eighth century BCE, before the devastations to be brought by the Assyrian armies had occurred (the fall of Samaria was in 722 BCE). There was prosperity in Israel, the northern kingdom, during this time of peace. But as often happens in situations of prosperity, there was a good deal of misery as well—in no small measure because the rich were increasing their wealth at the expense of the poor. The problems of wealth inequality are not limited to capitalist societies of the modern West. They may be more obvious to us living here and now, and they may seem more insidious (when one compares what a CEO of a major corporation makes in comparison with the lowest-paid workers). But in almost every economic system known on earth, the problems can be seen—and felt, if you are on the short end of the stick.

In any event, Amos took to task those who were acquiring and using their wealth in ways contrary to the will of the God, who was to be their guide in how to live. He condemned those "who sell the righteous for silver and the needy for a pair of sandals ... who trample the head of the poor into the dust of the earth and push the afflicted out of the way" (2:6–7). He maligned those who "trample on the poor and take from them levies of grain ... who afflict the righteous, who take a bribe, and push aside the needy in the gate" (5:1–11). He pointed in particular to a group of well-to-do women who lived in the capital city, Samaria, likening them to a herd of overfed and greedy cattle (Bashan was known for its abundant livestock):

> Hear this word, you cows of
>        Bashan
>     who are on Mount Samaria,
> who oppress the poor, who crush
>        the needy,
>     who say to their husbands,
>        "Bring something to
>        drink!" (Amos 4:1)

Every time I read this passage I imagine an heiress to millions sitting in a lounge chair by her outdoor pool, asking her "dawlin' husband" for another daiquiri.

Why are these "cows of Bashan" to take notice of Amos's reproach? Because their end will not be pleasant:

> The Lord God has sworn by his
>        holiness:
>     The time is surely coming upon
>        you,
>     when they shall take you away
>        with hooks,

even the last of you with
    fishhooks.
Through breaches in the wall you
    shall leave,
    each one straight ahead. (Amos 4:2–3)

Amos thinks that those who oppress the poor will be punished by God, when the enemy attacks the city, destroys its walls, and takes its wealthy inhabitants away, through the breaches in the wall, in single file, not linked together by chains around the wrists, but by massive hooks through their mouths. It is a vicious image, one that portrays the prophetic view of God's punishment graphically. But what about the *reasons* for the punishment? It is not God who oppresses the poor and needy. It is the rich. Suffering comes not only from God but also from others.

The other prophets we have examined agree. For Isaiah it is the rulers of the people who are especially culpable: "Your princes are rebels and companions of thieves. Everyone loves a bribe and runs after it. They do not defend the orphan, and the widow's cause does not come before them" (Isa. 1:23). Or again:

The LORD enters into judgment
    with the elders and princes of his people:
It is you who have devoured the
    vineyard;
    the spoil of the poor is in your
      houses.
What do you mean by crushing
    my people,
    by grinding the face of the
      poor? says the LORD GOD of hosts. (Isa. 3:14–15)

So too the prophet Jeremiah:

> For scoundrels are found among
>     my people;
>   they take over the goods of
>       others ...
> Like a cage full of birds,
>   their houses are full of
>       treachery;
> therefore they have become great
>     and rich,
>   they have grown fat and sleek.
> They know no limits in deeds of
>     wickedness;
>   they do not judge with justice
> the cause of the orphan, to make
>     it prosper,
> and they do not defend the
>     rights of the needy.
> Shall I not punish them for these
>     things?
>                 says the LORD. (Jer. 5:26–29)

God may get the last word, punishing the sinners. But in the meantime, the hungry go hungry, the needy are made needier, the poor get poorer, the defenseless have no one to defend them. This is suffering caused not by God but by people.

## The Consequences of Sin in the Historical Books

When people today say that the Bible is a "very human book," they tend to mean something about its authorship and ultimate authority—that rather than coming from the hands of God, it comes from human authors, authors with different views, perspectives, biases, ideas, likes, dislikes, and contexts. Others, of course, think that the

Bible is a "completely divine" book, meaning, in most cases, that ultimately it is God who is behind the writing of the various books of prophecy, history, poetry, and so on. Wherever people stand on that theological question, there is one sense in which I think everyone can agree that the Bible is a very human book. Its historical sections contain numerous accounts of people who act in all-too-human ways, sometimes living righteously but also sometimes sinning with gusto, not just striving to please God but also striving to oppose him with all their being, not just seeking to help others but also trying to hurt, oppress, maim, mutilate, torture, and kill others. The biblical authors did not shy away from presenting human existence as it is, and much of the time the resultant picture is not attractive.

Apart from religious faux pas like committing idolatry or breaking the sabbath, most "sins" in Scripture involve people harming other people. Most of the Ten Commandments involve personal relations: Israelites are not to murder one another (it is apparently all right to murder Canaanites), to steal from one another, or to want very much to steal (covet) someone's donkey or wife (these laws are patriarchally oriented, and women are often seen as the "property" of men). The historical narratives deal with violations of these laws and many others like them.

The first act of disobedience committed by human beings, of course, did not directly harm anyone else. Adam and Eve ate the forbidden fruit in the Garden of Eden. The results of this disobedience were bad: they were driven from the garden, the descendants of the woman were to experience excruciating pain during childbirth, and the descendants of the man were doomed to toil and labor with the sweat of their brow to provide adequate food. But these results were *punishments* for the sin; the sin itself had no effect on anyone else. Of course, there wasn't anyone else around to affect, but that's a different matter.

Also a different matter is what happened next. The primeval couple has two sons, Cain and Abel. Cain becomes a farmer and Abel a shepherd, and they both bring offerings to God from the fruit of their labor (Gen. 4). God prefers the animal sacrifice of Abel to the grain sacrifice of Cain (for some unexplained reason); Cain is angry (as one might understand) and decides to do something about it. Rather than make a second attempt with an animal sacrifice, he decides to sacrifice his brother, in a sense, and out of anger rises up and murders him (Gen. 4). In the context of the historical narrative of the Pentateuch, this can be seen as a kind of natural outcome of the first act of disobedience in the garden. Sin leads to sin, and the more heinous comes on the heels of the less. Why is Cain's fratricide more heinous than his parents' tasting of the fruit? Because Adam and Eve sinned against God, but Cain sinned against both God and his brother. Abel is the first direct victim of sin, brutally murdered by his own brother. The stage is set for the human drama. From here on out, sin will be a matter affecting not only human beings' relationship with God, but also their relationship with others, the objects of their willful and violent acts.

Such stories continue, of course, to the end of Genesis and on through the other historical narratives of Scripture. At the beginning of the next book, Exodus, when the twelve sons of Jacob have become a great nation in the land of Egypt, they are enslaved and put into forced-labor camps. They are under whip and lash, compelled to build cities of brick, eventually having to find their own building materials and being severely punished for not keeping production levels high. Jewish midwives are ordered to murder every newborn male to prevent the proliferation of the race (Exod. 1). All of this comes not as punishment for the sins of Israel but as a direct consequence of having "a Pharaoh who did not know Joseph" (Exod. 1:8), one who was ruthless in his designs.

It is not just the godless outsiders who cause suffering, though. Once the Israelites are brought out of their slavery in Egypt, they are given the promised land—a gift difficult to accept, of course, since someone already inhabited the land. To be "given" it meant taking it by force. And so the Israelite attack begins with the fortified city of Jericho, whose walls are demolished and whose entire population is slaughtered—every man, woman, and child in the city (Josh. 6). Now you might think that this is the judgment of God against the city and its inhabitants, but nothing in the text actually indicates this. The entire point of the narrative is that God wanted the children of Israel to inhabit the land, and to do so they had to get rid of the previous inhabitants. But what about the innocents in Jericho, the two-year-old girls toddling around their yards and their six-month-old brothers? Slaughtered on the spot. For the God of Israel, evidently, this was not a sin.

But the same cannot be said of the slaughter of other infants—for example, in the most famous instance from the New Testament, when the coming of the infant Lord into the world leads to the so-called slaughter of the innocents. The story is told only in Matthew (recall: I'm dealing here with biblical understandings of suffering—*not* with what "actually" happened; there is, in fact, no evidence that this event took place historically). After Jesus' birth the wise men come looking for him, led by a star (which evidently is giving them only general cues at first, since they have to make inquiries). When King Herod discovers that a new king has been born, he is understandably distressed; it is his throne, after all, that is up for grabs. In an attempt to circumvent the divine will, he sends for the troops and instructs them to murder every boy two years and younger in Bethlehem. They do as the king demands, and there was much weeping and wailing:

> A voice was heard in Ramah,
>     wailing and loud lamentation,
> Rachel weeping for her children;
>     she refused to be consoled, because they were no more.
>     (Matt. 2:18, quoting Jer. 31:15)

Originally, this saying referred to the time when the northern kingdom of Israel was destroyed and its inhabitants exiled by the Assyrians—a time of much wailing over the loss of human life. Matthew, however, sees the text as being "fulfilled" in the events surrounding

Jesus' birth. To that extent, one might look upon Herod's murderous actions as a kind of fulfillment of prophecy—that is, as according to the divine will. But there is nothing to suggest that these poor infants of Bethlehem had it coming to them. This is human brutality of the highest order.

One that matches it for sheer horror comes to us from the historical narratives of the Hebrew Bible, that infamous chapter 19 of Judges. There is a man from the tribe of Levi who lived in the northern part of the land, in Ephraim. He has a concubine—a kind of "wife" of secondary legal standing—who gets angry, apparently at how he has treated her, and returns to her home in Bethlehem in Judah. After four months, the man goes off to retrieve her, tracks her down, and stays for a few days in her father's house before heading home with her. On the way back, they need to find a place to stay the night and decide to try the town of Gibeah, north of Jerusalem, in the territory of Benjamin. They are taken in by a stranger, an old man who has seen them and offered hospitality.

And then the horror begins. After dark, "the men of the city, a perverse lot, surrounded the house, and started to pound on the door" (Judg. 19:22). They demand that the old man send his visitor outside so that they can gang-rape him. This would be not only a sexual crime but also a social one: by ancient codes of hospitality, by bringing the Levite under his roof the old man has responsibility for him and can't let him suffer. The concubine and the old man's virgin daughter are another story. They are, after all, merely women. The old man shouts to the townspeople through the door, "No, my brothers, do not act so wickedly. Since this man is my guest, do not do this vile thing. Here are my virgin daughter and his concubine; let me bring them out now. Ravish them and do whatever you want to them; but against this man do not do such a vile thing" (Judg. 19:23–24). The men outside, however, want the visitor. To save his own skin, the Levite grabs his concubine and thrusts her out the door. And then the unspeakable happens. The men of the city "wantonly raped her, and abused her all through the night until the morning." In the morning, she crawls up onto the doorstep and there, evidently, she dies of the abuse (or at least loses consciousness).

The Levite gets out of bed—we're not told, but evidently he had a decent night's sleep—and prepares to go on his way. He goes outside, sees his concubine there, and tells her, "Get up, we are going." When he sees that she is dead, he loads her on his donkey and returns to his home. And then the truly bizarre event of the narrative takes place. The Levite takes a knife and cuts the concubine into twelve pieces, limb from limb, and sends the pieces by messenger to the leaders of each of the twelve tribes of Israel, in order to show what has happened. This evidently is a call to war. The tribes gather together to attack the tribe of Benjamin, within which this crime has occurred, and in the ensuing war they nearly destroy the entire tribe (Judg. 20–21).

The Deuteronomistic historian who recounts this tale does so, in part, to show the rank immorality and unspeakable evil that transpired in the land "when there was no king in Israel" (Judg. 19:1). He will go on, in the chapters that follow, to show how God intervened to provide a king for his people, in part to control their sinful inclinations.

But not even the kings could bring sin under control. The degradation associated with human abuse of others continues under the kings—in fact, it is caused even by the kings themselves. And so there is the story of David and Bathsheba (2 Sam. 11). From the roof of his palace in Jerusalem David sees a beautiful woman, Bathsheba, bathing next door. He wants to have her, and since he is the king, no one can stop him. She is brought into the palace, they have sex, and as fate would have it, she becomes pregnant. The problem, of course, is that she is already married to someone else, and not only that, but this someone else, a man named Uriah, is off at war, fighting battles as a faithful soldier for his good king David, who has secretly seduced his wife. What is David to do? If word gets out, there will be a scandal, since Uriah himself is obviously not responsible for his wife's pregnancy (it's been a long war).

David hatches a plan to bring Uriah back from the front lines for a brief furlough—just long enough for him to have sex with Bathsheba. But faithful soldier that he is, Uriah refuses to enjoy the pleasures of the flesh while his colleagues are engaged in hand-to-hand combat. A frustrated David decides that Uriah has to die, and he makes an arrangement with the general in charge of the troops to put Uriah in the front line and to have everyone else pull back during an attack so that Uriah will be hacked apart by the enemy with no one to help him. It happens. Uriah dies. David marries Bathsheba. And life goes on. But not for Uriah, an innocent killed by a king who couldn't keep his pants buttoned.

David's son Solomon is another case in point. Solomon is best known for being the "wisest man ever to have lived" and for his amazing building projects—including most notably, the Temple in Jerusalem, his own palace, and other major undertakings in various cities throughout his realm (1 Kings 6–9). How exactly, though, does a king build so many fine structures? Does he find a subcontractor to hire out the jobs to the lowest bidder? No, not in ancient Israel. These projects are labor-intensive (no land-moving equipment, cranes, or electric tools), and for major work, one needs lots of bodies. And so Solomon provides lots of bodies—by enslaving large numbers of his own people for the job. For the Temple he "conscripted forced labor" to the tune of thirty thousand men, along with seventy thousand other laborers in the hill country, and eighty thousand stonecutters (1 Kings 5:13–18). Later we're told that these were not actually Israelites, but other peoples—Hittites, Perizzites, Hivites, and Jebusites—who had not been driven from the land when it was conquered (1 Kings 9:15–22). I think that is supposed to make us feel better about Solomon: he didn't enslave anyone descended from the tribes of Israel, just people of other ancestry.

## The Consequences of Sin in the New Testament

The Christian New Testament, of course, is no stranger to the effects of sinful human behavior on others. The central message of the New Testament is that Jesus brings a restored relationship with God, and nearly all of its authors understood that it was precisely the crucifixion of Jesus that brought this salvation. Authors like Paul focus on the significance of Jesus' crucifixion (1 Cor. 2:2; Gal. 3:1), but to the surprise of many modern readers, they say almost nothing about the event itself. Not even the Gospels, which tell stories of Jesus' life and death, indicate what happened at the crucifixion other than to say "and they crucified him" (see Mark 15:24). This seems odd to people who have seen movies about Jesus—most notoriously, Mel Gibson's *The Passion of the Christ*—that, we are told, give an "accurate account" of what the Gospels have to say about Jesus' death. But in precise *contrast* to the Gospels, such movies focus on the blood and gore, the torture and the torment, the pain and agony—exactly those aspects of Jesus' death that the Gospel writers never deal with, let alone explicate in long, detailed narratives that give a blow-by-blow account.

One reason the biblical authors do not explain what happened at the crucifixion may be that their readers knew full well what crucifixion meant and how it was done, and so didn't need to be told about it. It is striking that the Gospel writers are not alone in that. We have *no* detailed descriptions from the ancient world of what it meant for someone to be crucified. And so the modern ideas and portrayals of the crucifixion have to be based on scattered references and allusive statements found here and there in ancient sources.

What we do know is that death by crucifixion was not a happy sight. The Romans reserved this mode of execution for the lowest of criminals and seditionists, individuals they wanted to humiliate and publicly torture to the death as a kind of disincentive to crime and sedition. The Roman view of justice was very different from ours. We are concerned about due process, trial by jury, the possibility of appeal, and that sentences be carried out in private, away from the public eye. The Romans believed in public deterrents. If they had a problem with carjacking (which, of course, they didn't), they would simply round up a few of the culprits and nail them to crosses in public view, where they would hang for a couple of days before finally dying in excruciating agony. *Then* see how many people were inclined to rip off a car.

Crucifixion was evidently a death by asphyxiation, not blood loss. A criminal would be fastened either to a wooden upright or to a cross beam that would be attached to an upright, either tied or nailed through the wrists (not through the hands, or the nails might rip out) and sometimes through the feet. This naturally rendered the victim completely helpless against the elements, scavenging birds and animals, torments of thirst, and so on. Death came as the weight of the body forced the torso to distend, making it impossible to breathe. The crucified could relieve the pressure on the lungs by pulling up on the nails in the wrists or pushing up with the ankles. Sometimes a board was provided to sit on. That's why it could take days for crucifixion to work—and that's how the Romans wanted it (they, by the way, did not invent this method of execution, although they did use it a lot). The whole idea was to make death as painful, humiliating, and public as possible. Jesus' death, then, would have been like the death of many, many others in his time; two others were crucified just that morning with him in Jerusalem; we have no idea how many might have died that way at the same time throughout the empire. Or the next day or the day after. Altogether, there were many thousands who suffered the same fate.

In the New Testament, of course, Jesus' death is seen not simply as the evil workings of an unjust Roman state. It is seen also as the will of God. Nonetheless the New Testament authors were quite insistent that even though God effected something good out of the death of Jesus—something *very* good: the salvation of the world—the people who perpetrated the crime were still responsible. Sin has its ugly consequences in the suffering of others.

The same can be said of other instances of torturous treatments and horrible deaths in the New Testament. In the book of Acts, for example, the first Christian martyr is a man named Stephen who offends the Jewish authorities in Jerusalem and so is stoned to death (Acts 7). Stoning also was not—and is not (it is still practiced in some places)—a pleasant way to go. Rocks fly in, most of them missing anything vital but all of them causing enormous pain. They break bones and rupture organs, until some finally strike the head with enough force and accuracy to bring unconsciousness and then death.

We have one author who indicates that he was subjected to a stoning but lived to tell the tale—the apostle Paul. In the book of Acts there is a narrative account of Paul being stoned, but critical historians tend to doubt the historical accuracy of Acts' narratives, since they appear to have been constructed some thirty years after the events they describe by someone who had not witnessed those events. In the Acts account, Paul is preaching the gospel of Christ in the city of Lystra in Asia Minor (modern Turkey) when he incites the anger of his opponents among the non-Christian Jews. They stone him, drag him outside the city, and leave him for dead. After they leave, he gets up and goes on to the next city, as if nothing had happened to him (Acts 14:19–20). This account suits quite well the theological purposes of Acts—in this book nothing can stop Paul, because God is behind him and his mission. You can't keep a good man down.

Paul himself does allude to the event (or a similar one), but again without explicating the details. In one of the most interesting passages in his letters, Paul is trying to convince his converts in the city of Corinth that he is a true apostle, not because he is filled with supernatural power but because he suffers. A lot. For Paul, the more an apostle suffers, the more he is shown to be a true apostle. Jesus himself, after all, did not lead a charmed life with lots of luxury and popular acclaim. He was rejected, despised, and eventually crucified like a lowly criminal. For Paul, to be an apostle of Christ means to share his fate. He is writing this to the Corinthians because some of them are convinced that the power of God is at work in their midst making them rise above the petty concerns and cares of this world. For Paul, if they have it easy, they are not true apostles. And so Paul emphasizes his suffering:

> Are they [i.e., his Christian opponents, the counterapostles] ministers of Christ? I am talking like a madman—I am a better one: with far greater labors, far more imprisonments, with countless floggings, and often near death. Five times I have received from the Jews the forty lashes minus one. Three times I was beaten with rods. Once I received a stoning. Three times I was shipwrecked; for a night and a day I was adrift at sea; on frequent journeys, in ... danger from bandits, danger from my own people, danger from the Gentiles ... danger from false brothers and sisters. (2 Cor. 11:23–26)

And he goes on. His point is that suffering shows that he is closely aligned with Christ. For our purposes, his "suffering list" shows that for Paul there was a lot of evil in the world, and that people could not expect to be removed from the wicked and godless behavior of others.

Still other accounts of human pain and misery are intimated in the New Testament. Like the accounts of the crucifixion, they are not narrated at great length, in part because readers of the day may already have known enough for the mere mention of an incident to conjure up a mental image of suffering in extremis. Take, for example, Jesus' "prediction" in Luke's Gospel that Jerusalem would one day be besieged and conquered by the Romans:

> When you see Jerusalem surrounded by armies, then know that its desolation is near. Then those who are in Judea should flee to the mountains, and those inside the city must leave it, and those out in the country must not enter it; for these are days of vengeance that will fulfill everything that is written. Woe to those who are pregnant and those who are nursing children in those days. For great will be the distress upon the earth and the anger upon this people. They will fall by the edge of the sword and be led captive to all the nations, and Jerusalem will be trampled by the nations, until the times of the nations are fulfilled. (Luke 21:20–24)

Critical historians have long thought that this description was composed after the fact, that Luke, writing after the fall of Jerusalem in 70 CE, knew full well what had happened and what it was like. He does not, however, give a full account of the suffering inflicted upon the Jewish inhabitants of Jerusalem when the Roman general Titus laid the city under siege in an attempt to quell a violent uprising against Rome. We do have an account of what it was like during the siege, however, from an extrabiblical source, the Jewish historian Josephus, who was present at the siege and also knew Jews who survived it.

According to Josephus, things got very bad within the walls of the city: there were periodic bloody coups, daily murders, and massive starvation. The food shortage became so severe that family members were known to steal food from one another, from the very mouths of the weak. In the most horrendous account he provides, Josephus indicates that one woman, in the throes of desperate hunger, murdered her infant son and cooked him in her oven. She ate half of his body right away. When some men passing by the house smelled the roasting flesh, they came in to steal her meat. She showed them the half-consumed body and told them to go ahead and eat what was there. In horror they left her alone with the corpse of her partially eaten son, trembling as they went off to find food elsewhere.[1]

The siege of Jerusalem was cruel. This woman's heinous act was cruel. She suffered; her son suffered. And this is only one of millions of stories of unfathomable sufferings, brought on by human beings against human beings.

## Reactions to Suffering

How did writers of Scripture react when they, or others they knew, experienced horrible suffering at the hands of others? As you might imagine, there was a huge array of reactions, just as there is among people today: outrage, grief, frustration, helplessness. Some writers thought that suffering only made them stronger; some wanted God to avenge their pain by inflicting pain on others; others saw their misery as a test of their faith; and still others saw it as a sign that the end of time would soon arrive.

Some of the most striking reactions occur in the writings of Jeremiah, a prophet that we have already briefly considered. Jeremiah is often called "the suffering prophet"[2] because of the opposition and persecution he endured. Jeremiah wrote his prophecies, in part, during the time that the southern kingdom of Judah was under Babylonian attack. Many of the inhabitants of Jerusalem believed that the city was inviolable: that since God himself dwelt in the Temple in Jerusalem, the Temple built by Solomon some four hundred years earlier, God would protect it, and the people who worshiped in it, from any harm. Jeremiah took just the opposite view, arguing that the Temple would bring no security (see especially Jeremiah 7) and insisting that if the people wanted to survive the Babylonian onslaught, they should surrender to the enemy.

These were not popular teachings, and as a result Jeremiah suffered both verbal abuse and physical persecution. His reactions to his sufferings are found in a number of poetic "laments" scattered throughout chapters 11–20. Like others who have suffered horribly, Jeremiah sometimes wishes he had never been born (cf. Job 3):

Cursed be the day
    on which I was born!
The day when my mother bore
        me,
    let it not be blessed!
Cursed be the man
    who brought the news to my
        father, saying,
"A child is born to you, a son,"
    making him very glad.
Let that man be like the cities
    that the LORD overthrew
        without pity;

let him hear a cry in the morning
   and an alarm at noon,
because he did not kill me in the
      womb;
   so my mother would have been
      my grave,
   and her womb forever great.
Why did I come forth from the
      womb
   to see toil and sorrow,
      and spend my days in shame? (Jer. 20:14–18)

At other times, Jeremiah prays for divine wrath to descend upon his enemies, who schemed evil against him in his complete ignorance:

But I was like a gentle lamb
   led to the slaughter.
And I did not know it was against
      me
   that they devised schemes,
      saying,
"Let us destroy the tree with its
      fruit,
   let us cut him off from the land
      of the living,
   so that his name will no longer
      be remembered!"
But you, O LORD of hosts, who
      judge righteously,
   who try the heart and the mind,
let me see your retribution upon
      them,
   for to you I have committed my
      cause. (Jer. 11:19–20)

Such reactions will sound familiar to avid readers of the book of Psalms, which contains a number of "laments," that is, psalms that complain to God about the author's suffering and implore him to do something about it, or express a sense of trust that he will do so. Many of these psalms drip with pathos, making them favorite biblical passages of those who themselves are overtaken by personal adversity.

> Be gracious to me, O LORD, for I
>           am languishing;
>      O LORD, heal me, for my bones
>           are shaking with terror.
> My soul also is struck with terror,
>      while you, O LORD—how long?
> Turn, O LORD, save my life;
>      deliver me for the sake of your
>           steadfast love....
> I am weary with my moaning;
>      every night I flood my bed with
>           tears;
>      I drench my couch with my
>           weeping.
> My eyes waste away because of
>           grief;
>      they grow weak because of all
>           my foes.
> Depart from me, all you workers
>           of evil,
>      for the LORD has heard the
>           sound of my weeping.
> The LORD has heard my
>           supplication;
>      the LORD accepts my prayer.
> All my enemies shall be ashamed
>           and struck with terror;

they shall turn back, and in a
moment be put to shame. (Ps. 6:2–4, 6–10)

Some of these Psalms are even more explicitly prayers that God will inflict horrible judgments upon the author's enemies. These are not written by those who believe in turning the other cheek; they are eager for vengeance to be executed.

O God, do not keep silence;
do not hold your peace or be
still, O God!
Even now your enemies are in
tumult;
those who hate you have raised
their heads.
They lay crafty plans against your
people;
they consult together against
those you protect.
They say, "Come, let us wipe
them out as a nation;
let the name of Israel be
remembered no more." . . .
O my God, make them like
whirling dust,
like chaff before the wind.
As fire consumes the forest,
as the flame sets the mountains
ablaze,
so pursue them with your tempest
and terrify them with your
hurricane.
Fill their faces with shame,
so that they may seek your
name, O Lord.

Let them be put to shame and
dismayed forever;
let them perish in disgrace.
Let them know that you alone,
whose name is the LORD,
are the Most High over all the
earth. (Ps. 83:1–4, 13–18)

Nowhere is the pathos more gripping or the plea more vitriolic
than in Psalm 137, written at the time of the Babylonian exile by
one who desperately longed to return to his homeland and who
urged God to take vengeance on his enemies—even on their infant
children.

By the rivers of Babylon—
there we sat down and there we
wept
when we remembered Zion.
On the willow there
we hung up our harps.
For there our captors
asked us for songs,
and our tormentors asked for
mirth, saying,
"Sing us one of the songs of
Zion!"
How could we sing the LORD's
song
in a foreign land?
If I forget you, O Jerusalem,
let my right hand wither!
Let my tongue cling to the roof of
my mouth,
if I do not remember you,
if I do not set Jerusalem
above my highest joy.

Remember O LORD, against the
    Edomites
  the day of Jerusalem's fall,
how they said, "Tear it down!
    Tear it down!
  Down to its foundations!"
O daughter Babylon, you
    devastator!
  Happy shall they be who pay
    you back
  what you have done to us!
Happy shall they be who take
    your little ones
  and dash them against the rock! (Ps. 137:1–9)

Most of the laments, however, are not related to the national catastrophe of exile but to personal (almost never specified) anguish
caused by others. One of these psalms became particularly well
known in Christian circles because it was regarded as a messianic
prophecy of what would happen to Jesus at his crucifixion. As with
Isaiah 53, however, it is important not only to see how later readers
might have interpreted the psalm but also to think about what the
text might have meant in its own context—in this case the context
of an individual within Israel who felt forsaken by God and perse-
cuted by others.

My God, my God, why have you
    forsaken me?
  Why are you so far from
    helping me, from the
    words of my groaning?
O my God, I cry by day, but you
    do not answer;
  and by night, but find no rest....
... I am a worm, and not human;
    scorned by others, and despised

by the people.
All who see me mock at me;
      they make mouths at me, they
            shake their heads;
"Commit your cause to the LORD;
            let him deliver—
      let him rescue the one in whom
            he delights!"...
Many bulls encircle me,
      strong bulls of Bashan surround
            me;
they open wide their mouths at
            me,
      like a ravening and roaring lion.
I am poured out like water,
      and all my bones are out of
            joint;
my heart is like wax;
      it is melted within my breast;
my mouth is dried up like a
            potsherd,
      and my tongue sticks to my
            jaws;
      you lay me in the dust of death.
For dogs are all around me;
      a company of evildoers encircles
            me.
My hands and feet have
            shriveled;
I can count all my bones.
They stare and gloat over me;
they divide my clothes among
            themselves,
      and for my clothing they cast
            lots.

But you, O LORD, do not be far
> away!
O my help, come quickly to my
> aid!
Deliver my soul from the sword,
> my life from the power of the
> dog!
Save me from the mouth of the
> lion! (Ps. 22:1–21)

This notion that the hatreds, oppositions, and persecutions of others affect the faithful—so that suffering comes not only from God as a punishment, but also from human beings who violate his will—and the concomitant sense that God is the one who can save people from their suffering, is found not only throughout the pages of the Hebrew Bible, of course, but in the New Testament as well. As a concluding example I return to the writings of Paul, the apostle who suffered in order to be like his Lord, but who trusted in God to deliver him from his distress. As he tells his fellow Christians in the city of Corinth:

> Brothers, we do not want you not to know about the affliction that happened to us in Asia. For we were overwhelmed beyond all that can be imagined, so that we despaired even of life itself. But we held within ourselves a death sentence, so that we might not trust in ourselves, but in God, the one who raises the dead. He who delivered us from so great a death will save us yet again; it is in him that we hope, that he will save us again. (2 Cor. 1:8–10)

## The Consequences of Sin: An Assessment

While I've been writing this chapter, I've continually been thinking that it is all so obvious, and I've imagined my friends reading it and telling me that all these hours I've spent on it (there are only so many hours allotted to us in this life, after all) have been a complete waste of time. *Of course* people suffer because other people behave badly toward them. Where's the revelation in *that*?

At the same time, I know that there are lots of religious people in the world who think that everything that happens—the good and the bad—comes directly (or sometimes indirectly) from God. And on this some of the biblical authors would agree.

This latter view actually raises a rather paradoxical situation, well known to people who have wrestled with theological conundrums over the years: if people do bad things because God ordains them to do them, why are they held responsible? If Adam and Eve were foreordained to eat the fruit, why were they punished for it? If Judas betrayed Jesus and Pilate crucified him because that was God's will, how can they be held accountable? If the enemies of David or the enemies of Paul did what they did because of the divine oversight—who really is to blame?

As it turns out, none of the biblical authors deals directly with this kind of paradox. God is typically portrayed as the all-powerful Sovereign of this world who foreknows all things, yet human beings are portrayed as responsible for their actions. Even though the coming of the Antichrist is a preordained event, the Lake of Fire is being stoked up to await his arrival.

The fact that people are held responsible for their actions—from Adam and Eve, to Cain and Abel, to David and Solomon, to Judas and Pilate, to the Antichrist and his minions—shows that the biblical authors had *some* notion of free will. That is, this understanding of suffering as the result of sinful human behavior is the closest thing in the Bible to what is known in philosophical circles dealing with the problem of theodicy as "the "free-will" defense." In its simplest form, the philosophical argument goes something like this: If God had not given us free will, this would be a less-than-perfect world, but God wanted to create a perfect world, and so we have free will—both to obey and to disobey him, both to resolve suffering and to cause it. This is why there is suffering in a world controlled ultimately by a God who is both all powerful and all loving.

In discussions of theodicy, this free-will defense can be found as far back as there have been discussions of theodicy. It is the view, in fact, of the seventeenth-century polymath Leibniz, who coined the term *theodicy* in the first place. In modern discourse, the question of theodicy is, How can we possibly believe that an all-powerful and all-loving God exists given the state of the world? In ancient discourse, including the varieties of discourse found in the Hebrew Bible and the New Testament, that was never a question. Ancient Jews and Christians never questioned *whether* God existed. They knew he existed. What they wanted to know was how to *understand* God and how to *relate* to him, given the state of the world. The question of whether suffering impedes belief in the existence of God is completely modern, a product of the Enlightenment.

Enlightenment (and post-Enlightenment) theodicy derives from a modern set of assumptions about the world: for example, that the world is a closed nexus of cause and effect and runs more or less mechanistically following a set of natural "laws"—which, if they're not actually laws (as has become evident in modern studies of physics and the like), at least are highly reliable predictors of natural activity in the world. This modern view of the world probably explains why discussions of theodicy among modern philosophers is so very different from the discussions of suffering found in the biblical writings—or indeed in the writings and reflections of most human beings who think about suffering. I don't know if you've read any of the writings of the modern theodicists, but they are something to behold: precise, philosophically nuanced, deeply thought out, filled with esoteric terminology and finely reasoned explanations for why suffering does not preclude the existence of a divine being of power and love. Frankly, to most of us these writings are not just obtuse, they are disconnected from real life, life as lived in the trenches—the trenches of the First World War, for example, or the concentration camps of the Second World War, or the killing fields of Cambodia. I tend to agree with scholars like Ken Surin—who is easily as brilliant as any of the theodicists he attacks—that many of the attempts to explain evil can, in the end, be morally repugnant. I can even sympathize with theologians like Terrence Tilley, who argues that a believer's response to theodicy should be to renounce it as an intellectual project.[3] For Tilley, the attempt to justify the existence of suffering intellectually is to grapple with the problem on the wrong terms. Suffering, at the end of the day, should not lead merely to an intellectual explanation. It should also lead to a personal response.

Unlike Tilley, I am not a Christian believer. But I do think that there's something wrong with wrestling with problems of suffering as a purely intellectual exercise. Suffering calls for a living response, especially since so much of it is caused not by "natural" events— "acts of God," as they are ironically called by our insurance companies—but by other people. And not just by the Nazis and the Khmer Rouge, who lived in another time or a faraway place, but by people who live across the street from us, or work across the hall from us, people we see at the store and people whom we elect to office and people we pay to head the companies that provide us with our goods and services, people who exploit the workers in the world, and so on.

For me, at the end of the day, the philosophical problem called theodicy is insoluble. At the same time, while the so-called free-will defense can sometimes come across as a sterile philosophical argument, it can also be a powerfully practical one. Human beings hurt, oppress, torment, torture, violate, rape, dismember, and murder others. If ultimately there were a God involved in all this—especially if this God were responsible for all the wicked things that happen—then I suppose there is very little we could do about it. But I don't believe this for a second. The pain done to human beings by human beings is not caused by a superhuman entity. Since human beings misbehave and hurt others out of their free will (which does exist, even if God does not), then we need to intervene ourselves and do what we can to stop the oppression, torture, and murder—whether here at home or in developing countries, where the atrocities are both more blatant and less restricted—and so do what we can to help those who are subject to these abuses of human freedom.

# five

# The Mystery of the Greater Good: Redemptive Suffering

People who have gone through a kind of "deconversion" experience like mine understand how emotionally wrenching it can be. It may be easy to have a good sense of humor about it now that I'm well on the other side of the crisis (a friend of mine says that I went from being "born again" to being "dead again"), but at the time it was extremely traumatic. I went from being a hard-core and committed evangelical Christian who had spent his young adulthood in a fundamentalist Bible college, an evangelical liberal arts college, and a number of Bible-believing churches, to being an agnostic who viewed the Bible as a book produced entirely by human hands, who viewed Jesus as a first-century apocalyptic Jew who was crucified but not raised from the dead, and who viewed the ultimate questions of theology as beyond a human's ability to answer.

I don't know if there is a God. I don't call myself an atheist, because to declare affirmatively that there is no God (the declaration of atheists) takes far more knowledge (and chutzpah) than I have. How would *I* know if there's a God? I'm just a mortal like everyone else. I think what I *can* say is that if (IF!) there is a God, he is not the kind of being that I believed in as an evangelical: a personal deity who has ultimate power over this world and intervenes in human affairs in order to implement his will among us. It is beyond my comprehension that there could be a being like that—in no small part because, frankly, I don't believe that interventions happen. If God cures cancer, then why do millions die of cancer? If the response is that it is a mystery ("God works in mysterious ways"), that is the same as saying that we do *not* know what God does or what he is like. So why pretend we do? If God feeds the hungry, why are people starving? If God takes care of his children, why are thousands of people destroyed by natural disasters every year? Why does the majority of the earth's population suffer in abject poverty?

I no longer believe in a God who is actively involved with the problems of this world. But I used to believe in a God of that sort with all my heart and soul, and I was willing and eager to tell everyone around me all about him. My faith in Christ made me an amateur evangelist, one determined to convert others to belief as well. But now I've deconverted. And I have to say, the deconversion process was not easy or pleasant. As I pointed out in an earlier chapter, I left the faith kicking and screaming.

But what can else could I do? What can *you,* or anyone else, do when you're confronted with facts (or, at least, with what you take to be facts) that contradict your faith? I suppose you could discount the facts, say they don't exist, or do your best to ignore them. But what if you are absolutely committed to being true to yourself and to your understanding of the truth? What if you want to approach your belief with intellectual honesty and to act with personal integrity? I think all of us—even those of us who are agnostics—have to be willing to change our views if we come to think they were wrong after all. But doing so can be very painful.

The pain for me was manifest in lots of ways. One of the hardest things was that I was now at odds with many of those who were near and dear to me—members of my family and close friends—people with whom I had once shared an intimate spiritual bond, with whom I could, before, pray and talk about the big questions of life and death with the full assurance that we were all on the same page. Once I left the faith, that no longer happened, and friends and family started treating me with suspicion, wondering what was wrong with me, why I had changed, why I had "gone over to the dark side." Many of them, I suppose, thought that I had learned too much for my own good, or had opened myself up to the snares of the devil. It's not easy being intimate with someone who thinks you're in cahoots with Satan.

Probably the hardest thing for me to deal with personally involved the very core of what I had believed as an evangelical Christian. I had become "born again" because I wanted "to be saved." Saved from what? Among other things, from the eternal torments of hell. In the view that was given to me, Christ had died for the sins of the world, and anyone who accepted him in faith would have eternal life with him in heaven. All those who did *not* believe in him—whether out of willful refusal or sheer ignorance—would necessarily have to pay for their own sins in hell. Hell was a well-populated place: most people went there. And hell was a place of everlasting torment, which involved the spiritual agony of being separated from God (and hence, all that is good) and the physical agony of real torment in an eternal lake of fire. Roasting in hell was, for me, not a metaphor but a physical reality. No wonder I was so evangelistic in my faith: I didn't want any of my family or friends to experience the fires of hell for all eternity, and so I did everything I could to make sure they accepted Christ and received the free gift of salvation.

This view of hell was driven into me and deeply burned, so to say, onto my consciousness (and, probably, my unconscious). As a result, when I fell away from my faith—not just in the Bible as God's inspired word, but in Christ as the only way of salvation, and eventually from the view that Christ was himself divine, and beyond that from the view that there is an all-powerful God in charge of this world—I still wondered, deep down inside: could I have been right after all? What if I was right then but wrong now? Will I burn in hell forever? The fear of death gripped me for years, and there are still moments when I wake up at night in a cold sweat.

All of this is rooted in a sense of suffering, of course. The evangelical theology I had once held was built on views of suffering: Christ suffered for my sins, so that I would not have to suffer eternally, because God is a righteous judge who punishes for all time those who reject him and the salvation that he has provided. The irony, I suppose, is that it was precisely my view of suffering that led me away from this understanding of Christ, salvation, and God. I came to think that there is not a God who is actively involved with this world of pain and misery—if he is, why doesn't he *do* something about it? Concomitantly, I came to believe that there is not a God who is intent on roasting innocent children and others in hell because they didn't happen to accept a certain religious creed.

Another aspect of the pain I felt when I eventually became an agnostic is even more germane to this question of suffering. It involves another deeply rooted attitude that I have and simply can't get rid of, although in this case, it's an attitude that I don't really want to get rid of. And it's something that I never would have expected to be a problem when I was still a believer. The problem is this: I have such a fantastic life that I feel an overwhelming sense of gratitude for it; I am fortunate beyond words. But I don't have anyone to express my gratitude to. This is a void deep inside me, a void of wanting someone to thank, and I don't see any plausible way of filling it.

I began detecting this as a problem at about the time I was seriously considering becoming an agnostic, and, again, it happened in a way I wouldn't have expected. When I was growing up, my family always said grace before dinner. Often, it was just a little prayer that we kids took turns reciting when we were little: "God is great, God is good, and we thank him for our food." I still think this is a beautiful prayer for its simplicity, in saying just about all that needs to be said. As I got older, the thanks became more sophisticated and the praise more nuanced. But there came a time in my life when I found that I simply could no longer thank God for my food. And the irony is that it was because I came to realize (or, at least, came to think) that if I was thanking God for providing me with my sustenance, and acknowledging that I was fed not because of my own good efforts but because of his gracious actions toward me, then by *implication* I was saying something about those who didn't have food. If I have food because God has given it to me, then don't others lack food because God has chosen *not* to give it to them? By saying grace, wasn't I in fact charging God with negligence, or favoritism? If what I have is because of what he has given me, what about those who are starving to death? I'm surely not all that special in the eyes of the Almighty. Are these others less worthy? Or is he starving them, intentionally? Is the heavenly Father capricious? or mean-spirited? What would we think of an earthly father who starved two of his children and fed only the third even though there was enough food to go around? And what would we think of the fed child expressing her deeply felt gratitude to her father for taking care of her needs, when her two siblings were dying of malnutrition before her very eyes?

There is a lot of starvation in the world. According to reports released by the United Nations (see, e.g., www.wfp.org), about one out of every seven people in the world—that's 850 *million* people—does not have enough food to eat. Every five seconds a child dies of starvation in the world. Every five seconds. A child. I, on the other hand, have way too much to eat. Like most Americans, I'm a bit overweight, and every week I dig through the fridge and find some molding (and often unrecognizable) mass that I've left too long and it's gone bad. Elsewhere on the planet, people are malnourished, famished, starving for want of basic foodstuffs. Every day an average of twenty-five thousand people die because of hunger and poverty-related issues, while I debate whether to grill steaks or ribs, whether to open a microbrew or a nice bottle of Châteauneuf du Pape. There's something wrong with this world.

A natural reaction, of course, is that I should cut way down on what I eat, drink only water (it's clean, after all!), and give the money I save to charities that feed the poor. But the problems are far more complex and cannot be solved that way. If they could, that's certainly what we would do. And I absolutely agree that we—all of us—should give more, more to local charities dealing with homelessness and poverty in our communities, more to national charities dealing with relief efforts around the country, more to international organizations devoted to dealing with hunger on the worldwide scale. Absolutely, we should give more, lots more. And urge our government to give more. And vote to elect officials who see world hunger as a major problem. And on and on.

But even having said that, I'm left with my fundamental dilemma. How can I thank God for all the good things I have while realizing that other people don't have good things? How can I thank God without, by implication, blaming God for the state of the world?

I'm reminded of the scene we have all observed at one time or another on the televised news, when there has been a major airline disaster, a plane wreck with hundreds of people killed, and one of the survivors comes on the air thanking God for being with him and saving him. You wonder what people are thinking—or if they are thinking. God saved *you*? What about those other poor souls who had their arms and legs ripped off and their brains splattered all over the seat next to you? By thanking God for your good fortune, aren't you implicating him for the misfortunes of others?

I'm also reminded of something else you can see on television, not just occasionally but every Sunday morning: slick televangelists who are convinced that God wants the best for your life and who have a nifty twelve-step program—all based on a careful reading of Scripture, of course—that will enable you to enjoy the riches and prosperity that your heavenly Father has in store for you. The amazing thing is how easily people are convinced: God wants them to be rich! God has shown them how! They too, like Pastor X, can receive all the blessings God is eager to bestow on them! Millions of people buy this (or at least pay for it). Look at the megachurches in our country, where tens of thousands of people go every week to hear about God's secrets to successful and prosperous lives. And Jesus wept.

It may be important to remember that Jesus wept. And that Paul suffered. That, in fact, Jesus rebuked his disciples who thought that following him meant the pathway to glory; he told them that being his disciples meant taking up the cross and dying with him a painful and humiliating death. I suppose that message doesn't sell so well these days. Nor does Paul's insistence that the power of God is manifest in weakness, and that it was precisely because he had been flogged, and beaten, and subjected to stoning, shipwreck, and constant danger—that it was because of these things (not his nonexistent material prosperity) that he knew he was a follower of Christ.

The televangelists have it wrong from both a real-life point of view and a New Testament point of view. God doesn't make people rich. Being rich—or at least having enough food in the fridge (which for much of the world would count as incomprehensible prosperity)—is largely serendipitous: it is based on where you were born and the conditions of life that were handed to you, as well as what you do with the opportunities that come your way.

Some of us are lucky. The vast majority of people who have ever lived were and are not. Most have suffered from physical hardship and died without any resolution of the problem. How do we explain that? Or how do we explain the rampant suffering to which the human race has always been subjected?

We have already seen two ways the Bible explains suffering: sometimes suffering comes from God as a punishment for sin; and sometimes it comes from human beings as a consequence of sin. Now we can look at a third solution. Sometimes, for some biblical authors, suffering has a positive aspect to it. Sometimes God brings good out of evil, a good that would not have been possible if the evil had not existed. In this understanding, suffering can sometimes be redemptive. One of the first instances of this teaching is found in Genesis, in an extended passage that involves famine and starvation.

## Redemptive Suffering in the Story of Joseph

The final quarter of the book of Genesis (chapters 37–50) is largely about how God saved the family of the patriarch Jacob (the twelve brothers whose descendants would become the twelve tribes of Israel) from a famine that swept through the land, threatening to destroy its inhabitants, the forebears of the nation of Israel; had the famine succeeded it would have annulled the promise that God had given Jacob's grandfather Abraham, to make of him a great nation (the Jewish people). The story is a bit complicated but wonderfully told. It begins long before the famine with a tragic instance of familial discord in which one of the brothers is abused and sold into slavery—suffering, as we will see, that was all part of the divine plan.

Jacob (whose other name was "Israel") had twelve sons from a variety of wives, back in the days when there was more to worry about than a polygamous relationship here or there; his favorite was Joseph, upon whom he showered special favors, including "a "long robe with sleeves" (traditionally rendered as "a many-colored robe"). Jacob's favoritism stirred up some jealousy among the brothers, all of whom (except Benjamin) were older. The problem was exacerbated when Joseph had two dreams. In the first, he and his brothers were binding sheaves of grain in the field, and all the other sheaves bowed down to his. In the other dream, he saw the sun, moon, and eleven stars bowing down to him. His brothers got the point: Joseph was claiming that one day they (along with his mother and father) would all be subservient to him (Gen. 37:1–11).

The brothers did not much like this idea and, sweet-tempered fellows that they were, decided to kill Joseph (Gen. 37:18–20). Brother Reuben urged them, however, not to kill Joseph but to cast him into a pit. As it turned out, a caravan passed by, and another brother, Judah, convinced the others to sell Joseph to the Midianite traders as a slave. The traders took him off to Egypt, and the brothers took Joseph's special robe, dipped it in goat's blood, and brought it back to his father, who concluded with some agony that Joseph must have been eaten by a wild beast.

Meanwhile Joseph became successful as a slave in Egypt, because "the LORD was with him"; his owner, Potiphar, was a wealthy aristocrat, and Joseph was made the chief overseer of his entire estate. Potiphar's wife, however, developed a romantic crush on the handsome young slave. When he refused to sleep with her, she cried rape, and Joseph was hauled off to prison. He succeeded even in prison, however, because "the LORD was with him," and he was put in charge by the chief jailor (chapter 39). In prison, Joseph proved to be a remarkably reliable interpreter of dreams, so that after some years, when the Pharaoh of Egypt had a couple of disturbing dreams, his servants let him know that there was a prisoner who could interpret them for him.

Pharaoh had dreamed of seven "sleek and fat cows" grazing by the Nile who were devoured by seven "ugly and thin" cows; he also dreamed of a stalk with seven "plump and good" ears of grain that were devoured by seven "thin and blighted" ears of grain. Joseph had no trouble interpreting the dreams: they indicated that the land would experience seven years of bounteous crops followed by seven years of famine. The Pharaoh needed to appoint an administrator who could conserve resources during the seven abundant years as a provision against the seven lean years to come. Pharaoh realized that Joseph himself would be ideal for the job, released him from prison, and made him his right-hand man (chapter 41).

The famine that eventually came struck not just Egypt but the land of Israel as well, and it threatened massive starvation. Jacob sent his sons to Egypt to buy food, as it was widely heard that the Egyptians were well stocked with provisions. The brothers appeared before Joseph, not realizing who he was, of course, all these years later, and true to the dream of his youth, they bowed down in obeisance to him. After a number of intricate episodes in which Joseph tested their mettle, he eventually revealed himself to them, there was a happy reunion, and he promised deliverance for the famished families back home. These, along with their father Jacob, were sent for, and eventually all lived together in part of the land of Egypt under the protection of Pharaoh's chief administrator, Joseph. (This is how the people of Israel got to Egypt in the first place; this narrative, in other words, is used to set up their "exodus" four hundred years later under Moses.)

Jacob eventually died, and Joseph's brothers became nervous: would Joseph now turn on them for the evil that they did to him? After all, it was ultimately their fault that he had suffered so miserably: they had mocked him, threatened to kill him, kidnapped him, and sold him into slavery; he had served as a slave, had been wrongly convicted of attempted rape and spent years in prison, and so on. It had not been an entirely pleasant life, and it was all their fault. Knowing that his wrath could mean their deaths, they humbly approach him and ask for his forgiveness (Gen. 50:15–18). And then comes the key line of the text: "Joseph said to them, 'Do not be afraid! Am I in the place of God? Even though you intended to do harm to me, God intended it for good, in order to preserve a numerous people, as he is doing today'" (Gen. 50:19–20). Joseph promises then to tend to the needs of his brothers and their families, which he does until his death. And thus ends the book of Genesis. Through Joseph's suffering, God has saved his people.

This idea, that what human beings "intend for evil" God can "intend for good," can be found implicitly behind a large number of the biblical narratives of suffering. Sometimes, thanks to the intervention of God, suffering is redemptive. Some suffering, the biblical writers suggest, makes it possible for God to work his salvific purposes. The person who suffers may not realize it at the time; she or he may be completely ignorant of what God intends to do. But God sometimes brings good out of evil, salvation out of suffering.

## Other Examples of Redemptive Suffering in Scripture

The idea that human suffering can serve divine purposes is shown in the very next set of stories in the Hebrew Bible, those involving the exodus of the children of Israel out of their slavery in Egypt under Moses. When I was a young boy, and my mom would read Bible stories to me, I was always particularly enthusiastic about the accounts of the ten plagues against the Egyptians: the water-turned-to-blood, the frogs, the gnats, the flies, and so on. One of the reasons these stories fascinated me was that it always seemed like the plagues should have *worked:* if Moses says he'll bring a plague unless his demands are met, and then he brings a plague, you would think that after four or five times Pharaoh would get the point. But Pharaoh had a hardened heart. And the harder his heart became, the harder it was on the Israelite slaves, who continued to suffer the indignities of slavery while Moses put on a show for the aristocrats of Egypt.

One of the intriguing and much debated aspects of the plague stories, though, is just this business of Pharaoh's hardened heart. Sometimes the text indicates that it was Pharaoh himself who hardened his heart (e.g., Exod. 8:15, 32)—which makes some sense. When a plague ends, Pharaoh refuses to believe that it had anything to do with divine intervention and becomes more determined than ever to keep the Israelites enslaved. On other occasions, however, the text indicates that it is God who hardened Pharaoh's (or the other Egyptians') heart (Exod. 4:21; 10:1; 14:17; and so on). But why would God make Pharaoh not listen to reason or heed the nasty signs being done against him? On this the text is clear: God did not want Pharaoh to let the people go.

When he finally did let them go, he had a change of heart and chased after them. Then God himself performed a mighty act in order to show that he alone was the one who had delivered the people from their slavery. This is all made explicit in the narrative. Early on, God tells Moses, "I will harden his heart, *so that* he will not let the people go" (Exod. 4:21). He later explains the logic: "I have hardened his heart and the heart of his officials, in order that I may show these signs of mine among them, and that you may tell your children and grandchildren how I have made fools of the Egyptians ... so that you may know that I am the LORD" (Exod. 10:1–2). Somewhat later, when the children of Israel are prepared to cross through the sea on dry land, God says: "I will harden the hearts of the Egyptians so that they will go in after them [into the sea]; and so I will gain glory for myself over Pharaoh and all his army.... And the Egyptians shall know that I am the LORD ..." (Exod. 14:17–18). And of course that is what happens. The children of Israel cross through the sea with the water standing like a wall on either side of them. But when the Egyptians follow, the water returns and drowns the lot of them.

The suffering of the Israelites in slavery was prolonged so that God could show beyond any doubt that it was he—not a kind-hearted Pharaoh—who delivered them from their slavery. And the Pharaoh and all his armies suffered the ultimate punishment—resounding defeat in battle and death by drowning—in order for God to reveal to all that he was the mighty Lord who could bring deliverance to his people. Suffering can show forth the power and salvation of God.

In a kind of distant way, this story of the plagues against Egypt, in which God intentionally creates hardship and delays before helping his people, has long reminded me of a well-known story in the New Testament, perhaps Jesus' most famous miracle, the raising of Lazarus from the dead in John 11. I've found over the years when discussing this passage with groups of undergraduates that people tend to read quickly over the first part of the story to get to the juicy bits at the end. And to be sure, the ending is the high point: Jesus goes to the tomb of this man Lazarus, who has been buried for four days (and therefore is probably starting to putrefy rather noticeably), and in a rather theatrical voice calls out, "Lazarus, come forth"—after which the man rises from the dead in full view of the crowds. That climax is, of course, the point of the story. It shows that Jesus has the power over death. That's why Lazarus had to be dead for four days; otherwise, someone could say that he had just swooned, or that his spirit was still hanging around the grave. He was dead, really dead. Jesus, however, is the one who can overcome death. It is Jesus who is "the resurrection and the life" (John 11:25).

What is just as interesting to me, though, is the beginning of the story. It does not start with Lazarus's death, but with his illness. His sisters Mary and Martha send a message to Jesus—who is several days' journey away—that their brother is ill, asking Jesus to come heal him. But he refuses. And why? Because for Jesus, this illness "is for God's glory, so that the Son of God may be glorified through it" (John 11:4). And then comes the intriguing verse 6: "And so, because Jesus loved Martha and her sister and Lazarus, when he heard that Lazarus was ill, he stayed two days longer in the place he was." Students have a hard time believing that they're reading the text correctly. *Because* Jesus loved Lazarus, he stayed away for two days? Does that make any sense? If Jesus loved Lazarus, wouldn't he rush to heal him? No, not for the author of the Gospel of John. In this book, Jesus stays away precisely because he wants Lazarus to die. If Lazarus doesn't die, then Jesus can't raise him from the dead. And so Jesus doesn't start his journey for three days; and by the time he gets there, Lazarus has been dead four.

Why? "So that the Son of God might be glorified." The deliverance of God is intensified when the suffering is intensified. Jesus brings a resurrection, not just a healing.

And so, in some passages of Scripture, suffering is experienced *so that* God can be glorified by it. In other passages, suffering comes for other reasons, but God is able to bring good out of it. Suffering, in these passages, has a kind of silver lining. As an example of the latter we might return to the story of David and Bathsheba that I discussed in chapter 4. The king seduces his next-door neighbor, and when she becomes pregnant, he finds a way to have her husband murdered. As we have seen, the Deuteronomistic historian who tells this tale (2 Sam. 12) was firmly committed to the classical view of suffering, that sin brings punishment. And throughout this entire episode, David certainly sinned: seducing the wife of another, deceiving the cuckolded husband, and then arranging for him to be killed. Because there was a sin, there needed to be a punishment. In this case, David was punished by the death of Bathsheba's child: "The LORD struck the child that Uriah's wife bore to David, and it became very ill" (2 Sam. 12:15).

David prayed for God to spare the child, fasted, and spent the night on the ground, for seven days. Then the child died. This kind of "punishment" that David suffered should call into question the adequacy of the classical understanding of suffering: yes, David spent days in agony, and the outcome was not good for him. He suffered. But he didn't die. The *child* died. And the child hadn't done anything wrong. Killing one person to teach someone else a lesson—is that really how God acts? If we are to be godly people, does that mean we should act that way too? Kill someone's child to teach the parent a lesson?

In any event, the passage embodies another understanding of suffering as well, one more germane to our present discussion. For we are told that after the child's death, David "consoled his wife Bathsheba" and they eventually had another son. It was none other than Solomon. Out of evil, good can come. Solomon became one of the greatest kings in Israel's history, and the one through whom God promised to establish an eternal throne for his people (cf. 2 Sam. 7:14), a promise that later bearers of the tradition took to refer to the future messiah. For Christians, Jesus' royal lineage is traced back through Solomon (Matt. 1:6). In this reading of the text, David's suffering led to salvation.

## Direct Links Between Suffering and Salvation

The idea that God could make something good come out of something evil, that salvation could emerge from suffering, eventually took a turn in the thinking of some of the ancient writers, a turn toward the suggestion that salvation in fact *required* suffering. This turn had already been made by the time we reach Second Isaiah, the prophet of the Babylonian exile whom we met in chapter 3. As you'll recall, Second Isaiah speaks of "the servant of the LORD" who suffers on behalf of the people, and whose suffering in fact brings about God's salvation:

Surely he has borne our infirmities
  and carried our diseases;
yet we accounted him stricken,
  struck down by God, and
    afflicted.
But he was wounded for our
    transgressions,
  crushed for our iniquities;
upon him was the punishment that
    made us whole,
  and by his wounds we are
    healed. (Isa. 53:4–5)

As I tried to show earlier, the prophet himself identifies this "suffering servant" as the nation of Israel (e.g., Isa. 49:3: "You are my servant, Israel, in whom I will be glorified."). In its original context, Isaiah 53 was insisting that the suffering of the exiles in Babylon had "paid" for the sins of the nation and that, as a result, salvation could now come. The people would be forgiven and returned to their land, where they would enter into a restored relationship with God. The suffering of exile, then, was vicarious suffering: the pain and misery of one was counted as a kind of sacrifice for another.

This is the way the passage came to be read later by Christians, but with a decided twist. In their view, the "suffering servant" was not exiled Judah; it was an individual, the future messiah, whose suffering and death would be considered a sacrifice for the sins of others. Although none of the New Testament authors ever explicitly quotes Isaiah 53 to show that Jesus himself was the "suffering servant" who "was wounded for our transgressions," the *thought* of Isaiah 53 appears to stand very much behind the doctrines of atonement that we examined in chapter 3. Without citing the Hebrew Bible passage directly, for example, Paul speaks of "the redemption that is in Christ Jesus, whom God set forth as an atoning sacrifice that comes through faith in his blood" (Rom. 3:24–25).

An even more poignant statement can be found in 1 Peter 2:22–24, which speaks of Christ's passion as follows:

> He committed no sin, nor was deceit found in his mouth. When he was abused he did not abuse in return; when he suffered he uttered no threat. But he handed himself over to the one who righteously judges. He bore our sins in his body on the cross, so that we might be freed from sins and live for righteousness, for by his wounds you have been healed.

Here Isaiah 53 is clearly in mind and alluded to, although not explicitly quoted.

My point in looking at passages like this in chapter 3 was to stress that their logic of atonement is predicated on a classical model of sin leading to punishment; without a punishment, no reconciliation is possible for sin. Now we are examining a close corollary from a slightly different perspective. Not only does sin lead to punishment (hence Christ had to suffer if he was to deal with sin), but suffering can be redemptive (this suffering for sin brings about salvation).

This is Paul's teaching throughout his letters. As he states in 1 Corinthians: "For I handed over to you as of first importance what in turn I had received: that Christ died for our sins in accordance with the Scriptures" (1 Cor. 15:3). Paul was particularly committed to this idea that salvation could come only through the suffering and death of Jesus. As he reminded the Corinthians, for example, "I decided not to know anything among you except Jesus Christ—and this one crucified" (1 Cor. 2:2). In other words, in Paul's proclamation of the gospel, it was only the suffering death of Jesus that brought salvation.

To make sense of Paul's doctrine of salvation through Jesus' death, we need to dig a bit deeper into Paul's thought. Paul may be one of the favorite authors of many Christian readers today, but in fact he is very difficult to understand in places, even for professionals who devote their lives to interpreting his writings. Paul was a deep thinker, and occasionally an obtuse writer. All the same, one thing is patently clear from his letters: Paul was firmly convinced that a person could be put in a right standing before God not by keeping the prescriptions of the Jewish Law, but only by having faith in the death of Jesus.

One of the problems that Paul confronted in his life and ministry involved the numerous non-Jewish people converting to become followers of Jesus. Jesus himself, of course, was Jewish, as were his disciples. Jesus was born a Jew (as Paul himself admits; Gal. 4:4), he was brought up a Jew, he worshiped the Jewish God, kept the Jewish Law, followed Jewish customs, became a Jewish teacher, gathered Jewish followers, and taught them what he considered to be the appropriate interpretation of the Jewish Law. For many in the early church, then, it made sense that anyone who wanted to be a follower of Jesus first had to become Jewish. For Gentile men this meant that they had to be circumcised—since circumcision was required of all Jews by the Torah itself—and for both Gentile men and women, it meant keeping sabbath, observing Jewish food laws, and so on.

Paul, however, thought otherwise. For Paul, if a person could be made right with God by converting to Judaism and keeping the Jewish Law, there would have been no need for Jesus to have died in the first place (Gal. 3:21). The fact that Jesus—God's messiah—died must mean, in Paul's thinking, that God wanted him to die. And why was that? Because there needs to be a perfect sacrifice for sin: sin requires punishment, and Jesus bears the punishment. Out of pain comes salvation; Jesus' pain, our gain.

But there was more to it than that for Paul. In one passage of Paul's letters, he indicates that Jesus specifically had to be crucified. Why couldn't he just die of old age? Or if he had to be executed, why not by stoning? This is where it gets a bit complicated. Paul believed that even though the Law of God was a good thing—it was, after all, the law God himself had given—it had ended up bringing a curse upon people. People were controlled by forces of sin and were driven to violate the Law against their own (and God's) will. And so the Law, rather than bringing salvation, brought a curse. It commanded obedience but did not provide the power for obedience. As a result, everyone stood condemned, under the curse of the Law (see Rom. 7).

In Paul's thinking, Christ took the curse of the Law upon himself. He did this by being cursed by the Law. As Paul states it in one of his denser passages: "Christ redeemed us from the curse of the Law by becoming a curse for us—for it is written 'Cursed is everyone who hangs on a tree'" (Gal. 3:13). Paul is here quoting a passage from the Torah, Deuteronomy 21:23, which originally indicated that a person was under God's curse if his executed body was exposed by being hanged on a tree. Well, in a sense Jesus' body was hanged on a tree, precisely because he was crucified (rather than, say, subjected to stoning). The fact that he was hanged on a wooden cross (tree) showed that he was cursed. But he must not have been cursed for anything that he himself did—after all, he was God's messiah. Paul indicates, then, that Christ must have taken the curse of others upon himself, by being cursed on the tree. And so by suffering the death of crucifixion, Jesus removed the curse that lay upon others for their violation of the Law.

Salvation required suffering. For Paul, even more than that, it required the horrific suffering of crucifixion.

## A Vivid Portrayal of Salvation Through Suffering

Paul's letters predate by some fifteen or twenty years the first of our New Testament Gospels, Mark. Scholars have long wondered whether the Gospel writers were influenced by Paul's writings. At the end of the day, it is difficult to know for sure. Never do the Gospels quote Paul, obviously, and in many respects their views stand at odds with Paul's: Matthew, for example, appears to teach that followers of Jesus *do* need to keep the Law (see Matt. 5:17–20); and there is a real question of whether the Gospel of Luke teaches a doctrine of atonement.

But Mark's Gospel clearly does, as we have seen. In Mark, Jesus declares that "the son of man did not come to be served, but to serve, and to give his life as a ransom for many" (Mark 10:45; a verse that Luke omits).

Mark's view that the horrible suffering of death is itself redemptive can be seen with particular clarity in his account of the crucifixion itself. When I teach this passage to my students, I constantly remind them that when they are reading Mark's account, they are *not* reading Luke's or John's. Each author has his own way of portraying Jesus' passion, and we do a disservice to all of them if we pretend they are saying the same thing or have the same understanding of what the crucifixion meant, theologically.

The sheer pathos of the scene is striking in Mark (chapters 14–15). Jesus is silent during the entire proceeding (unlike, for example, in Luke). He has been betrayed by one of his disciples, Judas; he has been denied three times by his closest follower, Peter. He has been rejected by the Jewish crowds, condemned to death by the Roman governor, mocked, tormented, and tortured by the Roman soldiers. While he is being crucified, both of the criminals crucified beside him mock him, as do the leaders of his people and all those who pass by to see him hanging there. There is nothing in the scene to mitigate the sense that Jesus himself does not understand what is happening to him or why: betrayed, denied, mocked, forsaken, and abandoned. At the end, in despair, he cries out his only words in the entire proceeding: "My God, my God, why have *you* forsaken me?" (Mark 15:34). I take this to be a genuine question. At the end he felt forsaken by God, and he wanted to know why. He then utters a loud cry, and dies.

Even though, in Mark's account, Jesus may not have understood what was happening to him, the reader does. For immediately upon Jesus' death, Mark tells us, two things happen. The curtain in the Temple is torn from top to bottom, and the centurion who has just overseen the crucifixion cries out, "Truly this man was the son of God" (Mark 15:38–39). Both events are significant.

The curtain of the Temple that ripped in half was all that separated the Holy of Holies from the rest of the Temple precincts. The

Holy of Holies was the place where God himself was believed to dwell on earth, in this otherwise empty room into which no one could go, except once a year on the Day of Atonement (Yom Kippur) when the Jewish High Priest went behind the curtain to make a sacrifice for his own sins and then a sacrifice for the sins of the people. This curtain was what separated God from everyone else. And when Jesus died, according to Mark, the curtain was destroyed. In Jesus' death, God is now available to everyone.

And the centurion comes to realize it. Many people (as we will explore later in this chapter) had trouble believing that Jesus could be the messiah, the son of God, if he was crucified as a lowly criminal. Would God let that happen to his messiah, of all people? The centurion is the first person in all of Mark's Gospel to realize that yes, Jesus is the Messiah, the Son of God, not despite the fact that he was crucified but precisely *because* he was crucified.

Jesus' death, for Mark, is a redemptive event. It is probably significant that Mark portrays Jesus as somewhat uncertain before the end. People in Mark's own community may have been suffering persecution as Christians, and may have wondered if there could be any purpose, any divine intent behind it. For Mark there definitely is. Behind the scenes, God is at work in suffering. It is through suffering that God's redemptive action is performed. Suffering brings salvation.

## Salvation That Comes Through Rejection

Although the death of Jesus is the clearest instance in the New Testament of redemptive suffering, there are other instances as well, some of which have to do with the rejection and persecution of the early Christians.

The book of Acts, our earliest history of the Christian church, was written sometime near the end of the first century—it is often dated to 80–85 CE—by the same author who produced the Gospel of Luke.[1] Scholars continue to call this author Luke, even though his work is anonymous and there are good reasons for thinking that whoever he was, he was not the Gentile physician who was known to be a traveling companion of the apostle Paul. It is fair to say, though, that Paul is this author's ultimate hero; nearly two-thirds of Luke's account of the spread of Christianity throughout the Mediterranean (the theme of Acts) is devoted to the missionary exploits of Paul. (Some of the things he says about Paul's teachings and travels stand at odds with what Paul himself says in his letters; that is one reason for thinking that the book was not written by one of Paul's own companions.[2])

The idea that God can bring good out of evil is behind much of what the book of Acts has to say about the missionary activities of the early Christian church. Even before Paul appears on the scene—he is converted from being a persecutor of the church in chapter 9—the Christians are portrayed as preaching the message that God reverses the wicked actions of others. One of the key refrains of the apostolic sermons in the book is that the Jewish people are responsible for Jesus' death (this has been read as anti-Jewish, and understandably so), but that God acted on his behalf by raising him from the dead. The people should therefore feel remorse for what they have done, repent, and turn back to God. In other words, a very bad thing—the rejection of Jesus—can lead to a very good thing, salvation through repentance. A clear expression of this view comes in an early speech placed on the lips of the apostle Peter:

> Listen you Israelites ... The God of Abraham, the God of Isaac, and the God of Jacob, the God of our ancestors, has glorified his servant Jesus, whom you handed over and rejected before Pilate, though he had decided to release him. But you rejected the Holy and Righteous One and asked for a murderer to be given to you, and you killed the Author of life, whom God raised from the dead. To this, we ourselves are witnesses. (Acts 3:12–15)

For Luke, God reverses rejection and brings redemption out of suffering.

Luke shows this theme more subtly in his account of the persecution of the Christians. At the very beginning of Acts, Luke narrates a scene in which Jesus, after his resurrection and before his ascension, directs his disciples to be his "witnesses, in Jerusalem, in all Judea and Samaria, even to the ends of the earth" (Acts 1:8). You might think that the disciples would take his direction to heart and would start fanning out, telling people everywhere the good news of the resurrection. But they don't, at least at first. The disciples do start acquiring followers—in droves, in fact. Thousands of Jews in Jerusalem are said to have converted to belief in Jesus. But that's where the apostles and their converts stay—until they are driven out of town by persecution.

Persecution, of course, entailed a good deal of suffering—floggings, imprisonments, even executions, as indicated in Acts itself. But the author of Acts has a theological view of the progress of the early Christian mission, one in which suffering has a purpose. In particular, Luke thinks that the entire mission was driven by God through his Spirit, so that nothing that happened to the Christians could slow their progress. In fact, everything that happened simply contributed to the spread of the gospel. When the apostles Peter and John are arrested and taken before the Jewish council, they are released for lack of evidence of wrongdoing, and the disciples are emboldened to proclaim their faith more forcefully (chapter 4). When the apostles are imprisoned and flogged for causing trouble, they "rejoiced that they were considered worthy to suffer dishonor for the sake of the name" and preached the message all the more (chapter 5). When the first martyr, Stephen, is stoned to death for his blasphemous words about Jesus (chapter 7), he dies with a prayer on his lips. A very observant Jew standing nearby—Saul of Tarsus—will himself convert while on a mission to persecute the Christians, two chapters later.

Most significant, when persecution becomes severe in Jerusa-lem, all the believers scatter throughout Judea and Samaria (Acts 8:1). In other words, rather than shutting down the Christian mis-sion, the persecution forced the followers of Jesus to do what they had been directed to do—take the message outside Jerusalem to other parts of Judea and north into Samaria. The mission is fur-thered by the suffering inflicted on those who believe. This is Luke's way of saying that suffering can be redemptive, that good comes from evil.

The same theme drives the narratives of Paul's missionary activi-ties in Acts. For this book's author, the mission was to spread not only geographically but also ethnically: the salvation brought by Christ was not simply for Jews; it was for all people, Jew and Gen-tile. But how did the new religion breach the divide, how did it leap from being a strictly Jewish sect of Jewish followers of Jesus to become a religion of both Jew and Gentile? In no small measure it happened, according to Luke, because the Christian missionaries were rejected by the Jewish crowds, and so were more or less driven to take their message elsewhere. This is made explicit in several places, none more clear than in chapter 13, where Paul delivers a lengthy sermon to the Jewish congregation of a synagogue in the city of Antioch of Pisidia (Asia Minor).

> The next sabbath nearly the whole city came together to hear the word of the Lord. But when the Jews saw the crowds, they were filled with jealousy; and speaking blasphemies they contradicted everything preached by Paul. Then both Paul and Barnabas spoke out boldly, saying, "It was neces-sary that the word of God should be spoken first to you. But since you reject it and judge yourselves to be unworthy of eternal life, see—we are now turning to the Gentiles."....
> And the word of the Lord spread through the entire region.
> (Acts 13:44–49)

When the Jews sponsor a persecution against the apostles, they take their message to other lands. And so it goes. Rejection and persecution work to spread the gospel. For the author of Acts, God brings good from evil.

What did the historical Paul himself think?

## Rejection and Salvation in Paul

As mentioned earlier, when recounting the things that Paul said and did, the book of Acts does not always agree with Paul's letters. In his own descriptions of his missionary work, for example, Paul never mentions going to the synagogues in the various cities that he visited; and he does not talk about preaching to Gentiles only after Jews had rejected his message. This appears to be Luke's understanding of how the mission proceeded, but it may not be historically accurate. What is accurate is that Paul was principally a missionary to the Gentiles, and that he faced rejection by Jews who did not take kindly to his declaration that Gentiles who believed in Jesus—not Jews descended from Abraham—were the heirs of the promises that God had made to the patriarchs of Israel. Sometimes Paul is quite heated in speaking of the Jewish rejection of his message that Jesus' death is what puts a person into a right standing before God. As he says in his very first surviving letter:

> For you, brothers, became imitators of the churches of God in Christ Jesus that are in Judea, because you yourselves suffered the same things from your own compatriots as they did from the Jews, who killed both the Lord Jesus and the prophets and persecuted us; they are not pleasing to God and are opposed to all people, for they hindered us from speaking to the Gentiles, that they might be saved. As a result, they filled up their sins at all times. But wrath has come upon them at last. (1 Thess. 2:14–16)

Historically, this presents an interesting, but completely under-standable, situation. Paul's message was that the crucified Jesus was the messiah sent from God for the salvation of the world. Most Jews—I'm speaking historically now—considered this message lu-dicrous. Many Christians today have trouble understanding what the problem was. Doesn't the Hebrew Bible talk about the suffer-ing messiah? Doesn't it describe the crucifixion in such passages as Psalm 22 and Isaiah 53, looking forward to the fulfillment brought by Jesus? Wasn't the messiah *supposed* to be crucified and raised from the dead? Why can't Jews see that Jesus must be the messiah?

This is a source of genuine confusion among many Christians, but it doesn't really need to be. The fact is that if you simply read Psalm 22 and Isaiah 53, as I pointed out in my earlier discussions of these passages, you see that the word *messiah* never occurs. Jewish readers of these passages in antiquity did not think that they re-ferred to the messiah. They may have been referring to someone who was dear to God who suffered horribly, but this person was not the messiah. And why not? Because the messiah was not sup-posed to be someone who suffered and died, but someone who ruled in glory.

The term *messiah* comes to us from the Hebrew *mashiach,* which means "anointed one." The Greek equivalent is *christos,* from which we get the term *Christ.* I sometimes need to remind my students of this, that Christ was not originally Jesus' name. He was not "Jesus Christ, born to Joseph and Mary Christ." "Christ" is a translation of *messiah,* so that if someone says Jesus Christ they are saying "Jesus the messiah." But why was the term *anointed one* used of a future deliverer? It is probably because the kings in ancient Israel were anointed with oil during their inauguration ceremonies to show God's special favor upon them (see 1 Sam. 10:1; 16:12–13). For many Jews, the messiah would be God's *future* king, the one who, like King David, would rule Israel in a time of peace, undisturbed by rival nations, happy and prosperous.

Other Jews had other ideas of what the messiah would be like. Some anticipated that the future ruler would be a cosmic judge sent from heaven in judgment on the earth, come to overwhelm God's enemies with a supernatural show of force. Others thought that the future ruler would be a great man of God, a priest empowered by God to deliver the authoritative interpretations of his Law by which the nation would be governed.[3]

Whatever various Jews thought of the messiah, they agreed that he would be a figure of grandeur and power, one obviously chosen and favored by God. And who was Jesus? A crucified criminal. For most Jews, calling Jesus the messiah simply made no sense. He never raised an army, never attacked the Romans, never established his throne in Jerusalem; he certainly never came from heaven in a blaze of glory to overthrow God's enemies. Rather than defeating the enemy, Jesus was squashed by the enemy. He suffered the most humiliating and painful death the enemy could devise, reserved for the lowest of the low. Jesus was precisely the *opposite* of what people thought the messiah would be like.

Paul himself understood the problem full well—he indicates that the crucifixion of Jesus was the greatest "stumbling block to Jews" (1 Cor. 1:23). Nonetheless, as discussed earlier, for Paul, Jesus actually was the messiah, not despite the fact that he was crucified but precisely because he was crucified. He bore the curse of the Law (since he was hanged on a tree); but since he was God's chosen, he bore this curse not for any wrong he had done but for the wrong done by others. It is through his crucifixion, therefore, that one can escape from the curse of the Law and be set free from the power of sin that alienates people from God. For Paul, Jesus is not a messiah in a mere political sense but in a deep spiritual sense. He is the one favored by God who puts people into a right standing before God.

Still, most Jews didn't buy it, and this was a major source of pain to Paul. As he himself says: "I have great sorrow and endless anguish in my heart. For I would wish myself were accursed from Christ if it could help my own people, my kindred according to the flesh" (Rom. 9:2–3). Paul would rather suffer God's wrath himself than see his compatriots, the Jews, cut off from God. But in his view, cut off they were, because they rejected Christ. And this caused him deep emotional agony.

But even here, for Paul, the anguish could turn to joy. For eventually Paul came up with an explanation for why Jews had rejected the messiah, Jesus. This explanation is spelled out, in rather complicated fashion, in chapter 11 of his letter to the Romans. Here Paul reaffirms his belief that the gospel of Christ brings salvation to all people, Jew and Gentile. And why have the Jews rejected the message? For Paul, it is because this allowed the message then to be taken to the Gentiles. And what, for Paul, would be the net effect of the message of salvation going to the Gentiles? In one of his stranger arguments, Paul claims that when Jews see that Gentiles have come into the people of God, it will make them "jealous" (Rom. 11:11). That is why "a hardening has come upon part of Israel, until the full number of the Gentiles has come in. And thus all Israel will be saved" (Rom. 11:25–26). In other words, despite his agonizing over his compatriots who do not yet believe, Paul believed that God would bring something good to pass. Out of jealousy the Jews will eventually flock into the gates of salvation, and the entire world will be saved. Out of something bad, God makes something good.

## Other Suffering and Its Benefits

Paul has a lot of things to say about suffering and its benefits. Remember, he thought that it was only by suffering that he could be a true apostle of Jesus.[4] Rather than complain about suffering, then, Paul reveled in it. For one thing, Paul thought that suffering could build character:

> We even boast in our afflictions, knowing that affliction produces endurance, and endurance produces a proven character;

and a proven character produces hope; and hope is not put to shame, because the love of God is poured out in our hearts through the Holy Spirit that has been given to us. (Rom. 5:3–5)

So, also, he thought that by suffering he was better equipped to console others who suffered.

Blessed is the God and Father of our Lord Jesus Christ, the Father of all mercies and the God of all encouragement; the one who encourages us in our every affliction to enable us to encourage others who experience every affliction with the encouragement that we ourselves have received from God. For just as the sufferings of Christ abound in us, so also the encouragement we have through Christ abounds. If we are afflicted, it is for your encouragement and salvation; if we are encouraged, it is for your encouragement, which is manifest when you endure those sufferings we ourselves experience. We have an unshakeable hope in you knowing that as you are partners in our sufferings, so also you are partners in our encouragement. (2 Cor. 1:3–7)

Paul also felt that God brought suffering to induce humility and to help him, Paul, remember that the positive results of his ministry came from God, not from his own remarkable abilities. This is the point of the well-known passage in which Paul talks about having a "thorn in the flesh." In this passage, in 2 Corinthians, Paul has just described an exalted vision that he had of the heavenly realms, and he indicates that God did not want him to feel overly exultant in the fact that he had been privileged to have such a special revelation. And so God gave him a thorn in the flesh to induce humility:

In order that I might not be overly exultant, I was given a thorn in the flesh, a messenger of Satan, to harass me and to keep me from being overly exultant. Three times I asked the Lord about this, that he might remove it from me. And he said to me, "My grace is sufficient for you, for power is made perfect in weakness." And so I will be happy to boast instead in my weaknesses, that the power of Christ might rest upon me. Therefore I am satisfied with weaknesses, with insults, with constraints, with persecutions and hardships that come for Christ's sake. For when I am weak, then I am powerful. (2 Cor. 12:7–10)

There has been considerable debate about what Paul's "thorn in the flesh" actually was: some have suggested that Paul had epilepsy (that's allegedly why he fell from his horse when "blinded by the light" in Acts 9) or failing eyesight (that's why he mentions the "large letters" that he uses when he writes his epistles; Gal. 6:11), or some other physical ailment. The truth is that we'll never know. What we can know is that Paul came to see his suffering as a good thing. It did not come as a punishment for sin; it did not come simply because other people were behaving wickedly toward him. It came from God (even though it arrived through a messenger of Satan!), and in the end it was redemptive, because it allowed God's own power to show forth.

In all these ways, Paul thought that suffering, ultimately, was a good thing. Sometimes it had a silver lining; sometimes it was the will of God to keep his people humble; and sometimes it was the very essence of salvation.

## Redemptive Suffering: An Assessment

The idea that God can bring good out of evil, that suffering can have positive benefits, that salvation itself depends on suffering—all of these are ways of saying that suffering is and can be redemptive. This idea is found throughout the Bible, from the Jewish Scripture to the New Testament, starting with Genesis and continuing on all the way through the writings of Paul and the Gospels. In some ways it is the core message of the Bible: it is not simply despite suffering but precisely through suffering that God manifests his power of salvation, whether the salvation of the children of Israel from their slavery in Egypt at the exodus or the salvation of the world through the passion of Jesus.

A lot of people today resonate with this notion that suffering can have positive effects—sometimes highly positive, even salvific effects. I suppose all of us have had experiences that were miserable at the time but led to a greater good. I know I have, starting when I was fairly young. I've always attributed my entire career, indirectly, to an accidental and rather painful incident that occurred when I was a teenager.

It was the summer of 1972, before my senior year in high school, and I was playing baseball in an American Legion summer league, rather enjoying myself, when suddenly, back from a road trip we had taken to play in Bartlesville, Oklahoma, I started feeling lethargic and generally miserable. I went to a doctor and found that somehow or other I had contracted hepatitis A. So much for a summer of fun (and baseball). I was taken out of action, and it was not pleasant. But there was nothing I could do: I was stuck indoors with little to do but sit around and take care of myself.

It took about three days to become bored out of my skull. (I've always had a passion for the outdoors, especially when it's hot and sunny, as it often is during Kansas summers.) I decided that I needed to do something besides watch TV all day, and thought that maybe I could start working as much as my energy would allow on the high school debate topic for the coming year. I had been on the debate team both my sophomore and junior years and was decent enough at it but by no means one of the stars. My high school had one of the best debate programs in the state (we had won the state championship the previous two years, even though I had had little to do with it as a lowly underclassman), and I wasn't projected to be one of the leaders on the team. Each year a different debate topic was assigned, and teams had to be prepared to debate affirmative or negative on the resolution in tournaments that took place over a series of months in the autumn. The team's stars spent the summers preparing; I personally preferred playing baseball (and tennis and golf and anything else that was outdoors). But there I was, with nothing else to do and lots of time on my hands.

And so I arranged for books to be brought to the house, and I started doing research, and before I knew it, I was head over heels into the project, devoting almost every waking hour to it. It suddenly came to be a huge challenge, figuring out the intricacies of that year's resolution (it had to do with whether the federal government, rather than localities, should assume all funding for primary and secondary education)—as big a challenge as playing second base had been just weeks earlier.

When I got over the hepatitis, I was still hooked on doing research. My senior year was unlike any other school year I had had. I was still involved in sports, especially tennis in the spring; but in the fall I was completely inundated with work on the upcoming debates. My star began to rise, I was eventually chosen to be one of the team leaders, my colleague (who had been a star for years) and I won big tournaments, eventually I was chosen to be on the team representing the high school at regional and state tournaments, and we won the state championship.

The reason all that mattered in the long run was that it got me interested in doing academic research. When I went off to college, I threw myself into my studies more than I had ever done in high school. As a direct result, I became a scholar. No one—absolutely *no one!*—would have predicted that of me before my senior year in high school. I did well in school, but a career in the academy was as unlikely as a career in the Moscow ballet.

If I hadn't caught hepatitis, I'm still convinced, it never would have happened. I can't describe how happy I am that I got hepatitis. Sometimes something good can come out of suffering.

At the same time, I am absolutely opposed to the idea that we can universalize this observation by saying that something good *always* comes out of suffering. The reality is that *most* suffering is not positive, does not have a silver lining, is not good for the body or soul, and leads to wretched and miserable, not positive, outcomes.

I simply do not believe it's true that "Whatever does not kill us only makes us stronger." Would that that were true, but unfortunately it's not. A lot of times, what does not kill you completely incapacitates you, mars you for life, ruins your mental or physical well-being—permanently. We should never, in my view, take a glib view of suffering—our own or that of others.

I especially, and most vehemently, reject the idea that someone else's suffering is designed to help *us*. I know there are people who argue that recognizing the pain in the world can make us nobler human beings but, frankly, I find this view offensive and repulsive. Sure, our *own* suffering may, on occasion, make us better people, stronger, or more considerate and caring, or more humane. But other people do not—decidedly do not—suffer in order to make us happier or nobler. It is one thing to say that I enjoy the success I now have because for so many years I had bad luck or misfortune; that I enjoy the fine food I can eat now because for years I lived on peanut butter sandwiches; that I enjoy my vacations now because for years I could barely afford gas to drive to the store. It is a completely different thing to say that I better enjoy the good things in life because I see other people without them.

To think that other people suffer horrible diseases so that I can appreciate my good health is atrocious; to say that other people starve so that I can appreciate my good food is completely egocentric and coldhearted; to say that I enjoy life so much more now that I see people all around me dying is the self-centered raving of an adult who hasn't matured beyond childhood. On some occasions, my own misfortune may have something good come of it. But I'm not going to thank God for *my* food because I realize other people don't have any.

Moreover, there is a lot of suffering in the world that is not redemptive for *anybody*. The eighty-year-old grandmother who is savagely raped and strangled; the eight-week-old grandchild who suddenly turns blue and dies; the eighteen-year-old killed by a drunk driver on the way to the prom—trying to see good in such evils is to deprive evil of its character. It is to ignore the helplessness of those who suffer for no reason and to no end. It robs other people of their dignity and their right to enjoy life every bit as much as we do.

And so there must be yet other answers to why there is suffering in the world. Or perhaps, in the end, there is simply no answer. That, as it turns out, is one of the answers given by some of the biblical writers, as we will see in the next chapter. The answer is that there is no answer.

# six

# Does Suffering Make Sense?
# The Books of Job and Ecclesiastes

Everyone has experienced physical suffering and will experience still more before they die. From broken fingernails to broken bones, from hardened arteries to cancer to failed organs; diseases curable and incurable. My dad was taken by cancer eighteen years ago at the ripe young age of sixty-five. In August of that year we were together on a fishing trip, and he seemed fine. Six weeks later he was on his deathbed in the hospital, his physical appearance changed almost beyond belief, with cancer metastasized throughout his body. Six weeks later, after excruciating pain—one doctor didn't want to increase his morphine because he might get "addicted" (you wonder sometimes what people are *thinking*)—six weeks later, he was dead.

Just now, many years later, I was sketching this chapter in an airport in Pennsylvania, coming home from a memorial lecture I had given at Penn State University for a friend and colleague, Bill Petersen, a brilliant linguist and historian of early Christianity who had died of cancer at the peak of his career, aged fifty-nine. It can hit any of us anytime. Even the more prosaic sicknesses that drive us to our beds and make us think the world is surely going to end soon—flu, for example, so bad that it makes you want to die, or to think that you will.

Actually, many people do die of the flu. The worst epidemic in American history was the 1918 influenza epidemic, overshadowed in history by the First World War but far more deadly for American soldiers, not to mention civilians. In fact, it killed more Americans than all the wars of the twentieth century put together. It broke out in an army camp at Fort Riley, Kansas, in March 1918; doctors thought that it was a new strain of pneumonia. And then it seemed to disappear. But it came back with a vengeance, both among civilians and among the troops—who managed to take it over to Europe when transferred to the front lines, so that soldiers from other countries contracted it and took it back to their homelands. It ended up being a worldwide epidemic of apocalyptic proportions.

The symptoms were unlike anything anyone had ever seen. It seemed to attack the young and healthy—twenty-one- to twenty-nine-year-olds were most at risk—rather than the very young, the very old, or the very weak. Symptoms would appear without warning and worsen by the hour. The lungs would fill with fluid, making breathing difficult; body temperatures would soar so high the hair would begin to fall out; people would turn blue and black; they would eventually die by drowning in the fluid gathered in their lungs. All this might occur within twelve hours. Someone you saw healthy at breakfast could well be dead by dinner. And the numbers of those infected were extraordinary.

In September 1918 twelve thousand died in the United States—and then it got worse. There were army units in the war who lost 80 percent of their soldiers; Woodrow Wilson had to decide whether to send support troops, knowing that the virus could kill the majority of those on ship before they reached the war theater, with the impossibility of quarantine and the lack of any vaccine. Back home, places like New York City and Philadelphia were in high-crisis mode: by October 1918, New York was recording more than eight hundred deaths a day; in Philadelphia, eleven thousand died in a month. They ran out of caskets, and the ability to bury the caskets that were used.

Despite intense efforts, medical scientists could not come up with a vaccine (part of the problem: they assumed the disease was caused by a bacterium when, in fact, it was a virus). Eventually the disease ran its course and stopped the killing, mysteriously, on its own. But not before the majority of the human species had been infected. In the ten months of the epidemic, the influenza had killed 550,000 Americans and a whopping thirty million people worldwide.

How do we explain an outbreak like this? Do we appeal to a biblical answer? Many people did. Could God be punishing the world? Some people thought so and prayed for a respite. Was this a human tragedy inflicted on humans? There was a rumor that the Germans had started the flu by releasing a top-secret chemical weapon. Was there anything redemptive in the suffering? Some people saw it as a call to repentance before Armageddon, which was hastening to its completion in the European conflict.

Or maybe it was just one of those things. Maybe what happened had nothing to do with a divine being who intervenes for his people or against his enemies. There were, after all, numerous precedents in human history. The so-called plague of Justinian in the sixth century was even worse than the influenza outbreak of 1918, destroying something like 40 percent of the inhabitants of Constantinople, the capital of the Byzantine Empire, and as much as one-fourth of the population of the entire eastern Mediterranean. And there was the infamous Black Death, the bubonic plague of the mid-fourteenth century, which may have killed off as much as one-third of the population of Europe.

We ourselves are not exempt, as we know so well. Despite some improvements in treatment, the AIDS crisis continues as a hellish nightmare for millions. The numbers provided by ALERT, an international HIV and AIDS charity based in the United Kingdom, are staggering. Since 1981 more than twenty-five million people worldwide have died of AIDS. In 2006, some forty million people were living with HIV/AIDS (nearly half of them women). Three million people died in that year alone; more than four million were newly infected. Worldwide, still today, with all the awareness out there, some six thousand young people (under the age of twenty-five) become infected with HIV each day. At present, Africa has twelve million AIDS orphans. In the country of South Africa alone, more than a thousand people die of AIDS *every day*, day in and day out.

It is not only homophobic and hateful but also inaccurate and unhelpful to blame this epidemic on sexual preference or promiscuity. Unsafe practices might spread the disease—but why is there a disease in the first place? Are those who suffer the unspeakable emotional and physical agonies of AIDS more sinful and worthy of punishment than the rest of us? Has God chosen to punish all those AIDS orphans? I frankly don't see how the biblical answers to suffering that we've seen so far can be helpful for making sense of their plight—or the deaths of those struck down by influenza in 1918 or the bubonic plague in 1330. This isn't God who is creating excruciating pain and misery; it certainly isn't something human beings have done to other human beings; and I see nothing redemptive in the innocent young child who contracts AIDS, through absolutely no fault of her own, and who can expect nothing but the nightmarish torments that the disease produces. Are there other explanations for suffering in the world?

There are, and some of them are in the Bible. The best-known wrestling with the problem of suffering comes to us in the book of Job.

## The Book of Job: An Overview

Most people who read Job do not realize that the book as it has come down to us today is the product of at least two different authors, and that these different authors had different, and contradictory, understandings of why it is that people suffer. Most important, the way the story begins and ends—with the prose narrative of the righteous suffering of Job, whose patient endurance under duress is rewarded by God—stands at odds with the poetic dialogues that take up most of the book, in which Job is not patient but defiant, and in which God does not reward the one he has made to suffer but overpowers him and grinds him into submission. These are two different views of suffering, and to understand the book we have to understand its two different messages.[1]

As it now stands, with the prose narrative and the poetic dialogues combined into one long account, the book can be summarized as follows: it begins with a prose description of Job, a wealthy and pious man, the richest man in the eastern world. The action then moves up to heaven, where God speaks with "the Satan"—the Hebrew word means "the adversary"—and commends Job to him. The Satan claims that Job is pious toward God only because of the rewards he gets for his piety. God allows the Satan to take away all that Job has: his possessions, his servants, and his children—then, in a second round of attacks, his health. Job refuses to curse God for what has happened to him. Three friends come to visit him and comfort him; but it is cold comfort indeed. Throughout their speeches they tell Job that he is being punished for his sins (i.e., they take the "classical" view of suffering, which is that sinners get what they deserve). Job continues to insist on his innocence and pleads with God to allow him to present his case before him. At the end of the dialogues with the friends (which take up most of the book), God does show up, and overwhelms Job with his greatness, forcefully reproving him for thinking that he, God, has anything to explain to Job, a mere mortal. Job repents of his desire to make his plea before God. In the epilogue, which reverts to prose narrative, God commends Job for his upright behavior and condemns the friends for what they have said. He restores to Job all his former wealth and more; he provides him with another batch of children; and Job lives out his life in prosperity, dying at a ripe old age.

Some of the basic discrepancies between the prose narrative with which the book begins and ends (just under three chapters) and the poetic dialogues (nearly forty chapters) can be seen just from this brief summary. The two sources that have been spliced together to make the final product are written in different genres: a prose folktale and a set of poetic dialogues. The writing styles are different between these two genres. Closer analysis shows that the names for the divine being are different in the prose (where the name Yahweh is used) and the poetry (where the divinity is named El, Eloah, and Shaddai). Even more striking, the portrayal of Job differs in the two parts of the book: in the prose he is a patient sufferer; in the poetry he is thoroughly defiant and anything but patient. Correspondingly, he is commended in the prose but rebuked in the poetry. Moreover, the prose folktale indicates that God deals with his people according to their merit, whereas the entire point of the poetry is that he does not do that—and is not bound to do so. Finally, and most important, the view of why the innocent suffer differs between the two parts of the book: in the prose narrative, suffering comes as a test of faith; in the poetry, suffering remains a mystery that cannot be fathomed or explained.

To deal adequately with the book of Job, then, we need to look at the two parts of the book separately and explore at greater length its two explanations for the suffering of the innocent.

## The Folktale: The Suffering of Job as a Test of Faith

The action of the prose folktale alternates between scenes on earth and in heaven. The tale begins with the narrator indicating that Job lived in the land of Uz; usually this is located in Edom, to the southeast of Israel. Job, in other words, is not an Israelite. As a book of "wisdom," this account is not concerned with specifically Israelite traditions: it is concerned with understanding the world in ways that should make sense to everyone living in it. In any event, Job is said to be "blameless and upright, one who feared God and turned away from evil" (Job 1:1). We have already seen that in other Wisdom books, such as Proverbs, wealth and prosperity come to those who are righteous before God; here this dictum is borne out. Job is said to be enormously wealthy, with seven thousand sheep, three thousand camels, five hundred yokes of oxen, five hundred donkeys, and very many servants. His piety is seen in his daily devotions to God: early each morning he makes a burnt offering to God for all his children, seven sons and three daughters, in case they have committed some sin.

The narrator then moves to a heavenly scene in which the "heavenly beings" (literally: the sons of God) appear before the Lord, "the Satan" among them. It is important to recognize that the Satan here is not the fallen angel who has been booted from heaven, the cosmic enemy of God. Here he is portrayed as one of God's divine council members, a group of divinities who regularly report to God and, evidently, go about the world doing his will. Only at a later stage of Israelite religion (as we will see in chapter 7) does "Satan" become "the Devil," God's mortal enemy. The term *the Satan* here in Job does not appear to be a name so much as a description of his office: it literally means "the Adversary" (or the Accuser). But he is not an adversary to God: he is one of the heavenly beings who report to God. He is an adversary in the sense that he plays "devil's advocate," as it were, challenging conventional wisdom to try to prove a point.

In the present instance, his challenge has to do with Job. The Lord brags to the Satan about Job's blameless life and the Satan challenges God about it: Job is upright only because he is so richly blessed in exchange. If God were to take away what Job has, the Satan insists, Job would "curse you to your face" (Job 1:11). God doesn't think so, and gives the Satan authority to take everything away from Job. In other words, this is to be a test of Job's righteousness: can he have a disinterested piety, or does his pious relationship to God depend entirely on what he manages to get out of the deal?

The Satan attacks Job's household. In one day the oxen are stolen away, the sheep are burned up by fire from heaven, the camels are raided and carried off, all the servants are killed, and even the sons and daughters are mercilessly destroyed by a storm that levels their house. Job's reaction? As God predicted, he does not utter curses for his misfortune; he goes into mourning:

Job arose, tore his robe, shaved his head, and fell on the ground and worshiped. He said, "Naked I came from my mother's womb, and naked shall I return there; the LORD gave, and the LORD has taken away; blessed be the name of the LORD." (Job 1:20)

The narrator assures us that in all this "Job did not sin or charge God with wrongdoing" (Job 1:22). One might wonder what "wrongdoing" God could possibly do, if robbery, destruction of property, and murder are not wrong. But in this story, at least, for Job to preserve his piety means for him to continue trusting God, whatever God does to him.

The narrative then reverts to a heavenly scene of God and his divine council. The Satan appears before the Lord, who once again brags about his servant Job. The Satan replies that of course Job has not cursed God—he has not himself been afflicted with physical pain. But, the Satan tells God, "Stretch out your hand now and touch his bone and his flesh and he will curse you to your face" (Job 2:5). God allows the Satan to do so, with the proviso that he not take away Job's life (in part, one might suppose, because it would be hard to evaluate Job's reaction were he not alive to have one). The Satan then afflicts Job with "loathsome sores ... from the sole of his foot to the crown of his head" (Job 2:7). Job sits on a pile of ashes and scrapes his wounds with a potsherd. His wife urges on him the natural course, "Do you still persist in your integrity? Curse God and die." But Job refuses, "Shall we receive the good at the hand of God and not receive the bad?" (Job 2:10). In all this, Job does not sin against God.

Job's three friends then come to him—Eliphaz the Temanite, Bildad the Shuhite, and Zophar the Naamathite. And they do the only thing true friends can do in this kind of situation: they weep with him, mourn with him, and sit with him, not saying a word. What sufferers need is not advice but a comforting human presence.

It is at this point that the poetic dialogues begin, in which the friends do not behave like friends, much less like comforters, but insist that Job has simply gotten what he deserves. I will talk about these dialogues later, as they come from a different author. The folktale is not resumed until the conclusion of the book, at the end of chapter 42. It is obvious that a bit of the folktale was lost in the process of combining it with the poetic dialogues, for when it resumes, God indicates that he is angry with the three friends for what they have said, in contrast to what Job has said. This cannot very well be a reference to what the friends and Job said in the poetic dialogues, because there it is the friends who defend God and Job who accuses him. And so a portion of the folktale must have been cut off when the poetic dialogues were added. What the friends said that offended God cannot be known.

What is clear, though, is that God rewards Job for passing the test: he has not cursed God. Job is told to make a sacrifice and prayer on behalf of his friends, and he does so. God then restores everything that had been lost to Job, and even more: fourteen thousand sheep, six thousand camels, a thousand yokes of oxen, a thousand donkeys. And he gives him another seven sons and three daughters. Job lives out his days in peace and prosperity surrounded by children and grandchildren.

The overarching view of suffering in this folktale is clear: sometimes suffering comes to the innocent in order to see whether their pious devotion to God is genuine and disinterested. Are people faithful only when things are going well, or are they faithful no matter what the circumstances? Obviously for this author, no matter how bad things get, God still deserves worship and praise.

But serious questions can be raised about this perspective, questions raised by the text of the folktale itself. For one thing, many readers over the years have felt that God is not to be implicated in Job's sufferings; after all, it is the Satan who causes them. But a close reading of the text shows that it is not that simple. It is precisely God who authorizes the Satan to do what he does; he could not do anything without the Lord directing him to do it. Moreover, in a couple of places the text indicates that it is God himself who is ultimately responsible. After the first round of Job's sufferings, God tells the Satan that Job "persists in his integrity, although you incited me against him, to destroy him for no reason" (Job 2:3). Here it is God who is responsible for Job's innocent sufferings, at the Satan's instigation. God also points out that there was "no reason" for Job to have to suffer. This coincides with what happens at the end of the tale, when Job's family comes to comfort him after the trials are over, showing him sympathy "for all the evil that the LORD had brought upon him" (Job 42:11).

God himself has caused the misery, pain, agony, and loss that Job experienced. You can't just blame the Adversary. And it is important to remember what this loss entailed: not just loss of property, which is bad enough, but a ravaging of the body and the savage murder of Job's ten children. And to what end? For "no reason"—other than to prove to the Satan that Job wouldn't curse God even if he had every right to do so. Did he have the right to do so? Remember, he didn't do anything to deserve this treatment. He actually was innocent, as God himself acknowledges. God did this to him in order to win a bet with the Satan. This is obviously a God above, beyond, and not subject to human standards. Anyone else who destroyed all your property, physically mauled you, and murdered your children—simply on a whim or a bet—would be liable to the most severe punishment that justice could mete out. But God is evidently above justice and can do whatever he pleases if he wants to prove a point.

## Other Tests in the Bible

The idea that suffering comes as a test from God simply to see if his followers will obey can be found in other parts of the Bible as well. There are few stories that illustrate the view more clearly and more horribly than the "offering of Isaac" recounted in Genesis 22. The context of the story is this: The father of the Jews, Abraham, had long been promised a son by God, a son who would then become the ancestor of a great and mighty people. But it was not until he and his wife were in extreme old age that the promise was fulfilled. Abraham was a ripe, and obviously fertile, hundred-year-old when Isaac was born (Gen. 21:1–7). But then, when Isaac, the fulfillment of God's promise, is still a young man, or possibly even a boy, God issues a horrible directive to Abraham: he is to take his "only son Isaac" and offer him up as a "burnt offering" to God. The God who had promised him a son now wants him to destroy that son; the God who commands his people not to murder has now ordered the father of the Jews to sacrifice his own child.

Abraham takes his son Isaac and goes off to the wilderness with two servants and a donkey loaded with wood for the burnt offering (that is, the pyre on which he is to sacrifice his son's body). As they head to the specified place, Isaac wonders what is happening: he sees the wood and the fire, but where is the sacrificial animal? Abraham tells him that God will provide it, not letting his son know what is to transpire. But then he seizes his son, ties him up, lays him upon the wood, and prepares to knife him to death. At the last second, God intervenes, sending an angel to stay the knife before it strikes. The angel then tells Abraham, "Do not lay your hand on the boy or do anything to him; for now I know that you fear God, since you have not withheld your son, your only son, from me" (Gen. 22:12). Abraham looks up and sees a ram caught in a thicket; he captures the ram and offers it instead of Isaac as a burnt offering (Gen. 22:13–14).

It has all been a test, a horrible test, to see if Abraham will do what God asks, even if it means slaughtering his own son, the son God himself had promised to make the father of a great nation. The point of the story, like the point of Job's story, is that being faithful to God is the most important thing in life: more important than life itself. Whatever God commands must be done, no matter how contrary to his nature (is he or is he not a God of love?), no matter how contrary to his own law (is he opposed to murder—or human sacrifice—or not?), no matter how contrary to every sense of human decency. There have been many people since Abraham's day who have murdered the innocent, claiming that God told them to do so. What do we do with such people? We lock them up in prison or execute them. And what do we do with Abraham? We call him a good and faithful servant. I often wonder about this view of suffering.

Some people in the Bible are told to be faithful to God even though it leads to their own deaths. The model in the New Testament, of course, is Jesus himself, who is portrayed in the passion accounts as praying to God to "let this cup pass from before me" (Mark 14:36). In other words, Jesus did not want to have to die. But it was the will of God, and so he goes through his horrible passion (being rejected, mocked, flogged, and beaten to a pulp) and death by crucifixion—all because that is what God told him to do. But the end result—as was the case for both Job and Abraham—was good; these stories have happy endings. For Jesus, it led to his resurrection and exaltation to heaven. As one of our pre-Gospel sources tells us:

> Having been found in the form of a human, he humbled himself by becoming obedient unto death, even death on the cross. Therefore also God highly exalted him, and bestowed upon him the name that is above every name. (Phil. 2:7–9)

The followers of Jesus are to follow suit, being willing to suffer to prove their steadfast devotion to God. Thus as Christians are told in the book of 1 Peter:

> Beloved, do not be surprised at the fiery trial that has come upon you for your testing, as if something surprising has happened. But in so far as you partake of the sufferings of Christ, rejoice, so that you may also rejoice full of gladness at the revelation of his glory.... Therefore let those who suffer according to the will of God entrust their souls to the faithful creator by doing what is good. (1 Pet. 4:12–13, 19)

The suffering that Christians endure is a "test" to see if they can remain faithful to God to the very end, even to death. And so, rather than complaining in their misery, they are to rejoice, happy that they can suffer as Christ did. And for what reason? Because that's what God wants. But why does he want it? That, I'm afraid, is something that we can evidently never know for certain. It appears to be a test, a kind of final exam.

What, then, are we to make of this view of suffering, that suffering sometimes comes as a test of faith? I suppose people who have a blind trust in God might see suffering as a way of displaying their devotion to him, and this could indeed be a very good thing. If nothing else, it can provide inward fortitude and a sense that despite everything that happens, God is ultimately in charge of this world and all that occurs in it. But is this really a satisfying answer to the question of why people are compelled to endure pain and misery? Are we to imagine a divine being who wants to torment his creatures just to see if he can force them to abandon their trust in him? What exactly are they trusting him to do? Certainly not to do what is best for them: it is hard to believe that God inflicts people with cancer, flu, or AIDS in order to make sure they praise him to the end. Praise him for what? Mutilation and torture? For his great power to inflict pain and misery on innocent people?

It is important to remember that God himself acknowledged that Job was innocent—that is, that Job had done nothing to deserve his torment. And God did not simply torment him by taking away his hard-earned possessions and physical health. He killed Job's children. And why? To prove his point; to win his bet. What kind of God is this? Many readers have taken comfort in the circumstance that once Job passed the test, God rewarded him—just as God rewarded Abraham before him, and Jesus after him, just as God rewards his followers now who suffer misery so that God can prove his case. But what about Job's children? Why were they senselessly slaughtered? So that God could prove a point? Does this mean that God is willing—even eager—to take *my* children in order to see how I'll react? Am I that important, that God is willing to destroy innocent lives just to see whether I'll be faithful to him when he has not been faithful to me? Possibly the most offensive part of the book of Job is at the end, when God restores all that Job had lost—including additional children. Job lost seven sons and three daughters and, as a reward for his faithfulness, God gives him an additional seven sons and three daughters. What was this author thinking? That the pain of a child's death will be removed by the birth of another? That children are expendable and replaceable like a faulty computer or DVD player? What kind of God is this? Do we think that everything would be made right if the six million Jews killed in the Holocaust were "replaced" by six million additional Jews born in the next generation?

As satisfying as the book of Job has been to people over the ages, I have to say I find it supremely dissatisfying. If God tortures, maims, and murders people just to see how they will react—to see if they will not blame him, when in fact he is to blame—then this does not seem to me to be a God worthy of worship. Worthy of fear, yes. Of praise, no.

## The Poetic Dialogues of Job: There Is No Answer

As I indicated at the beginning of this discussion, the view of suffering in the poetic dialogues of Job differs radically from that found in the narrative framing story of the prologue and epilogue. The issue dealt with in the dialogues, however, is the same: if God is ultimately in charge of all of life, why is it that the innocent suffer? In the folktale, it is because God tests people to see if they can retain their piety despite undeserved pain and misery. In the poetic dialogues, there are different answers for different figures involved: for Job's so-called friends, suffering comes as a punishment for sin (this view appears to be rejected by the narrator). Job himself, in the poetic speeches, cannot figure out a reason for innocent suffering. And God, who appears at the end of the poetic exchanges, refuses to give a reason. It appears that for this author, the answer to innocent suffering is that there is no answer.

## The Overall Structure of the Poetic Dialogues

The poetic dialogues are set up as a kind of back-and-forth between Job and his three "friends." Job makes a statement and one of his friends replies; Job responds and the second friend replies; Job responds again and then the third friend replies. This sequence happens three times, so that there are three cycles of speeches. The third cycle, however, has become muddled, possibly in the copying of the book over the ages: one of the friend's (Bildad's) comments are inordinately short in the third go-around (only five verses); another friend's (Zophar's) comments are missing this time; and Job's response at one point appears to take the position that his friends had been advocating and that he had been opposing in the rest of the book (chapter 27). Scholars typically think that something has gone awry in the transmission of the dialogues at this point.[2]

But the rest of the structure is clear. After the friends have had their say, a fourth figure appears; this is a young man named Elihu who is said to be dissatisfied with the strength of the case laid out by the other three. Elihu tries to state the case more forcefully: Job is suffering because of his sins. This restatement appears to be no more convincing than anything the others have said, but before Job can reply, God himself appears, wows Job into submission by his overpowering presence, and informs him that he, Job, has no right to challenge the workings of the one who created the universe and all that is in it. Job repents of his desire to understand and grovels in the dirt before the awe-inspiring challenge of the Almighty. And that's where the poetic dialogues end.

## Job and His Friends

The poetic section begins with Job, out of his misery, cursing the day he was born and wishing that he had died at birth:

> After this Job opened his mouth and
> cursed the day of his birth. Job said:
> "Let the day perish in which I was
> born,
> and the night that said
> 'A man-child is conceived.' ...
> "Why did I not die at birth,
> come forth from the womb and
> expire?
> Why were there knees to receive
> me,
> or breasts for me to suck? ...
> Or why was I not buried like a
> stillborn child,
> like an infant that never sees the
> light?" (Job 3:1–3, 11–12, 16)

Eliphaz is the first friend to respond, and his response sets the tone for what all the friends will say. In their opinion, Job has received what was coming to him. God does not, they claim (wrongly, as readers of the prologue know), punish the innocent but only the guilty.

> Then Eliphaz the Temanite answered:
> "If one ventures a word with you,
> will you be offended?
> But who can keep from
> speaking? ...

"Think now, who that was
              innocent ever perished?
  Or where were the upright cut
              off?
As I have seen, those who plow
              iniquity
  and sow trouble reap the same.
By the breath of God they perish,
  and by the blast of his anger
              they are consumed." (Job 4:1–2, 7–9)

All three friends will have similar things to say throughout the many chapters of their speeches. Job is guilty, he should repent, and if he does so, God will relent and return him to his favor. If he refuses, he is simply showing his recalcitrance and willfulness before the God who punishes those who deserve it. (These friends seem well versed in the views of the Israelite prophets we considered in chapters 2 and 3.) And so Bildad, for example, insists that God is just and seeks Job's repentance.

Then Bildad the Shuhite answered:
  "How long will you say these
              things,
  and the words of your mouth
              be a great wind?
Does God pervert justice?
  Or does the Almighty pervert
              the right?
If your children sinned against
              him,
  he delivered them into the
              power of their
              transgression.

If you will seek God
    and make supplication to the
        Almighty,
if you are pure and upright,
    surely then he will rouse himself
        for you
    and restore to you your rightful
        place.
Though your beginning was
        small,
    your latter days will be very
        great." (Job 8:1–7)

Zophar too thinks that Job's protestations of innocence are completely misguided and an affront to God. If Job is suffering, it is because he is guilty and is getting his due; in fact, he deserves far worse (one wonders what could be worse, if the folktale is any guide).

Then Zophar the Naamathite answered:
"Should a multitude of words go
        unanswered,
    and should one full of talk be
        vindicated?
Should your babble put others to
        silence,
    and when you mock, shall no
        one shame you?
For you say, 'My conduct is
        pure,
    and I am clean in God's sight.'
But O that God would speak,
    and open his lips to you,
and that he would tell you the

secrets of wisdom!
 For wisdom is many-sided.
Know then that God exacts of you
  less than your guilt
   deserves." (Job 11:1–6)

And this is what Job's *friends* are saying! Sometimes they bar no holds in accusing Job, wrongly, of great sin before God, as when Eliphaz later declares:

"Is it for your piety that he
  reproves you,
 and enters into judgment with
  you?
Is not your wickedness great?
 There is no end to your
  iniquities.
For you have ... stripped the naked of their
  clothing.
You have given no water to the
  weary to drink,
 and you have withheld bread
  from the hungry....
"You have sent widows away
  empty-handed,
 and the arms of the orphans you
  have crushed.
Therefore snares are around you,
 and sudden terror overwhelms
  you." (Job 22:4–7, 9–10)

The word *therefore* in the final couplet is especially important. It is *because* of Job's impious life and unjust treatment of others that he is suffering, and for no other reason.

For Job, it is this charge itself that is unjust. He has done nothing to deserve his fate, and to maintain his personal integrity he has to insist on his own innocence. To do otherwise would be to lie to himself, the world, and God. He cannot repent of sins he has never committed and pretend that his suffering is deserved when in fact he has done nothing wrong. As he repeatedly tells his friends, he knows full well what sin looks like—or, rather, tastes like—and he would know if he had done anything to stray from the paths of godliness:

> Teach me, and I will be silent;
>> make me understand how I have
>>> gone wrong.
> How forceful are honest words!
>> But your reproof, what does it
>>> reprove? ...
> But now, be pleased to look at
>> me;
>> for I will not lie to your face....
> Is there any wrong on my tongue?
>> Cannot my taste discern
>>> calamity? (Job 6:24–25, 28, 30)

In graphic and powerful images Job insists that despite his innocence, God has lashed out at him and attacked him and ripped into his body like a savage warrior on the attack:

> I was at ease, and he broke me in
>> two;
>> he seized me by the neck and
>>> dashed me to pieces;
> he set me up as his target;
>> his archers surround me.

He slashes open my kidneys, and
      shows no mercy;
  he pours out my gall on the
      ground.
He bursts upon me again and
      again;
  he rushes at me like a warrior....
My face is red with weeping,
  and deep darkness is on my
      eyelids,
though there is no violence in my
      hands,
  and my prayer is pure. (Job 16:12–14, 16–17)


With violence he seizes my
      garment;
  he grasps me by the collar of
      my tunic.
He has cast me into the mire,
  and I have become like dust and
      ashes.
I cry to you and you do not
      answer me;
  I stand, and you merely look at
      me.
You have turned cruel to me;
  with the might of your hand
      you persecute me. (Job 30:18–21)

Job constantly feels God's terrifying presence, which he cannot escape even through sleep at night. He pleads with God to relieve his torment, to leave him in peace just long enough to allow him to swallow:

When I say, "My bed will comfort
            me,
    my couch will ease my
            complaint,"
then you scare me with dreams
    and terrify me with visions,
so that I would choose strangling
    and death rather than this body.
I loathe my life; I would not live
            forever.
    Let me alone, for my days are a
            breath....
Will you not look away from me
            for a while,
    let me alone until I swallow my
            spittle? (Job 7:13–16, 19)

In contrast, those who are wicked prosper, with nothing to fear
from God:

Why do the wicked live on,
    reach old age, and grow mighty
            in power?
Their children are established in
            their presence,
    and their offspring before their
            eyes.
Their houses are safe from fear,
    and no rod of God is upon
            them....
They sing to the tambourine and
            the lyre,
    and rejoice to the sound of the
            pipe.

They spend their days in
> prosperity,
and in peace they go down to
> Sheol. (Job 21:7–9, 12–13)

This kind of injustice might be considered less unfair if there were some kind of afterlife in which the innocent were finally rewarded and the wicked punished, but for Job (as for most of the Hebrew Bible's authors) there is no justice after death either:

As waters fail from a lake,
> and a river wastes away and
> > dries up,
so mortals lie down and do not
> rise again;
until the heavens are no more,
> they will not awake
or be roused out of their sleep. (Job 14:11–12)

Job realizes that if he tried to present his case before the Almighty, he would not have a chance: God is simply too powerful. But that doesn't change the situation. Job is in fact innocent, and he knows it:

God will not turn back his anger....
How then can I answer him,
> choosing my words with him?
Though I am innocent, I cannot
> answer him;
> I must appeal for mercy to my
> > accuser.
If I summoned him and he
> answered me,
> I do not believe that he would

> listen to my voice.
> For he crushes me with a tempest,
>     and multiplies my wounds
>         without cause ...
> If it is a contest of strength, he is
>         the strong one!
> If it is a matter of justice, who
>         can summon him?
> Though I am innocent, my own
>         mouth would condemn me;
>     though I am blameless, he
>         would prove me perverse. (Job 9:13–20)

In this, Job is prescient. For at the end of the poetic dialogues God does appear before Job—who is innocent and blameless—and cows him into submission by his fearful presence as the Almighty Creator of all. Still, though, Job insists on presenting his case before God, insisting on his own righteousness and his right to declare his innocence: "[M]y lips will not speak falsehood; ... until I die I will not put away my integrity from me" (Job 27:3–4). He is sure that God must agree, if only he could find him to present his case:

> Oh, that I knew where I might
>         find him,
>     that I might come even to his
>         dwelling!
> I would lay my case before him,
>     and fill my mouth with
>         arguments.
> I would learn what he would
>         answer me,
>     and understand what he would
>         say to me.

Would he contend with me in the
    greatness of his power?
No; but he would give heed to
    me.
There an upright person could
    reason with him,
    and I should be acquitted
    forever by my judge. (Job 23:3–7)

Would that it were so. Unfortunately, Job's earlier claims turn
out to be the ones that are true. God does not listen to the pleas of
the innocent; he overpowers them by his almighty presence. Still, at
the end of the dialogues Job throws down the gauntlet and demands a divine audience:

O that I had one to hear me!
    (Here is my signature! Let the
    Almighty answer me!)
    O that I had the indictment
    written by my adversary!
Surely I would carry it on my
    shoulder;
    I would bind it on me like a
    crown;
I would give him an account of all
    my steps;
    like a prince I would approach
    him. (Job 31:35–37)

This final demand receives a divine response. But not before another "friend" appears to state still more forcefully the "prophetic"
case against Job, that he is being punished for his sins. Elihu son of
Barachel appears out of nowhere and enters the discussion, delivering

a speech that separates Job's demand for a divine audience and the appearance of God himself on the scene. In this speech Elihu rebukes Job in harsh terms and exalts God's goodness in punishing the wicked and rewarding the righteous.

Job has no time—or need—to reply to this restatement of his friends' views. Before he can respond, God himself appears, in power, to overwhelm Job with his presence and cow him into submission in the dirt. God does not appear with a still, small voice from heaven, or in human guise, or in a comforting dream. He sends a violent and terrifying whirlwind and speaks to Job out of it, roaring out his reprimand:

> Who is this that darkens counsel
> > by words without
> > knowledge?
> Gird up your loins like a man,
> > I will question you, and you
> > shall declare to me.
> Where were you when I laid the
> > foundation of the earth?
> > Tell me, if you have
> > understanding.
> Who determined its
> > measurements—surely you
> > know!
> > Or who stretched the line upon
> > it?
> On what were its bases sunk,
> > or who laid its cornerstone
> when the morning stars sang
> > together
> > and all the heavenly beings
> > shouted for joy? (Job 38:2–7)

In his anger, God reproves Job for thinking that he, a mere mortal, can contend with the one who created the world and all that is in it. God is the Almighty, unanswerable to those who live their petty existence here on earth. He asks Job a series of impossible questions, meant to grind Job into submission before his divine omnipotence:

> Have you commanded the
>     morning since your days
>     began,
>   and caused the dawn to know
>     its place?...
> Have you entered into the
>     springs of the sea,
>   or walked in the recesses of the
>     deep?
> Have the gates of death been
>     revealed to you,
>   or have you seen the gates of
>     deep darkness?
> Have you comprehended the
>     expanse of the earth?
>   Declare, if you know all this....
> Have you entered the storehouses
>     of the snow,
>   or have you seen the
>     storehouses of the hail? ...
> Do you know the ordinances of
>     the heavens?
>   Can you establish their rule on
>     the earth?
> Can you lift up your voice to the
>     clouds,

> so that a flood of waters may
>      cover you?
> Can you send forth lightnings, so
>      that they may go,
>      and say to you, "Here we are"? ...
> Is it by your wisdom that the
>      hawk soars,
>      and spreads its wings toward
>           the south?
> Is it at your command that the
>           eagle mounts up
> and makes its nest on high? (Job 38:12, 16–18, 22, 33–35;
>      39:26–27)

This demonstration of raw divine power—it is God, not Job, who is the creator and ruler of this world—leads to the natural conclusion. If God is almighty and Job is a pathetically weak mortal, who is *he* to contend with God (40:1–2)? Job submits in humility (40:3–4). But God is not finished with him. He speaks a second time from the whirlwind.

> Then the LORD answered Job out
>      of the whirlwind:
> Gird up your loins like a man;
>      I will question you, and you
>           declare to me.
> Will you even put me in the
>           wrong?
>      Will you condemn me that you
>           may be justified?
> Have you an arm like God,
>      and can you thunder with a
>           voice like his? (Job 40:6–9)

No, obviously not. Job had predicted that if God ever were to appear to him, he would be completely overpowered by his divine majesty and driven to submit before him, whether innocent or not. And that's exactly what happens. When God's thundering voice is finally silent, Job repents and confesses:

> I know that you can do all
> > things,
> > and that no purpose of yours
> > > can be thwarted....
> I had heard of you by the hearing
> > of the ear,
> > but now my eye sees you;
> therefore I despise myself,
> > and repent in dust and ashes. (Job 42:2, 5–6)

Readers have read this climax to the poetic dialogues in a variety of ways.[3] Some think that Job got everything he had wished for—a divine audience—and was satisfied with that. Others think that Job came to realize his inherent guilt before the Almighty. Others think that once Job has recognized the enormity of God's creation, he can put his individual suffering in a cosmic perspective. Still others think that the point is that God has far too much on his hands—the governance of the entire universe, after all—to be all that concerned about Job's quibbles regarding innocent suffering.

I don't think any of these answers is right. Job did want a divine audience, but that was so he could declare his innocence before God—and he is never given a chance to get a word in. Nor is there any sense in which Job comes to realize that, in fact, he was guilty before God after all: when he "repents" he does not repent of any wrongdoing (he was, after all, completely innocent!); he repents of having thought that he could make his case before the Almighty. Nor does it seem fair to relativize a person's suffering because the world is, after all, a very big and amazing place. And it can't be true that the Lord God has too many other things to worry about other than Job's miserable little life: the entire point of Job's speeches is not that God is *absent* from his life but that he is far too *present,* punishing Job in ways that make no sense because he has done nothing wrong.

It cannot be overlooked that in the divine response from the whirlwind to Job's passionate and desperate plea for understanding why he, an innocent man, is suffering so horribly, no answer is given. God does not explain why Job suffers. He simply asserts that he is the Almighty and, as such, cannot be questioned. He does not explain that Job had committed sins of which he was simply unaware. He does not say that the suffering did not come from him but from other humans (or demonic beings) who were behaving badly toward Job. He does not indicate that it has all been a test to see if Job would remain faithful. His only answer is that he is the Almighty who cannot be questioned by mere mortals, and that the very quest for an answer, the very search for truth, the very impulse to understand is an affront to his Powerful Being. God is not to be questioned and reasons are not to be sought. Anyone who dares to challenge God will be withered on the spot, squashed into the dirt by his overpowering presence. The answer to suffering is that there is no answer, and we should not look for one. The problem with Job is that he expects God to deal rationally with him, to give him a reasonable explanation of the state of affairs; but God refuses to do so. He is, after all, God. Why should he have to answer to anybody? Who are *we,* mere mortals, to question GOD?

This response of God from the whirlwind seems to get God off the hook for innocent suffering—he can do whatever he pleases, since he is the Almighty and is not accountable to anyone. On the other hand, does it really get him off the hook? Doesn't this view mean that God can maim, torment, and murder at will and not be held accountable? As human beings, we're not allowed to get away with that. Can God? Does the fact that he's almighty give him the right to torment innocent souls and murder children? Does might make right?

Moreover, if the point is that we cannot judge the cruel acts of God by human standards (remember: Job was *innocent*!), where does that leave us? In the Bible, aren't humans made in the image of God? Aren't human standards given by God? Doesn't he establish what is right and fair and just? Aren't we to be like him in how we treat others? If we don't understand God by human standards (which he himself has given), how can we understand him at all, since we're human? Isn't this explanation of God's justice, at the end of the day, simply a cop-out, a refusal to think hard about the disasters and evils in the world as having any meaning whatsoever?

It may be that Job's problem is that he has read the Wisdom literature (Proverbs) and the Prophets, and thinks there must be a connection between sin and punishment—since otherwise it doesn't make sense to him that he is suffering. Maybe he should have read the book of Ecclesiastes instead.[4] For there we find the view that suffering does not come for known causes or known reasons. Suffering just comes, and we need to deal with it as best we can.

## Ecclesiastes and Our Ephemeral Existence

Ecclesiastes has long been one of my favorite books of the Bible. It is normally included among the Wisdom books of the Hebrew Scriptures, because its insights into life come not from some kind of divine revelation (in contrast, say, to the Prophets) but from a deep understanding of the world and how it works. Unlike other Wisdom books, such as Proverbs, however, the wisdom that Ecclesiastes imparts is not based on knowledge acquired by generations of wise thinkers; it is based on the observations of one man as he considers life in all its aspects and the certainty of death. Moreover, like the poetic dialogues of Job, Ecclesiastes is a kind of "anti-Wisdom" book, in the sense that the insights it gives run contrary to the traditional views of a book like Proverbs, which insists that life is basically meaningful and good, that evil is punished and right behavior rewarded. Not so for the author of Ecclesiastes, who calls himself the Teacher

(Hebrew: *Qoheleth*). On the contrary, life is often meaningless, and in the end, all of us—wise and foolish, righteous and wicked, rich and poor—all of us die. And that's the end of the story.[5]

There is no better way to identify the overarching message of the book than simply to consider its powerful opening lines. In them the author identifies himself as the son of David and the king in Jerusalem (Eccles. 1:1). The author, in other words, is claiming to be none other than Solomon—known from other traditions as the "wisest man on earth." Scholars are reasonably sure, however, that whoever wrote this book, it could not have been Solomon. Just on the linguistic level, the Hebrew of the book has been influenced by later forms of the Aramaic language, and it contains a couple of Persian loanwords—plausible only after the thinkers of Israel had been influenced by the thinkers of Persia (i.e., after the Babylonian exile). Usually this book is dated to about the third century BCE (some seven hundred years after Solomon himself). In any event, its opening statement virtually says it all:

> The words of the Teacher, the son
>     of David, king in Jerusalem.
> Vanity of vanities, says the
>     Teacher,
>     vanity of vanities! All is vanity.
> What do people gain from all the
>     toil
>   at which they toil under the
>     sun?
> A generation goes, and a
>     generation comes,
>   but the earth remains forever.
> The sun rises and the sun goes
>     down,
>   and hurries to the place where it
>     rises.

The wind blows to the south,
and goes around to the north;
round and round goes the wind,
and on its circuits the wind
returns....
All things are wearisome;
more than one can express;
the eye is not satisfied with seeing,
or the ear filled with hearing.
What has been is what will be,
and what has been done is what
will be done;
there is nothing new under the
sun.
Is there a thing of which it is said,
"See, this is new"?
It has already been
in the ages before us.
The people of long ago are not
remembered,
nor will there be any
remembrance
of people yet to come
by those who come after them. (Eccles. 1:1–6, 8–11)

The key term here is *vanity.* All of life is vanity. It passes by quickly, and then is gone. The Hebrew word is *hevel,* a word that can also be translated "emptiness," "absurdity," "uselessness." *Hevel* literally refers to a mist that evaporates, so that its root idea is something like "fleeting," "ephemeral." The word occurs about thirty times in this relatively short book. For this author, everything in the world is ephemeral and destined soon to pass away—even we ourselves. Placing ultimate value and putting ultimate importance in the things of this world is useless, vain; all things are fleeting, ephemeral.

In the guise of Solomon, this author indicates that he tried everything in order to make life meaningful. He sought for great wisdom, he indulged himself in pleasure, he engaged in large building projects, he accumulated masses of possessions (Eccles. 1:16–2:23); but then he reflected on the meaning of it all: "I considered all that my hands had done and the toil I had spent in doing it, and again, all was vanity and a chasing after wind, and there was nothing to be gained under the sun" (Eccles. 2:11). Despite being rich, wise, and famous, he "hated life" (Eccles. 2:17) and gave his "heart up to despair" (Eccles. 2:20). In the end he drew his conclusion: "There is nothing better for mortals than to eat and drink, and find enjoyment in their toil" (Eccles. 2:24). It is not that the Teacher (Qoheleth) had given up on God or on life; on the contrary, he thought that enjoying the simple things of life (your food and drink, your work, your spouse) comes "from the hand of God" (Eccles. 2:24). But even these things are fleeting and ephemeral: "vanity and chasing after wind" (Eccles. 2:26).

Here is a biblical author I can relate to. Look around and consider everything you work so hard for, everything that you hope to accomplish in life. Suppose you pursue wealth and become fabulously rich. In the end you die, and someone else inherits your wealth (Eccles. 6:1–2). Suppose you want to leave your wealth to your children. Well, that's fine. But they too will die, as will their children, and the children after them. What's the point of devoting your life to something you can't keep? Or suppose you decide to spend your life on intellectual pursuits. You will eventually die and your brain will stop working and then where will your wisdom be? Or suppose all you want in life is great pleasure. It too is completely fleeting—you can never get enough of it. And then your body grows old, wracked with pain, and eventually ceases to exist. So what, actually, is the point?

Moreover, for this author "traditional" wisdom was inherently flawed—another reason I like him so much. It simply is not true that the righteous are rewarded in life and the wicked perish: "In my vain life I have seen everything; there are righteous people who perish in their righteousness, and there are wicked people who prolong their life in their evil doing" (Eccles. 7:15); "there are righteous people who are treated according to the conduct of the wicked, and there are wicked people who are treated according to the conduct of the righteous. I said that this also is vanity" (Eccles. 8:14). The reason it is all *hevel* is that everyone dies and that's the end of the story: "Everything that confronts them is vanity, since the same fate comes to all, to the righteous and the wicked, to the good and the evil, to the clean and the unclean, to those who sacrifice and those who do not sacrifice. As are the good, so are the sinners ... the same fate comes to everyone" (Eccles. 9:1–3). Even in this life, before death, rewards and punishments are not meted out according to merit; everything is dependent on chance.

> Again I saw that under the sun the race is not to the swift, nor the battle to the strong, nor bread to the wise, nor riches to the intelligent, nor favor to the skillful; but time and chance happen to them all. For no one can anticipate the time of disaster. Like fish taken in a cruel net, and like birds caught in a snare, so mortals are snared at a time of calamity, when it suddenly falls upon them. (Eccles. 9:11–12)

Nor, for this author, should it be thought that there is a good afterlife for those who have been good, wise, faithful, and righteous or punishment for those who die in their sins. There are no rewards or punishments after death—life is all there is, and so it should be cherished while we have it. In the Teacher's memorable phrase, "a living dog is better than a dead lion" (Eccles. 9:4). And he explains why: "The living know that they will die, but the dead know nothing; they have no more reward and even the memory of them is lost. Their love and their hate and their envy have already

perished; never again will they have any share in all that happens
under the sun" (Eccles. 9:5–6).

You might think that all this thought about the fleeting character
of life would lead to utter depression and suicide. But not for this
author. It is true that he is pessimistic and claims that he "despairs"
of finding deeper, ultimate meaning. But suicide cannot be the
answer, because that puts an end to the only good thing we have:
life itself. Moreover, his constant refrain throughout the book is that
given the ultimate impossibility of understanding this world and
making sense of what happens, the very best thing we can do is
enjoy life while we have it. On seven occasions in the book he tells
his readers that they should "eat, drink, and be merry." And so he
says:

> This is what I have seen to be good: it is fitting to eat and
> drink and find enjoyment in all the toil with which one toils
> under the sun the few days of the life God gives us; for this is
> our lot. (Eccles. 5:18–19)

> So I commend enjoyment, for there is nothing better for
> people under the sun than to eat, and drink, and enjoy them-
> selves, for this will go with them in their toil through the days
> of life that God gives them under the sun. (Eccles. 8:15)

This strikes me as some of the best advice to be found in any ancient writing. Even though there are people (lots of people!) who
claim to know what happens to us when we die, the truth is that
none of us knows, and none of us ever will "know" until it's too late
for our knowledge to do us any good. My own suspicion is that the
Teacher was right, that there is no afterlife, that this life is all there
is. That should not drive us to despair of life, however. It should
drive us to enjoy life to the uppermost for as long as we can and in
every way we can, cherishing especially the precious parts of life
that can give us innocent pleasure: intimate relationships, loving

families, good friendships, good food and drink, throwing ourselves into our work and our play, doing what we enjoy.

But with this view of the world—what about suffering? For the Teacher, pain as well as pleasure is fleeting and ephemeral. He does not deal with the kinds of intense pain and misery found, say, in the book of Job. His concern is more with the pain of existence itself, the existential crises that all of us confront simply as part of being human. It is not difficult, though, to recognize how he would deal with suffering in extremis were he confronted with it. It too is *hevel*. To be sure, we should work to overcome suffering—in ourselves and others. Freedom from pain is a major goal for those of us living these fleeting lives of ours. But life is more than simply avoiding suffering. It is also enjoying what can come to us in our short stay on earth.

In some respects the Teacher appears to have had a view of suffering similar to that found in the poetic dialogues of Job—but decidedly *not* like the view in the folktale at the book's beginning and conclusion. The author of Ecclesiastes is explicit that God does not reward the righteous with wealth and prosperity. Why then is there suffering? He doesn't know. And he was the "wisest man" ever to have lived! We should take a lesson from this. Despite all our attempts, suffering sometimes defies explanation.

This is like the poetic dialogues of Job, where God refuses to explain to Job why he has inflicted such pain upon him. It differs from Job in that for Ecclesiastes God is not responsible for the pain in the first place. For Job, God inflicts pain and suffering but refuses to say why. As I pointed out, I find this view completely unsatisfying and almost repugnant, that God would beat, wound, maim, torture, and murder people and then, rather than explain himself, overpower the innocent sufferers with his almighty presence and grind them into silence. I find the Teacher's view much more amenable. Here too there is, ultimately, no divine answer to why we suffer. But suffering doesn't come from the Almighty. It is simply something that happens on earth, caused by circumstances we can't control and for reasons we can't understand. And what do we then do about it? We avoid it as much as we can, we try to relieve it in others whenever possible, and we go on with life, enjoying our time here on earth as much as we can, until the time comes for us to expire.

# seven

# God Has the Last Word: Jewish-Christian Apocalypticism

When I tell people that I'm writing a book about suffering, I typically get one of two responses. Some people immediately feel compelled to give me "the" explanation for why there is pain and misery in the world: almost always the explanation is that we have to have free will; otherwise, we would be like robots running around on perfect planet Earth; and since there is free will, there is suffering. When I respond by suggesting that free will can't solve all the problems of suffering—hurricanes in New Orleans, tsunamis in Indonesia, earthquakes in Pakistan, and so on—my discussion partner normally gets a kind of confused look and is either silent or decides to change the subject.

The other response, though, is actually more common. Some people, when they hear that I'm writing about suffering, want to talk about something else.

I used to think that I had the perfect conversation-stopper at cocktail parties. All I had to do was mention what I do for a living. Someone comes up to me, Chardonnay in hand, we make small talk, and he asks me what I do. I tell him I teach at the university. "Oh, what do you teach?" "New Testament and early Christianity." Long pause, and then, "Oh. That must be interesting." And then he heads off, without a single idea about how to ask a follow-up question. Now that I'm writing this book, I have an even better stumper.

"What are you working on these days?" "I'm writing a book about suffering." Pause. "Oh." Longer pause. "And what will you be doing next?" And so it goes.

The reality is that most people don't want to talk about suffering—except to give you an answer that explains all the pain, misery, and anguish in the world in fifteen seconds or less. This, of course, is completely human and natural. We don't want to occupy ourselves with pain but with its absence—or even better, with its opposite, pleasure! And it is very easy for those of us in comfortable American circumstances to keep far removed from the pain of the world. We don't have to deal with death very much: the funeral home makes all the arrangements. We don't even have to grapple with the death of the animals we eat—heaven forbid that we should actually have to observe the butcher cutting up the meat, let alone watch the poor beast get killed, the way our grandparents did.

We are particularly adept at keeping suffering around the world at bay—especially the suffering that does not make the headlines. But in some parts of the world it is there, every day, front and center, impossible to ignore. Most of us had not thought much about malaria until October 2005, when the Bill and Melinda Gates Foundation announced that it was funding three grants, totaling just over $250 million, to help find and develop an effective vaccine and to work out ways to control the spread of the disease, which occurs almost entirely through mosquito bites. Then some of us took notice.

Malaria is a horrible disease, with ravaging and widespread effects, and it is almost completely preventable, in theory. The extent of the misery it produces is breathtaking. The National Institute of Allergy and Infectious Diseases estimates that between 400 and 900 million children, almost all of them in sub-Saharan Africa, contract an acute case of malaria every year. An average of 2.7 million people dies of it, every year. That's more than seven thousand a day, three hundred people an hour, five every minute. Of malaria! Something that most of us never devote a second's attention to. Almost all the fatalities are children. Somehow—apparently—it just doesn't seem that significant to us, that all these African children are dying. But what would it be like if five children died of an epidemic in our own hometown, every minute, of every day, for years and years? Then I suppose we might be more motivated to do something about it.

It may be that the problem will eventually be solved with the generous funding of groups like the Gates Foundation. (How many of *us* can plop down $250 million to deal with a problem? On the other hand, if a million of us would plop down $250 each, it would have the same effect.) But the misery and suffering of the world sometimes seems like the many-headed Hydra that Hercules had to deal with: every time he lopped off a head, two more would grow back in its place. Every time one problem is solved, we come to realize that there are two more, just as severe. Solve malaria, and then you have the problem of AIDS. Solve AIDS and then you have the problem of drinking water. And so on.

Drinking water, as it turns out, is an enormous problem. Most of us, again, don't think that much about it. Our choices are tap or bottled. Some of us are far beyond drinking anything from the tap, thank you very much, and have our bottled water delivered every week. A good part of the world would give a right arm just for the clean tap water that we reject; in fact, millions of people are giving up their lives for not having it.

According to an organization known as Global Water, founded in 1982 by former U.S. ambassador John McDonald and Dr. Peter Bourne, a former United Nations assistant secretary, there are more than one billion men, women, and children in the world (something like one out of every five living human beings) who do not have safe water to drink. The situation such people typically face is dire. Many of them are malnourished to begin with, and the contaminated water they drink carries waterborne parasites that continuously multiply in their weakened bodies, robbing them of the nourishment and energy they need to sustain health. Global Water indicates that 80 percent of the fatal childhood diseases throughout the world are caused not by shortages of food and medicine but by drinking contaminated water. Something like forty thousand men, women, and children die *every day* from diseases directly related to the lack of clean water. Break it down again: that's more than twenty-five a minute. Every minute.

Surely there's a way to solve these problems. If I can drink bottled water delivered to my door every week, nice French wine, microbrewed beer, and Diet Cokes on demand, surely someone living somewhere else should be able to drink water without parasites in it. I admit, I don't much like thinking about this myself. When I turn on the NCAA basketball tournament tonight and pour out a Pale Ale or two, I probably am not going to be reflecting on the fact that during the time it takes me to watch the game, three thousand people around the world will die because they have only unsanitary water to drink. But maybe I should think about it. And maybe I should try to do something about it.

This book is not really meant to explain just what we should be doing. There are other authors far more qualified than I to talk about devising a solution. This book is designed to help us think, not about the solution, but about the problem. And the problem I'm addressing is the question of why. Why—at the deep, thoughtful level—is there such pain and misery in the world? I'm not asking the scientific question of why mosquitoes and parasites attack the human body and make it ill, but the theological and religious question of how we can explain the suffering in the world if the Bible is right and a good and loving God is in charge.

Different biblical authors, as we have seen, have different explanations for all the pain and the misery: some think that pain and suffering sometimes come from God as a punishment for sin (the prophets); some think that misery is created by human beings who abuse and oppress others (the prophets again); some think that God works in suffering to achieve his redemptive purposes (the Joseph story; the Jesus story); some think that pain and misery come as a test from God to see if his people will remain faithful to him even when it does not pay to do so (the folktale about Job); others think that we simply can't know why there is such suffering in the world—either because God the Almighty chooses not to reveal this kind of information to peons like ourselves (Job's poetry) or because it is information beyond the ken of mere mortals (Ecclesiastes). When I think about malaria, or parasites ingested through contaminated water, or other related forms of misery, pain, and death, I personally resonate much more closely with Ecclesiastes than with any of the other options we've seen so far. To think that God is punishing the population of the sub-Sahara for its sins strikes me as grotesque and malevolent. They certainly aren't suffering from malaria because other human beings are oppressing them (directly), and I see nothing redemptive in their deaths, or any indication that God is merely testing them to see if they'll praise him with dying lips, wracked with pain. Maybe it is simply beyond our ability to understand.

Still other solutions are proffered by the biblical writers, however, and we should consider these as well. Probably the most significant historically for the development of the Christian religion— and at one time for Judaism as well—is the view found in the last of the Hebrew Bible books to be written, as well as in many of the New Testament books. It is a view that scholars today call *apocalypticism*. I will explain its name and its basic overarching view later in this chapter. First, though, I need to indicate where the apocalyptic perspective came from. As it turns out, it originated among Jewish thinkers who had grown dissatisfied with the traditional answer for why there is suffering in the world, the answer of the prophets, that suffering came to God's people because they had sinned. Apocalypticists realized that suffering came even more noticeably to the people of God who tried to do God's will. And they had to find an explanation for it.

## The Background of Apocalyptic Thinking

As we have seen, the theology of the Hebrew prophets was ultimately rooted in a belief that God had, in the distant past, intervened in earthly affairs on behalf of his people Israel. Traditions of
God's interventions are at the core of both the Pentateuch and the
Deuteronomistic History. God himself created this world, formed
the first human beings, gave them their first directives, and punished them when they disobeyed. God destroyed the world by flood
when humankind became too wicked. God eventually called one
man, Abraham, to become the father of a great nation that would
distinctively be his people and he their God. God interacted with
the Jewish patriarchs—Abraham, Isaac, Jacob, Jacob's twelve
sons—in guaranteeing that his promises would be fulfilled. He
guided them to Egypt in a time of famine, and then four hundred
years later he delivered them out of Egypt, where they had become
slaves. It was especially through Moses that God was seen to work
mighty wonders for his people, by sending plagues upon the op-
pressive Egyptians, which in turn led to the exodus, the crossing of
the Red Sea (or sea of reeds), the destruction of the Egyptian armies,
the giving of the Law to Moses, and the bestowal of the promised
land on the children of Israel.

God's frequent and beneficent interventions for his people in the
past created a theological problem for Israelite thinkers in later years.
On the one hand, the traditions of these interventions formed the
basis of theological reflection on the nature of God and his relationship to his people: he would protect and defend them when they were
endangered. On the other hand, historical realities seemed to contradict these theological conclusions. For the nation suffered massively,
from time to time. It experienced drought, famine, and pestilence; the
crops sometimes failed; there were political upheavals; and most noticeably, there were enormous military setbacks, especially when the
northern kingdom was destroyed by the Assyrians in 722 BCE and
the southern kingdom by the Babylonians in 586 BCE.

The prophets, of course, had an answer ready to hand: the people were suffering *not* because God was powerless to do anything about it for his chosen ones, but precisely because God was all powerful. It was God himself who was bringing this suffering upon his people, and it was because they had disobeyed him. If they would return to his ways, they would also return to his good favor; suffering would then abate and the people would once again enjoy peace and prosperity. So taught the prophets, whether Amos, Hosea, and Isaiah in the eighth century, or Jeremiah and Ezekiel in the sixth century, or, well, any prophet writing at any time. This was the prophetic view.

But what happens when the prophetic view comes to be disconfirmed by the events of history? What happens when the people of Israel do exactly what the prophets urge them to do—return to God, stop worshiping idols and following other gods, commit themselves to following the laws of God given to Moses, repent of their evil ways and return to doing what is right? The logic of the prophetic solution to the problem of suffering would suggest that then things would turn around and life would again be good.

The historical problem was that there were times when the people did return to God and it made absolutely no difference in their lives of suffering. In fact, there were times when it was *because* they returned to following the ways of God that they suffered, when foreign powers oppressed them precisely because they insisted on following the laws that God had given Moses for his people. How could one explain suffering then? The people must not be suffering for their sins—they were now suffering for their righteousness. The prophetic answer could not handle that problem. The apocalyptic answer arose to deal with it.

At this point I should address a potential objection to my summary of what happened when Israel repented of its sins and returned to God. Many readers—especially those who come from a Christian Protestant background—will no doubt object to my claim that Jews began suffering precisely because they started living righteous lives. In some Christians' views, the Jews never could live righteous lives because they could never actually do everything that God commanded them to do in the Law. And since they could never obey God's Law, they were doomed to suffer. Sometimes when Christians reflect this view, it is nothing more or less than anti-Semitic: making a claim specifically about Jews as being a "hard-necked and sinful people." But more often this view is based on the Christian notion that no people, no matter how hard they try, can possibly do all that God wants them to do. According to this view, to say that the righteous suffer is a bit of nonsense: no one is righteous, so how can the righteous suffer?

I should stress that this is a Christian view that was not shared by most ancient writers—especially the vast majority of ancient Jewish writers. The book of Job, for example, is quite explicit that Job was righteous before God and suffered *even though* he was innocent. The entire point of the book would have been lost if Job had deserved what he got (then, for example, his so-called friends would have been right after all). He did not deserve it, and the book tries (in at least two different ways) to explain why, then, he suffered.

So too with ancient Jewish apocalypticists. They also recognized the historical reality that Jewish people sometimes behaved righteously but suffered nonetheless. These thinkers did not take the views of Job, however, that it was all a test or that it was not a matter that can be explained to mere mortals by God Almighty. These thinkers believed that God had, in fact, explained the matter to them. And that is why scholars today call them apocalypticists. The word comes from a Greek term, *apocalypsis,* that means a "revealing," or an "unveiling." Jewish apocalypticists believed that God had revealed or unveiled to them the heavenly secrets that could make sense of earthly realities. In particular, they believed that God had shown them why his righteous people were suffering here on earth. It was not because God was punishing them. Quite the contrary, it was because the enemies of God were punishing them. These were cosmic enemies. They were obviously not making people suffer for breaking God's law. Just the opposite: as God's enemies, they made people suffer for *keeping* God's laws.

For apocalypticists, cosmic forces of evil were loose in the world, and these evil forces were aligned against the righteous people of God, bringing pain and misery down upon their heads, making them suffer because they sided with God. But this state of affairs would not last forever. Jewish apocalypticists thought, in fact, that it would not last much longer. God was soon to intervene in this world and overthrow the forces of evil; he would destroy the wicked kingdoms of this world and set up his own kingdom, the Kingdom of God, one in which God and his ways would rule supreme, where there would be no more pain, misery, or suffering. And when would this kingdom arrive? In the words of the most famous Jewish apocalypticist of all, "Truly I tell you, some of those standing here will not taste death before they see the Kingdom of God having come in power" (Mark 9:1). Or as he says later—to those who were standing right in front of him—"truly I tell you, *this generation* will not pass away before all these things take place" (Mark 13:30). These are the words of Jesus. Like other apocalypticists of his day, Jesus believed that evil forces were causing suffering for the people of God but that God was about to do something about it—soon, within his own generation.

Before we discuss the views of Jesus himself, as portrayed in our earliest Gospels, it is important to see more specifically where apocalyptic views came from, historically, and to sketch out the major tenets of Jewish apocalyptic thought as a kind of ancient "theodicy," an explanation of how there could be suffering in the world if a good and powerful God was in charge of it.[1]

## The Origins of Apocalyptic Thought

By the days of Jesus, Jewish apocalyptic thought had become a widespread and highly influential perspective among Jews, especially those living in Palestine. We can trace its roots to a period some 150–170 years before the birth of Jesus, during the events known to history as the Maccabean Revolt. This was a period of intense persecution of the Jews of Palestine by its non-Jewish ruler, the monarch of Syria (who controlled the promised land at the time). To make sense of this persecution—and the Jewish response to it in the development of an apocalyptic worldview—we need to have a bit of background.[2]

As we have seen, little Israel was constantly at the center of international struggles for domination of the eastern Mediterranean. The country was overrun, and its armies defeated, by one superpower after another: the Assyrians (722 BCE), the Babylonians (586 BCE), the Persians (539 BCE), the Greeks. The Greek armies were led by Alexander the Great (356–323 BCE), who conquered the Persian Empire and helped spread Greek culture throughout much of the region east of the Mediterranean. When Alexander died an untimely death in 323 BCE, his large empire, which extended from Greece as far east as the Indus River, was divided among his generals. Palestine—the later name for the land area that today we think of as Israel—was ruled by the Egyptians until it was wrested from their control by the Syrians in 198 BCE.

It is hard to know how most Jews felt about foreign domination during this entire time: for more than half a millennium the "promised land" was not controlled by the chosen people but by foreigners. No doubt many Jews resented it, but we have few writings from the period and so it is hard to know. What is abundantly clear is that matters got progressively worse under Syrian domination, particularly when the ruler Antiochus IV, otherwise known as Antiochus Epiphanes, came to the throne. Antiochus was not a benevolent ruler with a live-and-let-live attitude toward the lands that he controlled. He was intent on extending his kingdom as far as possible—he added much of Egypt during his time on the throne—and on bringing a kind of cultural hegemony to the lands that he conquered. In particular, he was interested in forcing Greek culture—the form of culture thought to be the most advanced and civilized—on the peoples under his rule. This, of course, created enormous conflicts for Jews living in Palestine, who were trying to follow the Law of Moses, which stood seriously at odds with the dictates of Greek culture. Jewish males, for example, were circumcised, something that most Greeks thought was bizarre if not downright hilarious; food laws were observed; sabbath day and certain festivals were honored. And above all, only the God of Israel was worshiped—not the foreign gods found in Greek cults scattered around the Mediterranean.

Antiochus, however, wanted to change all that, in his effort to make all the lands under his control consistent in terms of religion and culture. The account of his interactions with Israel is recorded for us in a Jewish writing known as 1 Maccabees, which is a detailed description of the violent uprising that began among the Jews in Palestine in 167 BCE against the policies of Antiochus. The book is named after a Jewish family responsible for starting the uprising—the Maccabees, based on the nickname of one of their leading men, Judas Maccabeus (i.e., Judas the "hammerer," presumably because he was a tough guy); the family is also known as the Hasmoneans, based on the name of a distant ancestor. For our purposes, what matters is not so much the course of events that eventually led to a Jewish victory and the establishment of an independent Jewish state, after all these centuries, in the promised land (a state that would last nearly a century, until the land was conquered by the Romans in 63 BCE under the general Pompey); rather, what matters to us here are the events that led up to the revolt, the attempt of Antiochus to rid Israel of its religion and culture.

According to 1 Maccabees, when Antiochus IV assumed the throne in 175 BCE, some "renegade" Jews in Israel eagerly supported the idea of converting the people of Israel to the ways of Greece. These men pushed Greek culture on other Jews; they built a Greek gymnasium (a kind of Greek cultural center) in Jerusalem, and even had operations to "remove the marks of circumcision" so that they could participate in sports without the embarrassing sign of circumcision there for all to see (1 Macc. 1:11–15). Not everyone was happy with this state of affairs. Eventually, Antiochus came up against Jerusalem and attacked it, defiling the Temple and removing from it the furniture and utensils used by the priests in offering sacrifices to God as prescribed in the Torah (1 Macc. 1:20–23). As the author of the account tells us, Antiochus "shed much blood and spoke with great arrogance" (1 Macc. 1:24).

Two years later Antiochus attacked the city a second time, burning parts of it, tearing down houses, and taking captive women and children (1 Macc. 1:29–31). Then, in order to bring cultural unity to his entire kingdom, he sent out a message that everyone was to "give up their particular customs" (1 Macc. 1:42); in particular, the sacrificial practices of the Jewish Temple were forbidden, the Temple was defiled, Jewish parents were forbidden to circumcise their baby boys, and no one was allowed to follow the dictates of the Mosaic Law, on pain of death (1 Macc. 1:44–50). Then began a horrible persecution: pagan sacrifices were offered in the Temple, altars to pagan gods were built throughout Judah, books of the Torah were collected and burned, anyone found with a Torah scroll was executed. And worse: "According to the decree, they put to death the women who had their children circumcised, and their families and those who circumcised them; and they hung the infants from their mothers' necks" (1 Macc. 1:59–61).

How was one to make sense of this horrifying situation? Here was a case of people suffering not because God was punishing them for breaking the Law but because God's enemies were opposed to their *keeping* the Law. The old prophetic view seemed unable to accommodate these new circumstances. A new view developed, the one that scholars today call apocalypticism. This view is first clearly expressed in a book that was produced during the time of the Maccabean uprising, the final book of the Hebrew Bible to be written, the book of Daniel.

## Daniel's Night Vision

In some ways a complicated text, the book of Daniel contains a number of stories about the prophet and wise man Daniel, said to have lived in the sixth century BCE during the time of the Babylo-

nian exile and the Persian kingdom. Scholars are unified in thinking, however, that the book was not actually produced then. For one
thing, a good portion of the book is written in Aramaic and in a late
form of Hebrew—suggesting a much later date. More important,
the book's symbolism is directed, in no small part, against Antiochus
Epiphanes and his repressive measures against the Jews. And so the
book is normally dated to the mid-second century BCE.[3]

The first part of the book, chapters 1–6, tells stories about Daniel,
a Jewish exile in Babylon, and his three Jewish friends, all of whom
are supernaturally protected from harm during their various esca-
pades in a foreign land. The second part of the book records visions
that Daniel has, and it is this part of the book that especially interests those concerned with the rise of apocalyptic thought in ancient
Israel.

Possibly of greatest significance is the vision that Daniel reports
in chapter 7. In his vision Daniel sees the four heavenly winds "stir-
ring up the great sea" (Dan. 7:2), and then he sees four terrible
beasts arising out of the sea, one after the other. "The first was like a
lion and had eagles' wings" (Dan. 7:4); it eventually becomes like a
human. The second "looked like a bear" with three tusks coming
out of its mouth. This one is told to "arise, devour many bodies"
(Dan. 7:5). The third beast appears like a leopard with the wings of
a bird and four heads. We are told that "dominion was given to it"
(Dan. 7:6). And then Daniel sees the fourth beast, which he describes as "terrifying and dreadful and exceedingly strong" (as if the
others weren't). This beast "had great iron teeth and was devour-
ing, breaking in pieces, and stamping what was left with its feet"
(Dan. 7:7). It had ten horns, and then another horn appeared, up-
rooting three of the others; this horn had eyes and "a mouth speaking arrogantly" (Dan. 7:8).

Next the author sees a heavenly scene in which the Ancient of
Days (i.e., God) ascends to his spectacular and awe-inspiring throne,
with multitudes worshiping him. The divine "court sat in judgment and the books were opened" (Dan. 7:10). The final beast with
the arrogant talking horn is put to death and burned with fire. The

other beasts have their dominions taken away. And then Daniel saw "one like a human being [literally: one like a son of man] coming with the clouds of heaven." This one appears before the Ancient of Days and is given eternal dominion over the earth:

> To him was given dominion
>     and glory and kingship,
> that all peoples, nations, and
>         languages
>     should serve him.
> His dominion is an everlasting
>         dominion
>     that shall not pass away,
> and his kingship is one
>     that shall never be destroyed. (Dan. 7:14)

And that's the end of the vision. As you might imagine, Daniel wakes up terrified, wondering what it all means. He approaches an angelic being, who happens to be there and who interprets the dream for him. The interpretation is short and sweet: "As for these four great beasts, four kings shall arise out of the earth. But the holy ones of the Most High shall receive the kingdom and possess the kingdom forever" (7:17–19). In particular, though, the prophet wants to know about the fourth beast. The angelic interpreter tells him that it represents a fourth kingdom that "shall devour the whole earth, and trample it down, and break it to pieces." This beast has ten horns to represent the ten kings that will govern it, until the little horn appears, which "shall speak words against the Most High, shall wear out the holy ones of the Most High, and shall attempt to change the sacred seasons and the law" (7:25). In other words, this little horn will be a foreign ruler who tries to overthrow the worship of God, change the laws to be followed by the people of God, and persecute them to the death. If this sounds a lot like Antiochus Epiphanes, well, it is.

But the angel goes on to say that the dominion of this one "shall be taken away to be consumed and totally destroyed." And then the saints of Israel will inherit the kingdom of earth:

> The kingship and dominion
>> and the greatness of the
>>> kingdoms under the whole
>>> heaven
>> shall be given to the people of
>>> the holy ones of the Most
>>> High;
> their kingdom shall be an
>> everlasting kingdom,
>> and all dominions shall serve
>>> and obey them. (Dan. 7:27)

And that's where the angel's explanation of the vision ends.

## The Interpretation of the Vision

How are we to understand this vision and the explanation of it given by the angel? Scholars have long recognized that Daniel 7 presents us with one of the first instances (or arguably *the* first instance) of a Jewish "apocalypse." The term *apocalypse* refers to a kind of literature—a literary genre—that started becoming popular during the Maccabean period and continued to be popular for centuries afterward, among Jews and eventually among Christians. Most people today are aware of at least one apocalypse—the Apocalypse (or Revelation) of John, the final book of the New Testament. Like the vision of Daniel 7, the Apocalypse of John looks very odd indeed to modern eyes. But it would not have seemed at all odd to its ancient readers: it was an apocalypse that shared with other writings of the same genre certain well-recognized literary conventions. The genre seems odd to us only if we are not accustomed to reading ancient apocalypses; but a lot of them still exist (outside the Bible). We have apocalypses written in the names of Adam, Moses, Elijah, Enoch, Baruch, Isaiah, Peter, John, Paul, and others. As with any kind of literature, it is possible to analyze the apocalypse *as a genre* (i.e., a *kind* of literature) and to classify its various genre characteristics.

Apocalypses were literary works in which a prophet described visions he had seen. These visions are almost always couched in bizarre symbolism that is hard to interpret (horrifying wild beasts and the like). But invariably an angelic interpreter is nearby who can provide some of the keys of explanation. Some apocalypses describe a journey that the seer is given through the heavenly realms in which what he sees in heaven reflects what happens on earth (there is some of this in the book of Revelation). In other instances, the seer is shown a sequence of events that are interpreted as a kind of historical time line of what will happen in the future (as here in Daniel). As was true with the Hebrew writing prophets, the apocalyptic prophets are speaking to their own day—they are not crystal-ball-gazing into times thousands of years removed. In most instances (not all), the apocalyptic seers write their accounts pseudonymously—claiming to be some famous religious figure of the past. This provides some authority for their accounts—for to whom else would heavenly secrets be revealed than those closest to God, the great men of God of old? And so, as I've pointed out, we have apocalypses allegedly written by Moses, and Elijah, and even Adam; later we get apocalypses allegedly written by Isaiah, Peter, and Paul.

One of the virtues of having a famous person of the past write an apocalypse is that the future events that he sees are, in fact, from the time of the actual writer, already past. As a result, the "predictions" that the pseudonymous author allegedly makes are certain of being fulfilled: they have already happened!

The book of Daniel gives us, then, an apocalypse. It is written pseudonymously during the time of the Maccabean Revolt, when Antiochus Epiphanes was defiling the sanctuary, trying to force the Jews no longer to obey the Law, and persecuting those who refused to cooperate. It is a vision with bizarre symbolism, explained by an angel, in which the "future" is allegedly predicted to a sixth-century prophet; in reality, though, most of the "future" events that are described are *past* events for the actual second-century writer. The value of this kind of fictitious prediction is that when the author then goes on to describe what is to happen next, in his own time, it does not seem that he has shifted from talking about what has already happened, historically, to what he anticipates is going to happen now, in the future. The reader reads *everything* as a future prediction; and since everything else described has already come true (as well it should have, since the author knows what happened in the past), then the predictions of what comes next seem to be sure to come true as well.

The angel in this case explains that each of the beasts represents a king or a kingdom that will arise on the earth and do great damage to its inhabitants. Since the book is set in the time of the Babylonians, scholars have recognized the series of four kingdoms as Babylon, Media, Persia, and Greece. The fourth terrible beast has ten horns— these are rulers coming in the wake of Alexander the Great. The final little horn who "speaks arrogantly," attempts to change the sacred laws, and persecutes the saints (see Dan. 7:25) is none other than Antiochus Epiphanes, who, according to 1 Maccabees, "spoke with great arrogance," tried to force Jews no longer to observe the Law, and persecuted to the death those who disobeyed him.

Who, then, is this "one like a human being" (or "one like a son of man") to whom the eternal kingdom is given? Christians, of course, have traditionally taken this to refer to Jesus, who at his second coming will inherit the Kingdom of God and rule it as the future messiah. But it is important to ask not only how this passage in Daniel came to be interpreted in later times, but also how it was read in its own context. And here we are given considerable help, because the angel interpreter gives a clear indication of who the "one like a human being" is. The humanlike one is set up to contrast with the wild beasts. They are animals; this one is human.

They came from the turbulent sea (the realm of chaos); this one comes from heaven. If the contrast is between beasts and a human-like one, and if the beasts each represent a kingdom, what does the humanlike one represent? Probably a kingdom. And in fact the angel tells us who the "one" is who receives the eternal kingdom: it is the "people of the holy ones of the Most High" (Dan. 7:27; also in 7:18). In other words, it is the holy ones of Israel, previously perse-cuted and slaughtered by their bestial enemies, now exalted to the rulership of the earth.[4]

## Suffering in the Apocalyptic Tradition

It is interesting to compare the understanding of suffering pre-sented in Daniel's vision with the views of the classical writing prophets such as Amos, Hosea, and Isaiah. This can best be done by raising some of the fundamental questions of suffering.

Why do the people of God suffer? According to a passage like Amos 3–5 (to pick a classical example), horrendous suffering comes upon the people of God because they have violated his will and he is punishing them. According to Daniel 7, suffering comes to God's people because of evil forces in the world (the beasts), forces that are opposed to God and those who side with him.

Who causes the suffering? In Amos, God brings suffering. In Daniel, it is the forces opposed to God who bring it.

Who is at fault for suffering? For Amos, the people are respon-sible for their own suffering: they have sinned and God punishes them. For Daniel, it is the forces aligned against God who are at fault: they are persecuting those who do God's will.

What causes the suffering? In Amos, it is the sinful activity of God's people. In Daniel, it is the upright behavior of those who side with God.

How will the suffering end? For Amos, it will end when the people of God repent of their sin and return to God's ways. For

Daniel, it will end when God destroys the evil forces that oppose him in the world and sets up his good kingdom for his people.

When will it end? For Amos, it will end at some undisclosed future time, when the people of God see the error of their ways and repent. For Daniel, it will end very soon, when God intervenes in history to overthrow the forces of evil.

## The Underlying Tenets of Apocalypticism

At the time the book of Daniel was being written, Jewish thinkers and authors took up such ideas and developed an entirely new worldview that could explain why there is such pain and misery in a world allegedly ruled by the God who created it. In addition to being aware of the literary genre of "apocalypse," we need to become familiar with the worldview lying behind it, the worldview I have called "apocalypticism." For the sake of clarity I should emphasize that even though the Jews and Christians who produced literary "apocalypses" were all apocalypticists, not all apocalypticists produced apocalypses (any more than all Marxists have produced a Communist Manifesto). As we will see, two of the most famous apocalypticists of the ancient world—Jesus and the apostle Paul— did not do so. But they were nonetheless firmly committed to apocalyptic views. What can we say about these views, as expressed in apocalyptic writings both within the Bible and outside it?

Jewish apocalypticists, as a rule, subscribed to four major tenets.

(1) *Dualism*. Jewish apocalypticists maintained that there were two fundamental components of reality in our world, the forces of good and the forces of evil. In control of the forces of good, of course, was God himself. But God had a personal opponent, an evil power in control of the forces of evil—Satan, the Devil. We earlier saw that in the book of Job, "the Satan" was not God's archenemy but a member of his divine council, one who reported to God with the other "sons of God." It is with Jewish apocalypticists that Satan

takes on a different character and becomes the archenemy of God, a powerful fallen angel who has been forced out of heaven and wreaks havoc here on earth by opposing God and all that he stands for. It was ancient Jewish apocalypticists who invented the Judeo-Christian Devil.

For apocalypticists, everything in the world is divided into the two camps, good and evil, God and the Devil. On God's side are the good angels; on the Devil's are the wicked demons. God has the power of righteousness and life; the Devil has the power of sin and death. In the apocalyptic system, "sin" is not simply a human activity, a disobedient act. Sin is actually a power, a kind of demonic force, that is trying to enslave people, to force them to do what is contrary to their own interests and contrary to the will of God (and it is obviously succeeding). Why is it that some people just "can't help themselves" and do what they know is bad or wrong? For Jewish apocalypticists, it is because the power of sin has overwhelmed them. So too "death" is not simply something that happens when our bodies cease to function; it is a demonic power in the world that is trying to capture us. And when it succeeds, it annihilates us, removing us from the land of the living and from all that is good—and from the presence of God.

The world is filled with demonic forces aligned against God and his people; it is a stage for an ongoing cosmic conflict. Human suffering is created in the course of battle, as evil forces in the world have their way with relatively powerless human beings, who suffer horribly as a result. For some unknown reason, God has relinquished control of this world to the forces of evil—for the time being. Pain, misery, anguish, suffering, and death are the result.

This cosmological dualism between the forces of good and evil has a historical component as well. Apocalypticists thought of history itself in dualistic terms: there is a radical disjunction between this age and the age to come. This age—for unknown, mysterious reasons—is given over to the forces of evil: the Devil, his demons, sin, suffering, and death. Why are there so many disasters in this world, earthquakes, famines, epidemics, wars, deaths? Because the powers of evil are in control. But not forever. God is going to intervene in this world, overthrow the forces of evil, and set up a new kingdom on earth, in which everything opposed to him is destroyed and his people are given lives beyond pain and suffering.

(2) *Pessimism.* Apocalypticists did not think that we would be able to make progress in bringing in this Kingdom of God ourselves. We cannot, in fact, improve our lot in this age, an age of evil, misery, and anguish. God has relinquished control of this world to the forces of evil, and things are simply going to get worse and worse, until the end, when literally all hell breaks out. We should not think, therefore, that we can make things better by improving our welfare programs, placing more teachers in the classroom, or putting more cops on the beat; we cannot make matters better by developing new technologies for making life easier, devising new plans for implementing world peace, or devoting enormous resources to fighting malaria, cancer, and AIDS. We can *do* these things, of course, but they won't matter. Ultimately, it is the forces of evil that are in control of this world, and they will continue to assert their power and gain the ascendancy, until God himself intervenes.

(3) *Vindication.* But intervene he will, in a cataclysmic act of judgment on this world. God is the one who created this world, and he is the one who will redeem it. He will vindicate his holy name, and the people who call upon his name, in a show of cosmic force. He will send a savior from heaven—sometimes thought of as the "messiah"; sometimes called "the Son of Man"—who will execute judgment on the earth and all who live on it. Those who have sided with God and the powers of good will be rewarded when this day of judgment appears; they will be brought into the eternal kingdom, a world in which there is no more pain, misery, or suffering. But those who have sided with the Devil and the powers of evil will be punished, sent away to eternal torment to pay for their disobedience to God and the suffering that they caused for God's holy people.

Moreover, this judgment will affect not only those who happen to be alive when the end of this age arrives; it will affect *everyone*, living and dead. Jewish apocalypticists developed the idea that at the end of this age there would be a resurrection of the dead, when those who had previously died would be brought back to life in order to face judgment, the righteous to receive an eternal reward and the unrighteous to be subjected to eternal torment.

Throughout most of the Hebrew Bible there is no idea of a future resurrection. Some authors (most) thought that death led to a shadowy existence among the shades in Sheol; others seemed to think that death was the end of the story. But not the apocalypticists. They invented the idea that people would live eternally, either in the Kingdom of God or in a kingdom of torment. The first expression of this view comes, in fact, in the book of Daniel (chapter 12). The point of this view is clear: you shouldn't think that you can side with the forces of evil in this world, become rich, powerful, and famous as a result (who else can acquire power in this world other than those who side with the forces in charge of it?), and then die and get away with what you did. You can't get away with it. At the end of time God will raise you from the dead and make you face judgment. And there's not a sweet thing you can do to stop him.

(4) *Imminence*. And when is this end of the age to come? When will God vindicate his name? When will the judgment day arrive? When will the dead be raised? For apocalypticists the answer was clear and compelling: It will happen very soon. It is right around the corner. It is imminent.

The reason for asserting that the end was almost here is obvious. Apocalypticists were writing in times of terrible suffering, and they were trying to encourage their readers to hold on, for just a little longer. Do not give up the faith; do not abandon your hope. God will soon intervene and overthrow the forces of evil, the powers of this world that are bringing such misery and anguish upon the people of God, the cosmic enemies who are causing the droughts, famines, epidemics, wars, hatreds, and persecutions. Those who are faithful to God have just a little while to wait. How long will it be? "Truly I tell you, some of those standing here will not taste death before they see that the Kingdom of God has come in power.... Truly I tell you, *this generation* will not pass away before all these things take place" (Mark 9:1; 13:30).

Jesus of Nazareth was not unique in preaching that a good kingdom of God was coming very soon, that it had already "drawn very near" (Mark 1:15), that people of his own generation would see it arrive "in power." In the essence of his proclamation, Jesus was preaching an apocalyptic message of hope to those who were suffering in this world. They did not have much longer to wait until God intervened. This was a message preached by a range of Jewish (and, later, Christian) apocalypticists, both before Jesus' day and in the days after.

## Jesus as an Apocalypticist

Most Christians today, of course, do not think of Jesus principally as a Jewish apocalypticist. This is certainly not the view of Jesus taught in most Sunday schools or proclaimed from most pulpits. Nevertheless, this is how the majority of critical scholars in the English-speaking (and German-speaking) world have understood Jesus for more than a century, since the publication of Albert Schweitzer's classic study, *The Quest of the Historical Jesus* (in German it had the more prosaic title *Von Reimarus zu Wrede,* 1906). I will not be able here to provide a full discussion of all the evidence that has led scholars to understand Jesus in this way—that would take an entire book, or more.[5] And, in fact, for the point I'm trying to make, it does not much matter whether the historical man Jesus, himself, was an apocalypticist. What I'm trying to show is that the Bible contains apocalyptic teachings—and it is beyond doubt that throughout our earliest sources describing Jesus' life, the Gospels of Matthew, Mark, and Luke, Jesus is portrayed as delivering an apocalyptic message of the coming end and the need to remain faithful to God in anticipation of the judgment soon to occur.

In the New Testament Gospels, this apocalyptic view does not originate with Jesus, for it is already proclaimed by Jesus' forerunner, the prophet John the Baptist. According to one of our earliest sources, John had the following to say to his opponents:

> Who warned you to flee from the wrath to come? Bear fruits worthy of repentance.... Even now the ax is lying at the root of the trees; every tree therefore that does not bear good fruit is cut down and thrown into the fire. (Luke 3:7–9)

For John, the wrath of God was soon to appear. In a vivid image he likened this judgment scene to the cutting down of trees, which—like sinners—would be burned with fire. How soon would the chopping begin? The ax is already "lying at the root of the trees." In other words, it is ready to begin, now.

Jesus delivers a similar message throughout our earliest sources. In the oldest surviving Gospel, Mark, Jesus' very first words are an apocalyptic proclamation of the coming kingdom: "The time has been fulfilled, the Kingdom of God is very near. Repent and believe the good news!" (Mark 1:15). When Jesus says that the time has been "fulfilled," he is using an apocalyptic image: This age we live in now has a certain amount of time allotted to it. That time is almost up; it is like an hourglass that is full. God's kingdom is about to arrive, and people need to prepare for it.

Jesus repeatedly speaks about this coming "Kingdom of God" in the early Gospels. For Jesus, this is not the destination of souls that leave the body and "go to heaven." The Kingdom of God is a real place, here on earth, where God rules supreme over his people in a utopianlike state. But not everyone will be able to enter into it:

> And there will be weeping and gnashing of teeth when you see Abraham and Isaac and Jacob and all the prophets in the Kingdom, but you are cast out; and people will come from east

and west and from north and south and recline at table in the
Kingdom of God. (Luke 13:28–29)

In particular, Jesus taught that a cosmic figure, whom he called
the Son of Man, will bring in this kingdom in a cosmic act of judgment.[6] When Jesus refers to the Son of Man, he is probably alluding
to the passage in Daniel that we saw earlier, in which "one like a
son of man" comes on the clouds of heaven at the time of judgment
on the earth. Jesus too thought that someone (whom he appears to
have taken as an individual), called the Son of Man, would come on
the clouds of heaven in judgment. In fact, this one will judge people
based on whether they have listened to Jesus' proclamation, done as
he demanded, and repented in preparation.

Whoever is ashamed of me and my words in this adulterous
and sinful generation of that one will the Son of Man be
ashamed when he comes in the glory of his Father with the
holy angels. (Mark 8:38)

This appearance of the Son of Man will involve a worldwide
judgment, sudden and comparable in scope to the destruction of
the world in the days of Noah:

For just as the flashing lightning lights up the earth from one
part of the sky to the other, so will the Son of Man be in his
day.... And just as it was in the days of Noah, so will it be in
the days of the Son of Man. They were eating, drinking, mar-
rying, and giving away in marriage, until the day that Noah
went into the ark and the flood came and destroyed them
all.... So too will it be on the day when the Son of Man is revealed. (Luke 17:24, 26–27, 30)

This judgment will not be a happy time for the evildoers of earth,
but the righteous will be rewarded:

Just as the weeds are gathered and burned with fire, so will it be at the culmination of the age. The Son of Man will send forth his angels, and they will gather from his Kingdom every cause of sin and all who do evil, and they will cast them into the furnace of fire. In that place there will be weeping and gnashing of teeth. Then the righteous will shine forth as the sun, in the Kingdom of their Father. (Matt. 13:40–43)

This future kingdom will be an actual place, ruled, in fact, by the twelve followers of Jesus himself:

Truly I say to you, in the renewed world, when the Son of Man is sitting on the throne of his glory, you (disciples) also will be seated on twelve thrones, judging the twelve tribes of Israel. (Matt. 19:28)

The kingdom will be inhabited by the "chosen ones" (for Jesus: the ones who adhere to his teaching) and will come only after this world, which is controlled by the forces of evil, is done away with:

In those days, after that affliction, the sun will grow dark and the moon will not give its light, and the stars will be falling from heaven, and the powers in the sky will be shaken; and then they will see the Son of Man coming on the clouds with great power and glory. Then he will send forth his angels and he will gather his elect from the four winds, from the end of earth to the end of heaven. (Mark 13:24–27)

In our earliest Gospels Jesus teaches that when this judgment day comes, there will be a complete reversal of fortune for those on earth. Those who are powerful and exalted now will be destroyed; but those who are poor and oppressed will be rewarded. There is an apocalyptic logic to this way of thinking. How is it that people in the present age can become rich, powerful, and influential? It is only by siding with the powers that control this world; and those powers are evil. Who is suffering in this world? Who are the poor, the outcast, and the oppressed? It is those whom the powers of this world are afflicting. In the new age to come, everything will be reversed. The powers now in control will be deposed and destroyed, along with all those who sided with them. That is why the "first will be last and the last first" (Mark 10:31). This wasn't just a clever one-liner that Jesus came up with one day to give us something to say when we're trying to make the best of things while standing in a long line at the grocery store; it's something he actually meant. Those prominent now will be taken out of power; the oppressed now will be rewarded. "All those who exalt themselves shall be humbled and those who humble themselves shall be exalted" (Luke 14:11). That is why "whoever is least among you, this one in fact is great" (Luke 9:48); and it is why "whoever humbles himself as this small child, this is the one who is great in the kingdom of heaven" (Matt. 18:4).

The relevance of these teachings to the question of suffering should be obvious. For the Jesus of our earliest Gospels, those who are suffering in the present world can expect that in the world to come they will be rewarded and given places of prominence. Those who are causing pain and suffering, on the other hand, can expect to be punished. That is the point of the famous Beatitudes, which are probably given in their oldest form not in the well-known Sermon on the Mount in Matthew 5, but in the so-called Sermon on the Plain in Luke 6. There Jesus says: "Blessed are you who are poor, for yours is the Kingdom of God." One might wonder what is so great about being poor. Is poverty really to be celebrated, something to be happy about? The saying best makes sense in an apocalyptic setting. The poor are "blessed" because when the Kingdom of God comes, they are the ones who will inherit it.

The same interpretation applies to "Blessed are you who are hungry now, for you will be filled." It's not that it is inherently a good thing to be starving. But those who don't have enough to eat now will enjoy the fruits of the kingdom, when it arrives. Comparable are those who are wracked with other kinds of misery: "Blessed are you who weep now, for you will laugh." All things will be reversed in the coming kingdom. That is why you should rejoice "when people hate you, and when they exclude you, revile you, and defame you." There will be a reversal in the age to come. Among other things, this means that those who have it good now had better take heed: when the kingdom comes, they will face dire consequences for the actions in life that have produced such good results:

> Woe to you who are rich,
> for you have received your
> consolation.
> Woe to you who are full now,
> for you will be hungry.
> Woe to you who are laughing
> now,
> for you will mourn and weep;
> Woe to you when all speak well
> of you,
> for that is what their ancestors
> did to the false prophets. (Luke 6:24–26)

And when, for the Jesus of our earliest Gospels, will this time come, when the Son of Man arrives in judgment and brings a reversal of fortunes to all who dwell on earth? As we have seen, Jesus thought it would be very soon, before "this generation passes away," before his disciples "taste death." That is why he repeatedly says, "What I say to you I say to everyone: Watch!" (Mark 13:33–37); "Watch, therefore, for you do not know the day or the hour." That is also the point of many of his parables:

> If a servant [whose master has left town for a time] says to himself, "My master is not coming for a while," and begins to

beat the servants, both men and women, and to eat, drink, and carouse, the master of that servant will come on a day he is not expecting and in an hour he does not know, and he will cut him to shreds. (Luke 12:45–56)

No one knows when the day will come, says Jesus: but it is soon. That's why everyone must constantly "Watch!"

## The Relevance of an Apocalyptic View

How are we to evaluate this apocalyptic point of view, with its conviction that this rotten course of affairs, this miserable world we inhabit, is very soon to come to a crashing halt? We live nearly two thousand years after Jesus is said to have spoken these words, and, of course, the end has not come. Still, throughout history there have always been people who have expected it to come—within their own generation. In fact, nearly every generation of Jesus' followers, from day one until now, has had its self-styled prophets—there are many on the scene yet today—who believed they could predict that the end, this time, really was imminent.

One of the times that I saw this for myself, most graphically, was when I moved to North Carolina to take up my teaching position at the University of North Carolina at Chapel Hill. That was in August 1988, and there was a bit of a media frenzy at the time involving the imminent end of the world with the reappearance of Jesus. A former NASA rocket engineer named Edgar Whisenant had written a book in which he claimed that Jesus would soon return to earth and take his followers out of the world (the so-called rapture), leading to the rise of the Antichrist and the coming of the end. The book was entitled, cleverly enough, *Eighty-eight Reasons Why the Rapture Will Occur in 1988.*

There is no point in recounting all of Whisenant's eighty-eight reasons here, but I can mention one. In the Gospel of Matthew, Jesus explains to his disciples what will happen at the end of the age, and they want to know when it will happen. Jesus tells them: "From the fig tree, learn this lesson. As soon as its branch becomes tender and it puts forth leaves, you know that summer is near. So also you, when you see all these things, you should know that he is near, at the very gates. Truly I tell you, this generation will not pass away before all these things take place" (Matt. 24:32–34).

But what does all this mean? In his book, Whisenant points out that in Scripture the "fig tree" is often an image of the nation Israel. And what does it mean for the fig tree to "put forth its leaves"? This is referring to what happens every spring; the tree has lain dormant over the winter, as if dead, and then buds appear. When does that happen to Israel? When does Israel come back to life? When it is restored to the promised land and once again, after lying dormant for so long, becomes a sovereign nation. And when did that happen? In 1948, when Israel became a country once again. "This generation will not pass away before all these things take place." How long is a generation in the Bible? Forty years. And so there it is: add forty years to the year 1948 and that brings us to 1988.

Whisenant was convinced on the basis of this prophecy—and eighty-seven others—that the end of the world as we know it was going to occur in September of 1988, during the Jewish festival of Rosh Hashanah. When other Bible-believing Christians pointed out that Jesus himself had said that "no one knows the day or the hour" when the end would come, Whisenant was not at all fazed. He did not know "the day or the hour," he claimed; he just knew the week.

Whisenant, of course, was convincingly proved wrong. Jesus did not return. In response, Whisenant wrote a second book, claiming that he had made an error the first time around because he had failed to remember that there was no year "zero" in our calendar. As a result, all his calculations were off by a year. Jesus was to return in 1989. But, of course, he didn't.

Whisenant had two things in common with every other of the

many thousands of Christians over the centuries who thought they knew when the end would come. To a person, they have based their calculations on "undisputed" prophecies of Scripture (especially the book of Revelation, which we'll consider in the next chapter). And every one of them has been dead wrong.

But maybe the point of apocalyptic teaching in the Bible—even on the lips of Jesus—is not about the calendar, about the actual timing of the end. Maybe it's about something else.

Jesus and other apocalypticists in the ancient world were dealing with the very real problems of pain and suffering. They did not think that God was causing suffering—either to punish sinners or to test his people. At the same time, they believed that God was ultimately in control of this world. Why then is there suffering? For mysterious reasons, God has handed over control of the world, temporarily, to the powers of evil, who are wreaking havoc here, especially among God's chosen ones. But God in the end is sovereign. And evil is not the end of the story. Pain, misery, and death— these are not the last word. God has the last word. God will reassert himself and wrest control of this world from the forces that now dominate it. And those who suffer now will be rewarded then, in the good kingdom that God is soon to bring.

This may not be a view that people can accept today, without adopting an ancient, rather than a modern, view of the world. But it should not be ignored, for all that. As I will show in the next chapter, the apocalyptic view predominates throughout the New Testament, and it is a message designed to provide hope to those who suffer, a message designed to keep them from despair in the midst of the agony and misery that belong very much to a world that seems to be controlled by evil forces that are opposed to God and his people.

# eight

# More Apocalyptic Views: God's Ultimate Triumph over Evil

After preparing to write this chapter yesterday, I went off to lead an undergraduate seminar on the apocryphal Gospels—that is, the Gospels that did not make it into the New Testament. I am on sabbatical leave this year from my position at the University of North Carolina but had been asked to be a scholar in residence for a week at nearby High Point University. During the seminar, yesterday, a student asked if I was writing anything now, and I told her yes, I was writing a book on biblical answers to the problem of why there is suffering. As I expected, she was ready and eager to tell me "the" answer: "There's suffering," she said, "because we have to have free will; otherwise we would be like robots." I asked her my standard question: if suffering is entirely about free will, how can you explain hurricanes, tsunamis, earthquakes, and other natural disasters? She wasn't sure, but she felt pretty confident that it had something to do with free will.

As we have seen, the "free will" answer is not nearly the focus of attention for the biblical authors that it is for people today. But there are a lot of things that are not in the Bible (or are not the main point of the biblical writers) that people mistakenly *think* are in the Bible. I remember growing up thinking, along with just about everyone else, that one of the central verses in the Bible was "God helps those who help themselves." As it turns out, while the phrase may be ancient, it is not biblical. It was popularized, in America at least, in Benjamin Franklin's 1736 edition of *Poor Richard's Almanack*. So too the free-will argument—or maybe we should call it the robot argument. Very popular today, it was not heard nearly so often in biblical times.

The free-will argument can, of course, explain a good deal of the evil in the world around us, from the Holocaust to the disaster of 9/11, from sexism to racism, from white-collar crime to governmental corruption. But it also leaves a lot out of the equation.

I think I first realized this in a big way right around the time I was teaching my course on "The Problem of Suffering in the Biblical Traditions" at Rutgers in the mid-1980s. I had not paid an inordinate amount of attention to natural disasters before then; I was aware of them, felt sorry for those involved, wondered how a poor fellow like me could do anything to help, and that sort of thing. But they didn't really affect me too much personally. Then one happened that haunted me for weeks and months.

On November 13, 1985, we learned that a volcano had erupted in northern Colombia, South America. The mudslides that resulted blanketed and destroyed four villages. Nearly everyone in these villages was killed in his or her sleep, as the mud rushed down at something like thirty miles an hour, dwarfing the flimsy huts and suffocating the people inside. The total death toll was put at more than thirty thousand people. That number really stuck in my mind: thirty thousand people who were alive one minute and dead the next, killed in their sleep, horribly. That's more than ten times the number of people who died in the attacks on the World Trade towers on 9/11. The latter has occupied our thoughts—rightly so!—for the last several years since the terrorist attack. The other we barely remember and more or less shrug away. Poor souls; shouldn't have lived so near a volcano.

But natural disasters can't be passed over so lightly. The thousands, hundreds of thousands, of people affected every year, injured, maimed, killed; homes destroyed, unsettled with nowhere to go and no one to rely on; for many, a hell on earth. The ones closest to home, of course, are the ones we're most concerned about. But even with these, there are a lot of people who seem to be less than sympathetic. Take those who have suffered from the devastations of Hurricane Katrina. We mourn those who died and scratch our heads in wonder at the incompetence of the federal bureaucracy that makes it impossible for New Orleans to rebuild and for its people to get on with their lives. We seem to be able to send entire fleets of ships into the Persian Gulf without much problem, and that costs *tons* of money. Why can't we devote adequate resources to helping people living near our own gulf? Even though the Katrina aftermath continues to be in the news a year and a half later, the reality seems to be that most people wish that New Orleans would somehow just get solved. And some people are all too willing to blame other human beings for what happened. The levees were poorly constructed, and everyone knew it. What right did they have to build New Orleans there anyway? Surely people knew this was going to happen—why didn't they just move away? And so on. I suppose it's easier to blame the victims when we think mainly about ourselves: *I* would have gotten out of there!

That's easy to say when you can afford a bus ticket to anywhere in the country or can easily pack up and move without noticing a serious drop in income. It is harder to say when you can't afford to put food on the table, let alone go out for a nice meal once in a while—and how, exactly, is someone like that supposed to move to a safer place? And what place, really, is completely safe? I lived in Kansas for most of my early life, but it wasn't until I moved to North Carolina that I almost got nailed by a tornado. The point of natural disasters is that none of us is safe.

As devastating as Katrina was and continues to be, it pales in comparison with the other horrendous disasters that have hit our world in recent years. On December 26, 2004, a devastating earthquake struck in the Indian Ocean, its epicenter off the west coast of Sumatra, Indonesia. It triggered a tsunami (or rather, a series of tsunamis) along the coasts of most of the countries bordering the ocean and destroyed villages and towns and human life all across south and southeast Asia, especially in Indonesia, Sri Lanka, India, and Thailand. The body count will probably never be complete, but the best estimates put the total at around 300,000. If the Colombian mudslide destroyed ten times more lives than the terrorist attacks on 9/11, the tsunami destroyed ten times more lives than the mudslide. Not to mention the millions affected in other, extremely tangible ways, people forced, like those in New Orleans, to pick up the pieces but, unlike those in New Orleans, for the most part unable to yell and scream at governmental officials for their crass insensitivity and inability to deal with the situation. Most of the people affected are helpless and hopeless, dependent at best on the beneficence of international relief efforts.

And so it goes, one disaster after another. It's enough to make an apocalypticist out of you. These disasters—and the countless others like them, since time immemorial—are not created by human beings but by the forces of nature. Unless you want to think that God is the one who called forth the demons behind these attacks, it is hard to know what God had to do with them. One of the virtues of the apocalyptic perspective embraced by many (most?) of the New Testament authors is that it insists quite vociferously that God does not bring disasters; his cosmic enemies do. Not just earthquakes and hurricanes and tsunamis, but sickness and disease, mental health problems, oppression and persecution: it is the Devil and his minions, the demons, who are at fault. This is an age in which they have been given virtually free rein. To be sure, God sometimes intervenes for good—for example, in the ministry of Jesus or of his apostles. But the evil forces of this world will not be taken out of the way until the end, when God unleashes his wrath upon them and those who have sided with them. And then there will be hell on earth in ways that have never been seen before.

This is the message delivered by Jesus in the Gospels, as we saw in the preceding chapter; it is also the message of the Gospel writers as they remembered the key events of his life, of the apostle Paul living after Jesus, and of the author of the book of Revelation, a book that provides a fitting apocalyptic climax to the writings that form the canon of the New Testament.

## Remembering the Apocalyptic Life of Jesus

Jesus' life as it was remembered by the Gospel writers of the New Testament was all about suffering—suffering of others that he relieved, and suffering of his own that he endured. In some ways the essence of Jesus' life is summed up in the mocking words spoken against him by the Jewish leaders as he was hanging from the cross in Mark's Gospel—words that, for Mark, tell the truth in ways that the speakers appear not to have understood: "He saved others, but he is not able to save himself" (Mark 15:31). The word *saved* here does not have the connotation that it does to many modern evangelical Christians, who ask "Are you saved?" in order to know whether you have done what you need to do to go to heaven when you die. The Greek word for "save," in this and other contexts, refers to restoring a person to health and wholeness. Jesus "saved" others because he healed them when they were sick or demon-possessed. He is unable to save himself—not because he lacks the ability to come off the cross (in Mark's view) but because he must do the Father's will, which is to suffer and die for the sake of others. In other words, to bring about salvation, Jesus cured those who are suffering by what he did in his life; ultimately, he cured them by what he did in his death.

With respect to his life, the Gospels recount one miracle after another in which Jesus dealt with the ailments, misery, and suffering that he saw around him. The earliest traditions of Matthew, Mark, and Luke are quite clear that Jesus did not do miracles for his own benefit, to help himself out. That is, in part, the point of the temptations that Jesus experiences in the wilderness when the Devil tries to get him to satisfy his own hunger by turning stones into bread (Matt. 4:1–11). No, his miracle-working abilities are not meant for his own good, but for the good of others. And so the Gospels record his miraculous life as he goes about during his ministry in Galilee restoring people to physical and mental health—"saving" them. So much does his miracle-working ability characterize his ministry that you can scarcely look at any page of the Gospels without reading about him healing one person or another.

He heals a man who has spent his life paralyzed, making him stand up and walk away from the crowd, carrying his pallet; he heals a man who has a withered hand; he gives sight to those who are blind, even to those blind from birth; he makes the lame walk; he heals a woman who has been hemorrhaging blood for twelve years; he gives the mute the ability to talk; he cures lepers. Sometimes his miracles demonstrate his power over nature: he stills a storm at sea; he walks on water. Sometimes his miracles demonstrate his divine character, as when he turns the water into wine. Often his miracles are done on complete strangers; at other times he does them for his friends. On occasion they are done for the crowds: once he feeds five thousand who are hungry in the wilderness; at another time he feeds four thousand. His miracles deal not only with physical ailments but with what we might think of as mental disease as well: he casts out demons from people, demons that create schizophrenia or demented personalities, or demons that drive people to harm themselves.

His most spectacular miracles are probably his resuscitations of the dead—a twelve-year-old girl whose parents are grieving; a young man whose mother is now left alone; his close friend Lazarus, whom he raises theatrically before a large crowd in order to show that he, Jesus himself, is the "resurrection and the life" (John 11:25).

For the Gospel writers, Jesus' life-giving miracles show that he is the long-awaited messiah. When John the Baptist sends messengers to Jesus from prison, wanting to know if he is the One who was to come, Jesus replies: "Go, report to John the things you have seen and heard: the blind see again, the lame walk, lepers are cleansed, the deaf hear, the dead are raised, and the poor hear the good news. And blessed is the one who does not stumble because of me" (Luke 7:22–23). This is an apocalyptic message. For apocalypticists, at the end of the age God will once again intervene on behalf of his people who are suffering; he will deliver them from the powers of evil that have been unleashed on this world. It is the Devil and his demons who create such hardship—blinding, mutilating, paralyzing, over-powering people. Jesus is portrayed as God's intervention, who has come at the end of the age to defeat the powers of evil, in anticipation of the imminent arrival of God's good kingdom in which there will be no more sin, sickness, demons, Devil, or death.

Although Jesus relieves suffering, his own life climaxes in a moment of intense suffering. Throughout the Gospels he repeatedly tells his followers that he must go to an excruciating and humiliating death on the cross, a death that is necessary for the salvation of the world. He did "save" others, but he "cannot save himself." To do so would be to fail his ultimate mission, which was not to bring temporary health and well-being to people who would, after all, eventually grow frail and die anyway. His ultimate mission was to suffer himself, so that he might restore all people to a right standing before God and give them "salvation" in the ultimate sense. For the Gospel writers, those who "believe in" Jesus as the one who was sacrificed for others would be restored to a right standing before God, so that they might enter the Kingdom of God that was soon to appear. His suffering would substitute for their own; his death would be a sacrifice for the sins of others. Jesus shows that he has the power over sin by healing those who are sick. But ultimately he overcomes the power of sin by himself dying for sin. He suffers the penalty of sin that others might be forgiven and given eternal life in the kingdom that is soon to arrive. That is the ultimate message of the Gospel writers who remember Jesus' life.

## Suffering in the Writings of Paul

The Gospel writers' ultimate message is also the apostle Paul's ultimate message. Next to Jesus, it is Paul who dominates the pages of
the New Testament. Of the twenty-seven books in the New Testament, fully thirteen claim to be written by Paul; one other, the book
of Acts, is largely written about Paul; and another, the letter to the
Hebrews, was accepted into the canon because it was believed
(wrongly) to have been written by him. That makes fifteen of the
New Testament books directly or indirectly related to Paul. And
who was Paul? Above all else, he was a Jewish apocalypticist who
had come to believe that the death and resurrection of Jesus restored people to a right standing before God here at the climax of
the age, before the apocalyptic day of judgment arrived and the end
of the world as we know it occurred.

We have already seen some of Paul's views of suffering. To an
extent, he agreed with the prophets of the Hebrew Bible that suffering comes as a punishment for sin. That is why Christ had to die
on the cross: sin brings a penalty, and Christ paid the penalty owed
by others. Christ obviously was not paying the penalty for sins that
he himself had committed: he was perfect and without sin. The
reason he was crucified was that the Law of God indicates that
anyone who "hangs on a tree is cursed" (Gal. 3:13; quoting Deut.
21:23). By taking the curse of the Law upon himself, Jesus was able
to remove the curse from others who believed in him. And so Paul
also agreed with those biblical authors who saw suffering as redemptive. For Paul, Christ's death brings the ultimate redemption;
through his death and resurrection, people who are cursed through
their sins can be delivered from their sins. Jesus paid the price for
others.

But there is more to Paul's thought than this. To understand Paul
fully, it is important to recognize that at heart he was an apocalypticist.[1] In fact, Paul was probably an apocalypticist even before he was
a follower of Jesus. It was Paul's apocalyptic assumptions about the

world that most affected his theology. To make sense of his theology—a theology rooted in the idea of suffering—we have to understand what it meant for him to be an apocalypticist. And for that we need some historical background.[2]

## Paul as a Pharisee

Paul does not tell us a great deal about his life before he became a follower of Jesus; but he does tell us a few things, in a couple of passages from his letters (Gal. 1–2; Phil. 2). He tells us that he was a very righteous Jew, trained in the traditions of the Pharisees, and that he was an avid persecutor of the followers of Jesus. His conversion, then, was from being an opponent of the early church to becoming one of its greatest advocates, missionaries, and theologians.

What did it mean for Paul to be an upright Pharisee? Sometimes people—even trained scholars—speak almost glibly about the Jewish party known as the Pharisees, as if we knew all about them and what they stood for. The reality is that we do not know much about the Pharisees from Jesus' or Paul's day, since our sources of information are for the most part later—in most instances, well over a century later.[3] We have the writings of only one Jewish Pharisee produced before the catastrophic destruction of Jerusalem in 70 CE; strikingly enough, these are the writings of Paul, written *after* he had converted to faith in Christ. One thing we do know with relative certainty is that Pharisees, unlike other Jewish groups and people (like the Sadducees), were firm believers in the future resurrection of the dead. This shows that Pharisees were by and large apocalypticists, thinking that at the end of the age people would be raised from the dead to face judgment and to be rewarded if they had sided with God or to be punished if they had sided with the forces of evil. This appears, then, to have been Paul's belief *before* his conversion to being a follower of Jesus.

This raises an interesting question. What is the significance of Jesus' resurrection? I find that when I ask my students this question, they rarely have very good ideas about it, even though they firmly believe that Jesus was raised. But what does it mean, I ask? What's the *significance* of the resurrection? Some students have a fairly vague idea that somehow the resurrection showed that Jesus was the messiah (to which I point out that there were no Jews prior to Christianity who believed that the messiah was supposed to die and be raised from the dead); others have an even vaguer idea that somehow the resurrection showed that Jesus was righteous before God (you can't keep a good man down).

I think a more precise answer is possible. What would it mean for a Jewish apocalypticist to come to believe that someone had been raised from the dead? Remember, apocalypticists maintained that this world was controlled by cosmic forces of evil, which, for some mysterious reason, had been given virtually free rein to wreak havoc on earth; but apocalypticists also believed that God was soon to intervene in this course of affairs and vindicate his good name by overthrowing the forces of evil to set up his good kingdom here on earth. At the very end of this age—before the coming of the new age—there would be a resurrection of the dead to face judgment.

If that was Paul's belief as a Pharisee—a Jewish apocalypticist—what was he to think if he came to believe that someone had *already* been raised from the dead? If the resurrection was to come at the end of this age, then the theological conclusion would be both certain and significant. If someone has been raised, then the resurrection has started! We are living at the very end of time. This age is nearly over, the new age is ready to appear. The end has begun.

## Paul's Teaching of the Resurrection

And that is exactly what Paul did think. The resurrection of Jesus for Paul was not merely God's vindication of a good man. It was the clear sign that the expected, imminent end of history as we know it had come, and that humankind was living in the very last days. This wicked age with all its pain and misery was nearly over; its days were numbered; the perfect Kingdom of God, in which there would be no more agony, suffering, and death, was soon to appear.

That this is what Paul thought is clear from his own writings, especially in the one chapter (1 Cor. 15) that he devotes almost exclusively to the question of the resurrection, both of Jesus and of his followers.[4] Paul begins this chapter by emphasizing the teaching that was the core of his gospel message:

> For I handed over to you as of first importance that which I also received, that Christ died for our sins in accordance with the scriptures, and that he was buried; and that he was raised on the third day in accordance with the scriptures, and that he appeared to Cephas and then to the twelve. (1 Cor. 15:3–5)

Paul goes on to indicate that after Jesus' resurrection, he appeared to a large number of people:

> Then he appeared to more than five hundred brothers at one time, from whom many are still alive until now, though some have fallen asleep; then he appeared to James, then to all the apostles. And last of all as to one untimely born, he appeared also to me. (1 Cor. 15:6–8)

A lot of readers of 1 Corinthians have mistakenly thought that by giving this list of people who saw the resurrected Jesus, Paul is trying to convince the Corinthians that the resurrection of Jesus really took place. But that's not the case at all. Paul is *reminding* them of what they already know and believe (see verses 1–2: "I am reminding you, brothers, of the gospel that I preached to you, which you also received and in which you stand"). Why then does he stress that Jesus appeared to all these people after his death—including to five hundred people at one time (an incident not mentioned in the Gospels of the New Testament), some of whom are still alive to testify? It is because Paul wants to remind his followers that Jesus actually, really, physically was raised from the dead. Paul needs to stress this point because there are some people in the congregation in Corinth who deny that there is going to be a future, physical resurrection of all who have previously died (verse 12).

There were Christians in the Corinthian church who had come to believe that they were already experiencing the full benefits of salvation, that they had experienced some kind of spiritual resurrection, and that in some way they were already ruling with Christ now, in the present. Paul in 1 Corinthians 15 wants to stress that the doctrine of the resurrection had to do with an actual, physical resurrection. Jesus was not simply raised spiritually. He had a kind of body when he was raised. It could be seen—and was seen, by lots of people. Since Jesus was the first to be raised, everyone else would be raised like him, in physical bodies.

That's why Paul calls Jesus the "first fruits" of the resurrection (verse 20). This is an agricultural image: the first fruits were the crops brought in on the first day of the harvest. Farmers would celebrate the event, in anticipation of going out and gathering in the rest of their crops. And when would the rest of the harvest be gathered in? Right away—not in some distant future. By calling Jesus the first fruits, Paul was indicating that the rest of the resurrection was imminent; it was to happen right away. The resurrection of believers was not a past, spiritual event; it was a future, physical event. The proof was in the resurrection of Jesus himself. He was physically raised from the dead, and others would be as well.

The fact that the resurrection was a physical, not just a spiritual, event was what showed Paul the resurrection of the dead had not yet occurred. No one else had yet experienced a transformation of the body the way Jesus had. A large number of interpreters have misread 1 Corinthians 15 because of what Paul says in verse 50: "I tell you this, brothers, that flesh and blood cannot inherit the kingdom of God, nor will the perishable inherit the imperishable." Because of this verse, these (mis)interpreters insist that Jesus was not bodily raised from the dead, because flesh-and-blood bodies, allegedly, do not enter into the kingdom. On this basis they say that Jesus was raised spiritually, not physically.

But that is completely missing the point Paul is making. For Paul, it is decidedly a physical body that enters into the kingdom. But it is not a normal physical body. It is a body that has been transformed and made immortal. That's why people could see Jesus after his resurrection. It actually was his body. But it was a transformed body. Paul likens it to a tree: it is an acorn that goes into the ground, but it is an oak tree that emerges from the ground. The resurrection is like that. Bodies go into the ground as mortal, weak, and sickly; they come up out of the ground completely transformed (verses 36–41). The bodies that will emerge at the resurrection will be glorious bodies, like the resurrected body of Jesus. They will be intimately connected with the bodies that go into the ground (i.e., that are buried). The oak grows out of an acorn, not out of nothing. But the raised bodies will be transformed in marvelous and spectacular ways: what grows from the ground is not a giant acorn but an oak tree.

As a Jewish apocalypticist, Paul believed that this physical world we dwell in is controlled by evil forces, and that our bodies are themselves subject to these forces. That is why we get sick, that is why we age, that is why we die. But God will intervene and overthrow these forces. And when that happens our bodies will be transformed, no longer subject to the ravages of disease, aging, and death. We will have eternal bodies and dwell with God forever. For Paul, this was an event that was very soon to take place. In fact, just as Jesus had predicted to his disciples that "some of those standing here will not taste death before they see that the Kingdom of God has come in power," so too Paul predicted that the end of the age, the resurrection of the dead and the transformation of bodies, would happen while some—himself included—were still alive to see it happen.

See, I tell you a mystery. Not everyone will fall asleep [i.e., die], but all will be changed, in a moment of time, in the twinkling of an eye, at the last trumpet. For the trumpet will sound and the dead will be raised as imperishable; and we also will be changed. For this perishable body must be clothed in imperishability and this mortal body must be clothed in immortality. (1 Cor. 15:51–53)

This resurrection of the dead, in which our weak, mortal, suffering bodies are transformed and re-created so as no longer to be subject to the ravages of pain and death, will mark the end of history as we know it:

When this perishable body is clothed with imperishability and this mortal body is clothed with immortality, then will this word that is written come to pass:
"Death is swallowed up in
    victory.
Where is your
    victory, O Death?
And where is your sting, O Death?" (1 Cor. 15:54–55)

For Paul, the solution to the pain and suffering of the world comes at the end of the age, when all are transformed and brought into the glorious Kingdom of God in which there will be no more misery, anguish, or death. This is a future event, but it is imminent. The evidence? Jesus has been raised from the dead, so the resurrection has already begun.

## Paul and the Imminence of the End

Throughout his writings Paul presupposes that the end of the age has begun with the resurrection of Jesus, and that it is soon to be brought to a climax. This climax will involve Jesus himself returning from heaven, inaugurating the resurrection of the dead. Nowhere is this taught more clearly than in the earliest surviving letter from Paul's hand, the book of 1 Thessalonians.[5] In part, Paul wrote this letter because members of the church he had founded in the city of Thessalonica were growing confused. At the time of their conversion, Paul had taught them that the end was coming right away with the return of Jesus from heaven in judgment on the earth. But it never came. Meanwhile, some people in the congregation had died, and those who were left were upset: did this mean that those who had died would miss out on the glorious rewards to be bestowed when Christ returned in glory? Paul's letter assures them that all is going according to plan and that "the dead in Christ" have not lost out on the eternal rewards. Indeed, they will be the first to be rewarded at Christ's return. This is stated clearly in Paul's most graphic comments about what will happen at the end of this age:

> For this we say to you by a word of the Lord, that we who are alive, who remain until the appearance of the Lord, will not precede those who have fallen asleep [i.e., died]. For the Lord himself, with a shout, with the voice of an archangel, and with the trumpet of God, will descend from heaven; and the dead in Christ will rise first. Then we who are living who remain will be snatched up together with them in the clouds, to meet the Lord in the air. And so we will be with the Lord forever. (1 Thess. 4:15–17)

An amazing passage this. Several points about it are worth emphasizing. First, Paul appears to think that he will be one of those still living when this cataclysmic event takes place (he includes himself among "we who are alive, who remain"). Second, the entire passage presupposes an ancient cosmology in which the universe we live in consists of three levels (sometimes called the three-storied universe). There is the level where we human beings now live, on the flat earth. There is the realm below us where the dead exist (e.g., in Sheol). And there is the realm above us, where God—and now Christ—lives. In this understanding, Christ was once with us on our level, then died and went to the lower level. But he was raised from the dead, to our level, and then ascended to the level above us. He is coming back down here, though, and when he does, those below us will go up, and we too will be caught up with them, to meet the Lord above, in the air.

That's how Paul thought—completely like an ancient person who didn't realize that this world is round, that it is simply one planet in a large solar system of planets circling a single star out of billions of other stars in our galaxy, which is only a moderately sized galaxy among billions of others. In *our* cosmology, there is no such thing as up and down, literally speaking. And God certainly doesn't live "up there" or the dead "down below." We have a different universe from Paul's. It's hard to imagine how he would have conceptualized his apocalyptic message if he had known what we know about planet Earth.

## Suffering in the Meantime

For Paul, then, as an apocalypticist, suffering as we experience it now will end when the final resurrection occurs and this world and our mortal bodies are transformed into what is imperishable and impervious to pain, suffering, and death. But what happens in the meantime? For Paul, what happens is a lot of suffering.

Paul's letters to the Corinthians (both 1 and 2 Corinthians) were written against those who supposed that they were already experiencing the benefits of the resurrected life in the present. For Paul, nothing could be further from the truth. Christ's resurrection was the beginning of the end, but the end of the end had not yet come, and until it did, this was a world of pain and misery. As he says elsewhere, in his letter to the Romans:

> I think that the sufferings of the present time are not worthy to be compared to the glory that is about to be revealed to us.

For the creation waits with eager expectation for the revealing of the sons of God [i.e., for the transformation that will happen at the future resurrection].... This creation itself will be set free from its slavery to corruption when it obtains the freedom of the glory of the children of God. For we know that the entire creation is groaning, experiencing labor pains until now. And not only the creation, but we ourselves, who have the first fruits of the Spirit—even we ourselves groan while we await our adoption as sons, which will come with the redemption of our bodies. (Rom. 8:18–23)

Life in the present is a life of pain and suffering, as we groan like women who are going through the agonies of childbirth. That, for Paul, is the way that it has to be. The future redemption has not yet taken place, and we are still experiencing life in our mortal bodies.

Paul emphasizes that Christ himself did not lead a painless existence in this life. To be sure, Paul, as has frequently been noticed, says very little about Jesus' actual life in his letters. Paul never mentions any of Jesus' great miracles, his healings, his exorcisms, his raising of the dead. He does not dwell on the spectacular things that Jesus did or experienced. He dwells on one and only one aspect of Jesus' life: his crucifixion. For Paul, this was a symbol of what it means to live in this world. Life in the present is a life wracked with pain and agony, just as Christ experienced the agony of the cross. That is why, for Paul, the "super-apostles" as he calls them—the self-styled apostles who appeared in the church of Corinth—had seriously misunderstood the message of the gospel (see 2 Cor. 11).

These so-called apostles believed that Christ had given them the power to rise above the miseries of life here on earth, and that anyone who followed their teachings would be able to do the same. Not according to Paul. Life in this world was miserable, and those who followed Christ would fully participate in the misery that he experienced at the cross. That's why, for Paul, being an apostle in this age meant suffering—and so he proudly displays his own suffering for Christ, his imprisonments, floggings, beatings; his being subject to stoning and shipwreck and constant danger and hardship; his hunger, thirst, and homelessness (2 Cor. 11:23–29). These were the marks of the true apostle, in this age of suffering, in the days before Jesus returned in glory and brought about the resurrection of the dead, when those who were faithful to him now would be rewarded and made perfect and whole, as they entered into the great Kingdom of God that he was bringing from heaven.

## The Apocalypse of John

When I teach my class on the New Testament at Chapel Hill, I always begin the first week by asking students to hand in a list of three things they would like to learn from the course before the semester is over. In part I do this to help them start thinking about what it is they are interested in; in part I do it to see what, or if, they are already thinking. Some of the responses I get are truly bizarre: "I want to learn more about why Buddhists don't believe in God" or "I want to learn whether Moses really parted the Red Sea." For a class on the New Testament. And so it goes. But there's one item I can always count on getting, many times over: "I want to learn what the book of Revelation says about the end of the world."

For some reason the vast majority of people who think about the book of Revelation suppose that it is concerned with our own future, that it is about what will happen when history as we know it comes to a screeching halt. Most people seem to think that the book was written explicitly with us in mind: all of history has been moving toward us, we are the climax of all that has so far happened, the prophecies are being fulfilled in our own day. In other words, it's all about us. Or it's all about me.

When we finally get to the book of Revelation—which I save till the end of the course, naturally—some students are upset that I don't talk about the current conflict in the Middle East as a fulfillment of the ancient prophecies, or about how Russia is predicted to launch a nuclear attack on Israel, or about how the European commonwealth is soon to be headed by a political leader who will turn out to be none other than the Antichrist. But the sad reality is that I don't think the book of Revelation—or any other book of the Bible—was written with us in mind. It was written for people living in the author's own day. It was not anticipating the rise of militant Islam, the war on terror, a future oil crisis, or an eventual nuclear holocaust. It was anticipating that the end would come in the author's own time. When the author of Revelation expected that the Lord Jesus "was coming soon" (Rev. 22:20), he really meant "soon"—not two thousand years later. It was only a later bit of sophistry that devised the idea that "soon" with God meant "the distant future"—that "with the Lord a day is as a thousand years and a thousand years as a day," as the author of 2 Peter put it (2 Pet. 3:8). This redefinition of what "soon" might mean makes sense, of course. If the author of Revelation, and other ancient Christian prophets like Paul, thought the end was to come right away, and it never did come, what else *could* one do but say that "right away" meant by God's calendar, not by earthly calendars?

For critical scholars of the New Testament, interpreting the book of Revelation means understanding what it might have meant in its own context. And one thing is clear about that context: this author, who calls himself John, thought that things were going badly on earth and that they were only going to get worse, until the end, when all hell would break out. There is no book of the Bible more focused on suffering than the book of Revelation. Here we read of war, famine, epidemics, natural disasters, massacres, martyrdoms, economic hardship, political nightmares, and, eventually, Armageddon itself. No wonder people have always—from day one—assumed it was referring to their own time. For every generation, it sounds precisely *like* their own time.

In the preceding chapter I talked about the literary genre of the "apocalypse," which began to be popular at about the time of the Maccabean Revolt. The genre actually takes its name from the book of Revelation, which describes itself as an "Apocalypse [or Revelation] of Jesus Christ" (Rev. 1:1). This book is the one full-fledged apocalypse of the New Testament, in many ways like the book of Daniel in the Hebrew Bible and, like other apocalypses both Jewish and Christian, written at about the same time. Like other apocalypses it discusses the visions of a prophet who is given a guided tour of heaven and shown the heavenly truths—and future events—that make sense of earthly realities. These visions are often couched in bizarre symbols that include, as in the book of Daniel, wild beasts who wreak havoc on earth; and the symbols are often interpreted by an angelic companion who lets the prophet, and his reader, know what they actually mean. Like other apocalypses the book of Revelation has a kind of triumphalist march: just as the book of Daniel stresses that after all the catastrophes that strike the earth God will give the ultimate rulership of earth over to his chosen ones, so too the book of Revelation. Following chapter upon chapter of earthly disasters there comes a final battle and there arrives a utopian state, in which there will be no more pain, sorrow, or suffering. God's kingdom will arrive, and those destined to inhabit it will lead glorious lives forever. But there is hell to pay first.[6]

## The Flow of the Narrative

After the book opens with the author identifying himself as John and indicating that Christ was soon to return from heaven (Rev. 1:1, 7), he describes a symbolic vision of Christ as "one like the Son of Man" who appears in the midst of "seven golden lamp stands" (Rev. 1:12–13). It is an overpowering vision: Christ is a mighty figure who wears a long robe with a gold sash (showing his royalty), he has hair "white as snow" (showing his eternity), with eyes like "a flame of fire" (showing him as judge), and his voice sounds "like the sound of many waters" (showing his power). He holds seven stars in his hand (which represent the guardian angels of the seven churches of Asia Minor that the book is addressed to—they are in

Christ's hand), and sticking out of his mouth is a "two-edged sword" (showing that he speaks the word of God, which in Scripture is sometimes called a sword with two edges [see Heb. 4:12] because it is the word of judgment). Understandably, when the prophet sees all this, he faints.

Christ raises John up, however, and tells him to "write the things you have seen, and the things that are, and the things that are about to take place after these things" (Rev. 1:19). This command provides the structure of the book. What John has already seen is the vision of Christ who controls, ultimately, the churches among which he is present. The "things that are" refers to the current situation of the seven churches of Asia Minor; each of which is sent a letter from Christ (in chapters 2–3) in which their successes and failures are indicated and they are exhorted to do what is right and to remain faithful here at the end of time. The "things that are about to take place" refers to the vast bulk of the book, chapters 4–22, in which the prophet has a series of visions about the future course of earth's history. It is these visions that have most enthralled readers of this book over the years.

The visions begin with the prophet looking up and seeing a doorway in the sky (like Paul, this author thinks of the universe in three stories: up above the sky is where God dwells). He is told to "come up here" so that he can be shown "what must take place after these things" (Rev. 4:1). Somehow the prophet shoots up into the sky and through the door, and finds himself in the throne room of God, where the Almighty with his dreadful power is being worshiped and adored eternally by twenty-four elders (the twelve patriarchs of Israel and the twelve apostles?) and four living creatures (which appear to represent all life-forms). The author then sees a scroll in God's right hand, a scroll "sealed with seven seals" (Rev. 5:1). He begins to weep when he realizes that there is no one worthy to break the seals of the scroll. But then he sees a "lamb standing as if it had been slain" (Rev. 5:6)—obviously an image of Christ, who elsewhere in the New Testament is referred to as "the lamb of God who takes away the sins of the world" (John 1:29). This one, we learn, is worthy to open the scroll by breaking its seals.

The lamb receives the scroll, to much praise and adoration of the elders and living creatures. And then the action begins. The lamb breaks the seals one at a time, and each time he breaks a seal, a horrendous set of disasters strikes the earth—war, slaughter, economic hardship, death, martyrdom, and widespread destruction. With the breaking of the sixth seal come massive upheavals in heaven and earth:

> And I saw when he opened the sixth seal, and there was a great earthquake, and the sun became black as sackcloth and the entire moon became like blood, and the stars of the sky fell to earth … and the sky disappeared like a scroll that is rolled up, and every mountain and island was removed from its place. (Rev. 6:12–13)

You would think that now, with the destruction of the sun, moon, stars, and earth, we have come to the end of all things. But it is not so: we are only in chapter six! Two more rounds of disasters are yet to hit. With the breaking of the seventh seal, there is a great silence, and then the appearance of seven angels who are each given a trumpet (Rev. 8:1–2). As the angels blow their trumpets, new catastrophes strike: the earth is burned to a crisp, the waters of earth become blood and poisoned, the sun, moon, and stars are darkened, wild beasts are set loose upon the inhabitants of earth, violent wars and plagues strike. Along with other disasters is the appearance of the great beast—the Antichrist—who wreaks yet greater havoc on earth. And then, after the seventh trumpet is blown, seven more angels appear, each carrying an enormous bowl filled with God's wrath (Rev. 16:1–2). Each angel pours out his bowl upon the earth, leading to yet further catastrophes—until we reach a climax with the destruction of the great city that is the enemy of God, "Babylon the great" (Rev. 18:2).

Finally there is a last battle, in which Christ appears from heaven on a white horse (Rev. 19:11); he wages war with the Antichrist and his armies, leading to their eternal destruction in a lake of fire (Rev. 19:17–21). There follows a thousand-year period of utopia on earth, when the Devil himself is hidden away in the bottomless pit so that he can do no harm (Rev. 20:1–6). After the thousand years the Devil is released for a brief time, and then the end, finally, comes. All the dead are raised and forced to face judgment. Those written "in the book of life" are given an eternal reward; those whose names are in "the other books" are sent off to eternal punishment. Then Death is thrown into the lake of fire, as is the realm of the dead, Hades (Rev. 20:11–15).

And then the eternal kingdom appears. Heaven and earth are remade and a heavenly city, the holy Jerusalem, descends from heaven, a city with gates of pearl and streets of gold (Rev. 21:9–27). There the redeemed live forever, a blessed existence of joy and peace, where there is no more pain, anguish, misery, death, or suffering. There God reigns supreme, through the victorious "Lamb," who is worshiped forever and ever.

The prophet ends the book by indicating that Christ is "coming soon" to bring all this to pass (Rev. 22:12). He urges Christ to do so: "Amen, Come Lord Jesus!" (Rev. 22:20).

## The Audience of the Book

Since Revelation describes the disasters that will happen at the end of time and the glorious, utopian Kingdom of God that will then arrive, and since none of this, obviously, has yet happened, it is no wonder that readers over the centuries have interpreted the book as referring to what is yet to take place. But there are clear indications in the book that the author is not concerned with the distant future, say, the twenty-first century, but that he is symbolically referring to what will happen in his own time.[7]

As I have indicated, the visions found in ancient apocalypses are typically interpreted by an angelic companion, and this is the case with the book of Revelation as well. Let me give just two examples. In chapter 17, we are told that one of the angels with the bowls of God's wrath takes the prophet off into the wilderness to show him a vision of the great enemy of God who will appear at the end of time. This is the famous "Whore of Babylon." John sees a woman sitting on a scarlet beast, which has seven heads and ten horns (this is to remind the reader of the fourth beast in Daniel, also with ten horns). The woman is bedecked with gold, jewels, and pearls—that is, she is fabulously wealthy. She is said to be one with whom the "kings of earth" have "committed fornication." She holds in her hand a gold cup filled with her abominations and fornications. And on her forehead is "written a mystery: Babylon the great, the mother of whores and earth's abominations." The woman is said to be "drunk with the blood of the holy ones and the blood of the martyrs of Jesus" (Rev. 17:6).

Who or what is this great abomination, this great enemy of God? The first thing to note is that she is said to be a city: Babylon. Anyone familiar with the Hebrew Bible, of course, knows that the city of Babylon was the ultimate enemy of God and his people Israel. But what city could be the enemy of God for this prophet, since the real, historical Babylon was no longer a threat at the end of the first century when the prophet was writing? It must be a city that has "committed fornication" with other kings—that is, a city on earth that has had scandalous and flagrantly sinful relations with other empires. Most significant, we are told that the seven heads of the beast symbolize seven kings who have ruled the city, but also that they represent the "seven mountains on which the woman is seated" (Rev. 17:9). Any astute reader knows by now what the woman represents. What city in the ancient world was built on seven mountains? It was the city of Rome (you've probably heard of the "seven hills of Rome"; it was a city built on seven hills). And to clinch this interpretation, the prophet is told that the woman is in fact "the great city that has dominion over the kings of earth" (Rev. 17:18). What city held sway over the author's world, in the first century? Rome, or the Roman Empire. This was the great enemy of God, the one who persecuted the Christians (she is drunk with their blood). This was the enemy that would be overthrown by God. This is the enemy that the book of Revelation is written against.

Or take another image. In chapter 13 we read about another beast, one that rises from the sea (recall the fourth beast of Daniel again). And once more, it is said to have ten horns and seven heads. It has terrifying power over the earth. One of its heads (i.e., one of its rulers) is said to have received a "mortal wound" that then healed. All the earth worships the beast, but it speaks "haughty and blasphemous words" (remember the small horn of the beast in Daniel). Moreover, it "makes war against the holy ones and conquers them." If this sounds a lot like the beast of chapter 17, it is. It too is Rome. But here we are told that the beast has "the number of a person" and that the number—the mark of the beast—is 666.

Who is this Antichrist, whose number is 666? Over the years, of course, people have come up with all kinds of speculation about who it could be. In the 1940s it was sometimes thought to refer to Hitler or Mussolini. When I was in college there were books written to show that it was Henry Kissinger, or the pope. Recently people have written yet other books claiming it was Saddam Hussein or some other notorious figure in our own time.

An intelligent ancient reader would not have had difficulty knowing who was being referred to. Ancient languages like Greek and Hebrew used letters of the alphabet for their numerals (we, on the other hand, use roman letters but arabic numerals). The first letter was "one," the second was "two," and so on. The author of Revelation is indicating that if you take the letters of this person's name, they will add up to 666. On one level, this is highly symbolic. The perfect number, of course, the number of God, is seven. One less than seven is six; this is the number of a "human." Triple six is someone far from the perfection of God; it is a number that symbolizes what is most distant from God. But who is it?

If the beast of chapter 17 with seven heads and ten horns is Rome, it seems likely that this beast of chapter 13 is as well. This is the great enemy of the saints. Who in Rome was thought of as the great enemy of the Christians? The first emperor to persecute the Christians, of course, was Caesar Nero. As it turns out, there were rumors throughout the Roman East that Nero was going to return from the dead to wreak even more havoc on the world than he had done while alive the first time. That sounds like someone who receives "a mortal wound" but then recovers, as is said of this beast. But what is most striking is the number of the beast itself. When you spell the name Caesar Nero in Hebrew letters and add them up, they total 666.

## Suffering in the Book of Revelation

The book of Revelation was not predicting what is going to happen in our own time. Its author was concerned with what was happening in his time. His was a time of persecution and suffering. Christians had been put to death in Rome by the emperor Nero. And the world at large looked like it was in a terrible state. There were earthquakes, famines, and wars. Surely, thought this author, things were about as bad as they were going to get.

But things were going to get worse. This world was filled with evil, and God was going to judge it. The wrath of God was soon to break on this world, and woe to the one who lived to see it happen.

At the end of the terrible times ahead, however, God would finally intervene on behalf of his people. He would destroy all the forces of evil—the evil empires aligned against him and the cosmic forces of the Devil and his minions who supported them. Christ would return from heaven and in a cosmic show of strength annihilate every power opposed to God and every human being, from the emperor on down, who had cooperated with them. God's people would be vindicated, and a new kingdom would come to earth, a kingdom symbolized by the heavenly Jerusalem, with gates of pearl and streets lined with gold. All that is hateful and harmful now would be done away with then. There would no longer be any persecution, pain, anguish, misery, sin, suffering, or death. God would rule supreme once and for all. And his people would live a heavenly existence, forever and ever.

## The Transformation of Apocalyptic Thinking

What happens to an apocalyptic worldview when the expected apocalypse never comes? In Mark's Gospel Jesus indicates that some of his disciples "will not taste death" before they see the "Kingdom of God having come in power" (Mark 9:1). Even though he says that no one knows the precise "day or the hour," he does indicate that the end of all things is sure to come "before this generation passes away" (Mark 13:30). Paul himself seems to have expected to be among those "who are alive, who are left" until the Lord appeared in fiery judgment from heaven. The prophet John, in the book of Revelation, heard Jesus say that he was "coming soon," and so he prayed, "Yes, come Lord Jesus." But what happens when he doesn't come?

The earliest Christians believed they were living "in the last days." Their Lord had himself been an apocalypticist who warned the people of Israel to repent before it was too late, for "the Kingdom of God is very near" (Mark 1:15). And Jesus had been a follower of John, who indicated that the "ax is already laid at the root of the tree"—in other words, that the apocalyptic judgment was soon to begin. Jesus' own followers thought that he would be the one to bring that judgment, that he had ascended to heaven but would soon return to judge the earth and bring in the Kingdom of God as the messiah. They expected it all to be imminent.

But the days of waiting turned into weeks, then into months, then into years, and then into decades. And the end never came. What happens to a belief that is radically disconfirmed by the events of history?

What happened in this instance was that the followers of Jesus transformed his message. In some ways the apocalyptic hope can be understood as a kind of divine time line in which all of history is divided into two periods, this wicked age controlled by the forces of evil and the coming age in which evil will be destroyed and God's people will rule supreme. When the end did not come as expected, some of Jesus' followers transformed this temporal dualism (this age versus the age to come) into a spatial dualism, between the world below and the world above. Or put differently, they shifted the horizontal dualism of apocalyptic expectation of life in this age versus life in the age to come (horizontal dualism because it all takes place on this plane, here on earth) into a vertical dualism that spoke instead of life in the lower world versus life in the world above (with an up and down). In other words, out of the ashes of failed apocalyptic expectation there arose the Christian doctrine of heaven and hell.

Apocalypticism is nothing so much as an ancient kind of theodicy, an explanation of why there can be so much pain and suffering in this world if a good and powerful God is in charge of it. The apocalyptic answer is that God is indeed completely sovereign, and that he will reassert his sovereignty in the future when he overthrows the forces of evil and vindicates everyone who has sided with him (and therefore suffered) in this age. Why do the wicked prosper now? Because they side with evil. Why do the righteous suffer? Because they side with good. But God will reverse the order of rewards and punishment in the age that is coming. The first will be last and the last first; the exalted will be humbled and the humble exalted.

When that didn't happen—when the world never was transformed—Christians began to think that judgment was not something that would happen here, on this earthly plane, in some future cataclysmic event. It would happen in the afterlife, after each of us dies. Judgment day is not something that will take place in the by-and-by. It is something that happens all the time. It happens at death. Those who have sided with the Devil will be given their eternal reward by being sent off to live forever with the Devil, in the flames of hell. Those who have sided with God will be given their eternal reward by being granted eternal life with God, forever enjoying the bliss of heaven. In this transformed view, the Kingdom of God is no longer thought of as a future kingdom here on earth; it is the kingdom that God currently rules, in heaven. It is in the afterlife that God vindicates his name and judges his people, not in some kind of transformation of this world of evil.

There are already traces of this "de-apocalypticized" version of Christianity in the New Testament itself. The last of our Gospels to be written was John, written by someone other than the John who wrote the book of Revelation.[8] It is striking that in John's Gospel Jesus no longer talks about the coming Kingdom of God as a place where God will rule here on earth. What matters for John's Gospel is not the future of the world. What matters is eternal life in heaven, which comes to those who believe in Jesus. In John, Jesus does not urge the people of Israel to repent because "the Kingdom of God is near." He urges people to believe in him as the one who has come down from heaven and is returning to heaven to his heavenly Father (note the vertical dualism). Those who believe in him will themselves experience a rebirth, a birth "from above" (the literal meaning of John 3:3). Those who are born from above can expect to return to their heavenly home when they leave this life. That is why Jesus is leaving his disciples, according to John, so that he "can prepare a place" for them, an abode in heaven where they will go at death (John 14:1–3).

For John the world is still an evil place, ruled by the Devil. But salvation will not come when the Son of Man arrives in judgment on the world, bringing in the Kingdom of God within the lifetime of his disciples. It will come to each individual, who will have eternal life when he or she believes in the one who came down from the Father and has returned to him. Here, in John, we find the horizontal dualism of apocalyptic expectation transformed into the vertical dualism of heaven and earth.

Christians later developed in greater detail the doctrine of heaven and hell as places that individual souls go when they die. This teaching is not much found in the Bible. Most of the authors of the Hebrew Bible, if they believed in an afterlife at all, thought that the afterlife was a shadowy existence in Sheol for all human beings, whether wicked or righteous. Most of the authors of the New Testament thought that the afterlife involved a resurrected existence on earth in the coming Kingdom of God. The Christian notions of heaven and hell reflect a development of this notion of a resurrection, but it is a notion that has been transformed—transformed because of the failed apocalyptic expectations of Jesus and his earliest followers.

## The Apocalyptic Solution to Suffering: An Appraisal

At the heart of the apocalyptic answer to suffering is the notion that the God who created this world is going to transform it. The world has grown wicked; forces of evil are in control of the world and will grow increasingly powerful until the very end, when God will intervene once and for all, destroy all that is evil, and re-create the world as a paradise for his people.

I must say that there are aspects of this apocalyptic vision that I find very powerful and attractive. This is a view of the world that takes evil seriously. Evil is not simply something bad that people do to one another—although it is certainly at least that. But the evil people do to one another can be so massive, so wicked, so overwhelming that it is hard to imagine it as simply people doing bad things. The Holocaust, the genocide in Cambodia, the ethnic cleansing in Bosnia—these are somehow bigger than the individuals who did them. Human catastrophes can be cosmic in proportion; evil is sometimes so far beyond palpable that it is demonic. Apocalypticism argued that in fact it is demonic, caused by forces larger than human beings and more powerful than anything we ourselves can either muster or imagine.

Moreover, the apocalyptic view takes into account the horrendous sufferings experienced by people who fall prey to natural disasters: hurricanes that devastate entire cities; earthquakes that leave more than three million people homeless and helpless with winter barreling down upon them in the Himalayas; mudslides that destroy villages in a matter of minutes; tsunamis that kill hundreds of thousands in one very foul swoop. The apocalyptic view acknowledges that there is genuine evil in the world and that it isn't simply a matter of bad people doing bad things.

It is also a view designed to give hope to those experiencing suffering that otherwise seems too much to handle, suffering that seems to be completely nonredemptive, suffering that tears not just at the body but at the very core of our emotional and mental existence. The hope provided by an apocalyptic view is the hope in ultimate goodness. It says that even though evil is on the ascendancy now, its days are numbered. The people who experience pain, misery, and suffering in the world will all be vindicated. God will intervene and reassert his good power over this world gone awry. Evil does not have the last word; God has the last word. Death is not the end of the story; the future Kingdom of God is the end of the story.

I find all this powerful and moving. At the same time, I have to admit that the apocalyptic view is based on mythological ideas that I simply cannot accept. For ancient thinkers, like the writers of the Bible, the very notion of what would happen at the end of the age was predicated on an understanding of the world as a three-storied universe in which God above had relinquished control of earth down here but would soon come down and bring the world above to our world here below. But there is no God up there, just above the sky, waiting to come "down" here or to take us "up" there.

Moreover, the fervent expectation that we must be living at the end of time has proved time after time—every time—to be wrong. It is true that those who suffer can find hope in the expectation that soon all things will be transformed, that the evil they experience will be destroyed, and that they will be given their just reward. But it is also true that this expected end never has and never will come until, for whatever reason, the human race simply ceases to exist.

To be sure, there have always been prophets to tell us that it is sure to come very soon. Every time there is a major world crisis, these prophets arise in force. They write books (many of them make lots of money doing so, which has always struck me as ironic). They tell us that events in the Middle East, or in Europe, or in China, or in Russia, or in our own country are fulfilling what was predicted by the prophets of long ago. But then time goes on, nothing changes except the rulers in power and their policies and, often, the borders of the countries they control. And a new crisis arises: instead of Nazi Germany it is the Soviet Union; instead of the Soviet Union it is Islamic fundamentalism; instead of Islamic fundamentalism it is ... whatever comes next. Each new crisis generates a new set of books, which again assure us that recent events are now fulfilling the prophecies. And so on, ad infinitum, world without end.

There are problems with these points of view. Most obvious is the problem that everyone who has ever made a prediction of this sort—every single one of them—has been absolutely and incontrovertibly wrong. Another problem is that this kind of perspective tends to breed a religious complacency among those who "know" what the future holds and are unwilling to examine their views critically. There are few things more dangerous than inbred religious certainty.

Still another problem is that "knowing" that all things will eventually be made right by a supernatural intervention can lead to a kind of social complacency, an unwillingness to deal with evil as we confront it in the here and now, since it will be dealt with later by Someone far more capable of handling it than we are. But complacency in the face of real suffering surely is not the best approach to dealing with the world and its enormous problems. There must be a better way.

# nine

# Suffering: The Conclusion

I decided this morning to pick up the newspaper and take a look at the world. How are we doing today, in the suffering department? Frankly, it is not heartening. Here are some of the stories that I ran across. (I looked only at the first section of my Sunday paper, the Raleigh *News and Observer.*)

Pain hits even the rich and famous. Presidential hopeful John Edwards, a hometown boy (he lives in Chapel Hill, where I teach), has announced that he will continue his campaign even though his wife, Elizabeth, has been diagnosed with bone cancer. They found a malignancy. It's incurable. They have had four children. The second child, Wade, tragically died at age sixteen in a car accident eleven years ago. Two of the others are just eight and six. No one knows how long Elizabeth will last, but she's in good spirits and still on the campaign trail.

A twenty-one-year-old student at my school, the mascot for the athletic events, was struck by an SUV; he is in a coma with serious head injuries and brain swelling. He was to graduate in a month and a half; he will probably not live that long.

A tornado struck Logan, New Mexico, wrecking or destroying about one hundred homes and businesses and three schools, sending thirty-five people to the emergency room.

Residents of New Orleans are beginning to arm themselves at all-time high rates. Gun sales are thriving there. The reason? In the wake of Katrina, the homicide rate has grown to the highest in the nation. The sheriff has sent armored vehicles into some neighbor-hoods, and National Guardsmen and police are patrolling the streets. But people there don't trust the system and so are arming themselves.

Yesterday, North Korea's negotiators broke off six-nation talks regarding their nation's nuclear program. Now *that's* just what the world needs: more nuclear threats.

The war in Iraq has this week entered its fifth year. So far the war has claimed the lives of 3,230 U.S. troops. God knows how many Iraqis have died; we're never given those statistics.

The war so far has cost at least $400 billion. What the govern-ment is not saying, of course, is that that's $400 billion that could have been used on other things, like feeding the hungry or provid-ing housing for the homeless.

Suicide bombings killed forty-six in Iraq yesterday (this little news item was buried on page 18). One U.S. soldier was killed on patrol. Four Iraqis were killed by a mortar shelling. Ten bodies of men shot to death were found in Baghdad; ten others were found in the city of Fallujah, all killed execution-style. Things are not going well.

There was a kind of human interest story about Staff Sgt. Daniel Gilyeat, injured in Iraq. He was riding in an armored Humvee when it hit a tank mine. After the explosion he looked down and saw his pants shredded, but he didn't now how bad it was—until he saw two of his friends remove his leg from the truck, and some-one else remove his foot. He's now back home, trying to learn how to walk with an artificial leg.

Another story from Iraq. There is a woman—one of many hun-dreds—whose brother had been kidnapped. The kidnappers were demanding $100,000. She and her family could raise only $20,000. They were told that would be enough. They dropped off the money and were told that they would be contacted about where to find their brother. But they didn't hear from the kidnappers again. In desperation, they made the rounds of the morgues to try to find his body. They finally tracked down an independent burial contractor with pictures of all the bodies he had buried. The woman's brother was one of them. The picture showed him with hands tied over his head; his face was terribly bruised; his torturers had used an electric drill to put a hole through his forehead.

At this point, I stopped reading. Yesterday's paper had similar reports, and the paper the day before. And so it goes. The paper didn't mention the number of people who died yesterday of starvation, cancer, AIDS, malaria, and waterborne parasites, or the people who are perennially homeless or hungry, the wives who were physically or emotionally abused by their husbands or the children abused by their parents, the victims of racist or sexist violence, and on and on and on.

What are we to make of this mess? I should say that I'm not one of those people who is all gloom and doom, who wakes up every morning depressed and despondent about the state of the world. I'm actually very cheerful, with a good sense of humor, a zest for life, and a sense that there is an unbelievable amount of good in the world—some of which I personally enjoy, every day of my life. But what are we to make of all the tragedy in the world, all the misery, the pain, the suffering?

Just about every day I receive e-mails from people I don't know; they have read something I've written and heard that because I have difficulty explaining the suffering in the world, I have become an agnostic. These e-mails are always well meaning and many of them are very thoughtful. I try to respond to all of them, if nothing else just to thank the person for sending along his or her thoughts. It is a *little* surprising to me, though, that so many people have such a simple understanding of suffering and want to share it with me as if I hadn't heard or thought of that one before. Still, it's all kindhearted and innocent, and so I appreciate it. One of the most common explanations I get is that we have to understand that God is like a good parent, a heavenly father, and that he allows suffering into our lives as a way of building our character or teaching us lessons about how we should live. There is, of course, biblical precedent for this view:

> My child, do not despise the
>      LORD's discipline
> or be weary of his reproof,
> for the LORD reproves the one he
>      loves,
>      as a father the son in whom he
>           delights. (Prov. 3:11–12)

I haven't devoted an entire chapter to this view, because I don't think it's one of the most common explanations found in the Bible, but it is there on occasion, as we have already seen. In the book of Amos, for example, when God punishes the people for their sin, it is precisely as a kind of discipline, to teach them a lesson: they need to return to him and his ways. That is why, according to Amos, the nation has experienced famine, drought, pestilence, war, and death: God was trying to get his people to "return to me" (Amos 4:6–11).

This view would make sense to me if the punishment were not so severe, the discipline so harsh. Are we really to believe that God starves people to death in order to teach them a lesson? That he sends epidemics that destroy the body, mental diseases that destroy the mind, wars that destroy the nation, in order to teach people a lesson in theology? What kind of father is he if he maims, wounds, dismembers, tortures, torments, and kills his children—all in the interest of keeping discipline? What would we think of a human father who starved a child to death because she did something wrong, or who flogged a child nearly to death to help him see the error of his ways? Is the heavenly father that much worse than the worst human father we can imagine? I don't find this view very convincing.

From the e-mails I get, I realize that a lot of people think that the suffering experienced in this world is a mystery—that is, that it cannot be understood. As I've said before, this is a view that I resonate with. But many think, at the same time, that one day we will be able to understand and that it will make sense. In other words, God ultimately has a plan that we cannot, at present, discern. But in the end we will see that what happened, even the most horrendous suffering experienced by the most innocent of people, was in the best interests of God, the world, the human race, and even of ourselves.

This is a comforting thought for many people, a kind of affirmation that God really is in control and really does know what he's doing. And if it's true, I suppose we'll never know, until the end of all things. But I'm not sure that it's a convincing point of view. It is a view that reminds me very much of an episode in one of the greatest novels ever written, *The Brothers Karamazov* by Fyodor Dostoevsky. The most famous chapter of this very long novel is entitled "The Grand Inquisitor." It is a kind of parable, told by one of the book's main characters, Ivan Karamazov, to his brother Alyosha, in which he imagines what would happen if Jesus were to return to earth as a human being. In his parable Ivan argues that the leaders of the Christian church would have to arrange to have Jesus killed again, since what people want is not the freedom that Christ brings but the authoritarian structures and answers that the church provides. I think the leaders of our world's megachurches should sit up and take notice—leaders who much prefer providing the certainty of right answers to guiding people to ask difficult questions.

In any event, even though the chapter on the Grand Inquisitor is the novel's best-known chapter, it is the two chapters immediately before it that I have always found the most compelling. In these chapters it is again Ivan and Alyosha who are talking. Alyosha is a bright but inexperienced young novice at the local monastery; he is deeply religious but still displays some (at times delightful) naïveté. Ivan, his older brother, is an intellectual and a skeptic. Ivan admits that he thinks God exists (he is not an atheist, as interpreters have sometimes claimed), but he wants nothing to do with God. The pain and suffering in the world are too great, and ultimately God is at fault. Even if God were to reveal at the end of time the secret that made sense of all that had happened here on earth, it would not be enough. Ivan wants no part of it. As Ivan says: "It's not God that I do not accept, you understand, it is this world of God's, created by God, that I do not accept and cannot agree to accept" (page 235).[1]

He does not accept the world because even if God were to reveal at the end the one thing that made sense of it all, Ivan would still find the suffering in the world too horrible. Ivan likens his rejection of the world to a mathematical problem. The ancient Greek mathematician Euclid indicated that two parallel lines cannot meet (otherwise they would not be parallel). But Ivan notes that there are "some geometers and philosophers" who think that this rule applies only in the realm of finite space, that somewhere in infinity in fact the two parallel lines do meet. Ivan doesn't deny that this might be true, but he rejects it—his mind can't grasp it and so he refuses to believe it. It is like that with suffering for him. If in the end God showed that it all served some greater, nobler purpose, it still would not be enough to justify it. As Ivan says:

> I have a childlike conviction that the sufferings will be healed and smoothed over, and ... that ultimately, at the world's finale, in the moment of eternal harmony, there will occur and be revealed something so precious that it will suffice for all hearts, to allay all indignation, to redeem all human villainy, all bloodshed; it will suffice not only to make forgiveness possible, but also to justify everything that has happened.... Let all of this come true and be revealed, but I do not accept it and do not want to accept it! Let the parallel lines even meet before my own eyes: I shall look and say, yes, they meet, and still I will not accept it. (page 236)

This then launches Ivan into a discussion of his view of suffering, in the key chapter of the book, called "Rebellion." In it he explains that, for him, the suffering of innocent children can *not* be explained, and that if an explanation from the Almighty ever is forthcoming, he simply won't accept it (that's why the chapter is called "Rebellion"—for his pious brother Alyosha, this kind of attitude toward God is rebellious).

Much of the chapter involves Ivan agonizing over the suffering of the innocent. He talks about the violence of Turkish soldiers in the wars in Bulgaria who "burn, kill, rape women and children, [and] nail prisoners by the ears to fences and leave them like that until morning, and in the morning they hang them." He objects to anyone calling this animal behavior, because that "is terribly unjust and offensive to animals," who could never behave with this kind of cruelty. He continues:

These Turks, among other things, have also taken a delight in torturing children, starting with cutting them out of their mothers' wombs with a dagger, and ending with tossing nursing infants up in the air and catching them on their bayonets before their mothers' eyes. The main delight comes from doing it before their mothers' eyes. (page 238)

He then comes up with another horrible scenario:

Imagine a nursing infant in the arms of its trembling mother, surrounded by Turks. They've thought up an amusing trick: they fondle the baby, they laugh to make it laugh, and they succeed—the baby laughs. At that moment a Turk aims a pistol at it, four inches from its face. The baby laughs gleefully, reaches out its little hands to grab the pistol, and suddenly the artist pulls the trigger right in its face and shatters its little head.... Artistic, isn't it? (pages 238–39)

Ivan's stories are not just about wartime atrocities. They involve the everyday. And what is frightening is that they ring true to real-life experiences. He is obsessed with the torture of young children, even among well-educated, "civilized" people living in Europe:

> They have a great love of torturing children, they even love children in that sense. It is precisely the defenselessness of these creatures that tempts the torturers, the angelic trustfulness of the child, who has nowhere to turn and no one to turn to—that is what enflames the vile blood of the torturer. (page 240)

He tells then the story of a five-year-old girl who was tormented by her parents and severely punished for wetting her bed (a story that Dostoevsky based on an actual court case):

> These educated parents subjected the poor five-year-old girl to every possible torture. They beat her, flogged her, kicked her, not knowing why themselves, until her whole body was nothing but bruises; finally they attained the height of finesse: in the freezing cold, they locked her all night in the outhouse, because she wouldn't ask to get up and go in the middle of the nights (as if a five-year-old child sleeping its sound angelic sleep could have learned to ask by that age)—for that they smeared her face with her excrement and made her eat the excrement, and it was her mother, her mother who made her! (page 242)

Ivan notes that some people have claimed that evil is necessary so that we human beings can recognize what is good. With the five-year-old girl with excrement on her face in mind, he rejects this view. With some verve he asks Alyosha:

> Can you understand such nonsense [i.e., such evil acts], my friend and my brother, my godly and humble novice, can you

understand why this nonsense is needed and created? Without it, they say, man could not even have lived on earth, for he would not have known good and evil. Who wants to know this damned good and evil at such a price? (page 242)

For Ivan, the price is too high. He rejects the idea that there can ever be a divine resolution that will make all the suffering worthwhile, a final answer given in the sky by-and-by that will justify the cruelty done to children (not to mention others; he restricts himself to children just to keep the argument simple): "Listen: if everyone must suffer, in order to buy eternal harmony with their suffering, pray tell me what have children to do with it?" (page 244). Ivan takes his stand in the here and now to say that whatever is revealed later, whatever can bring "ultimate harmony" to this chaotic world of evil and suffering, he rejects it, in solidarity with the suffering children:

While there's still time, I hasten to defend myself against it, and therefore I absolutely renounce all higher harmony. It is not worth one little tear of even that one tormented child who beat her chest with her little fist and prayed to "dear God" in a stinking outhouse with her unredeemed tears! (page 245)

In a sense Ivan is reacting against the old Enlightenment view of Leibniz, that despite all its pain and misery, this is the "best of all possible worlds." The only way one could recognize that this is the best world is if what happens in it is finally explained and justified. But for Ivan, nothing can justify it. He prefers to stand in solidarity with the suffering children rather than to be granted a divine resolution at the end that provides "harmony" to the world—that is, a sense of why all things worked together for the good purposes of God and all humanity.

I'd rather remain with my unrequited suffering and my unquenched indignation, *even if I am wrong*. Besides, they have put too high a price on harmony; we can't afford to pay so much for admission. And therefore I hasten to return my ticket. And it is my duty, if only as an honest man, to return it as far ahead of time as possible. Which is what I am doing. It's not that I don't accept God, Alyosha, I just most respectfully return him the ticket. (page 245)

Here Ivan likens the final act of history, in which God reveals why all innocent suffering was "necessary" for the greater good—the harmony of all things—to a stage play, wherein the conflicts of the plot are resolved in the end. Ivan admits that the conflicts may be resolved, but he is not interested in seeing the play. The conflicts are too real and damning. And so he returns his ticket.

I first read *The Brothers Karamazov* more than twenty-five years ago when I was a graduate student (for years I read nothing but nineteenth-century novels, and this was one of my favorites). This passage has stayed with me all those years. I'm not sure I completely agree with Ivan. I think that if, in fact, God Almighty appeared to me and gave me an explanation that could make sense even of the torture, dismemberment, and slaughter of innocent children, and the explanation was so overpowering that I actually could *understand,* then I'd be the first to fall on my knees in humble submission and admiration. On the other hand, I don't think that's going to happen. Hoping that it will is probably just wishful thinking, a leap of faith made by those who are desperate both to remain faithful to God and to understand this world, all the while realizing that the two—their views of God and the realities of this world—are at odds with each other.

Other people, of course, have dealt with suffering by insisting that we change our views of God. This is what Rabbi Harold Kushner urges in his best-selling book *When Bad Things Happen to Good People.*[2] I have to admit, when I first read the book, in preparation for my course on suffering in the biblical traditions at Rutgers in the mid-1980s, I didn't like it at all and started calling it

"When Bad Books Are Written by Good People." My problem with it was that Kushner wanted to argue that God is not all powerful and cannot control the bad things that happen to people. What I found most unsettling was that Kushner took this to be the teaching of the Bible itself, specifically the book of Job. I thought that interpretation was outrageously bad, in fact just the *opposite* of the view of Job (and of almost all the other biblical writers). Job's entire point is that God is the Almighty who created and runs this world, and that mere mortals have no right to question him for what he does, even when he makes the innocent suffer. Kushner had not simply gotten an interpretation wrong—he had gotten it precisely reversed.

I reread Kushner a couple of months ago, and I must say that now that I'm older (and generally less irritable), I had a very different reaction to the book. It is, in fact, a wise book written by a wise man that can speak to people who are experiencing personal tragedy. I suppose that now—twenty years later—I'm not nearly as concerned as I used to be about having the "correct" interpretation of the Bible. I've seen a lot over the past two decades, and biblical interpretation no longer strikes me as the biggest concern on the face of the planet. Moreover, Kushner's view has a lot to be said for it. Not that it's a correct interpretation of Job—it's not even close. But it is a helpful view, one that has in fact helped many thousands of people, maybe even millions.

For Kushner, God is not the one who causes our personal tragedies. Nor does he even "permit" them when he could otherwise prevent them. There are simply some things that God cannot do. He can't intervene to keep us from suffering. But what he can do is equally important. He can give us the strength to deal with our suffering when we experience it. God is a loving Father who is there for his people, not to guarantee miraculously that they never have hardship, but to give them the peace and strength they need to face the hardship.

I now find this a powerful view, and it is understandable that so many people have been affected by it. If I still believed in God, it is probably the view I would eventually want to take. But for a biblical scholar like me, I have to admit that it still seems problematic. Most of the Bible's authors are completely unequivocal about the power of God. It is not limited. God knows all things and can do all things. That's why he is God. To say that he can't cure cancer, or eliminate birth defects, or control hurricanes, or prevent nuclear holocaust is to say that he's not really God—at least not the God of the Bible and of the Judeo-Christian tradition. Believing in a God who stands beside me in my suffering, but who cannot actually do much about it, makes God a lot like my mother or my kindly next-door neighbor, but it doesn't make him a lot like GOD.

Kushner is a Jewish rabbi, and he has found his views helpful in his pastoral ministry. There are other views, advanced by Christian thinkers, that have also proved helpful to people over the years. One of the classic discussions of suffering from the early 1980s, a book that a lot of seminarians used to read, is called *Suffering: A Test of a Theological Method* by Arthur McGill.[3] This too is a very wise book—written, though, not for popular audiences like Kushner's, but for pastors and theologians who don't mind thinking deeply about a complicated subject. McGill's book is explicitly Christian and would be of almost no use to someone who was not already a Christian. He insists, in fact, that Christian theology presupposes Christian faith and is an intellectual exercise engaged in and suitable for Christians alone. His view of suffering is completely Christocentric (i.e., focused on Christ). For McGill, Christ himself is the incarnation, the embodiment, of God. If we want to know what God is like, we look to Jesus.

And what do we see when we look to Jesus? We see one who spent his entire life, and went to his death, in self-giving love. This was not a love that expected anything in return. This was a love that was costly. It cost Jesus everything while he was living, and at the end it cost him his life. Jesus is the one who paid the ultimate price for his love. And if Christians want to be his followers, they will follow his example. They too will give everything for the sake of others. This is what Jesus did, and in doing it he showed us the true character of God. God is one who suffers with us. His power is made manifest in suffering. His character is shown when his followers give of themselves for others, even unto death.

This may seem like a severe religious view, and it is. It is serious Christianity. It is not the kind of Christianity that sells books (this was never a best-seller); it is not the kind of Christianity that builds megachurches (which prefer and preach success rather than suffering, thank you very much). But it is rooted in a carefully thought-out position on what it means to be a Christian—a true Christian, as opposed to the plastic model—in the world.

As moving as I find this point of view, I'm afraid that—as an outsider—I find it nonetheless problematic. There have been lots of other theologians who, along with McGill, have argued that Christ is God's solution to suffering, because in Christ God himself suffered. This view, I think, has proved comforting to Christian people who suffer, realizing that God too has gone through pain, agony, torture, humiliation, and death. But again I'm left wondering. Most of the Bible, of course, does not portray God as suffering. He is the one who causes suffering. Or who uses suffering. Or who prevents suffering. The idea that God himself suffers is based on the theological view that Jesus was God and that since he suffered, therefore God suffered. But the view that Jesus was himself God is not a view shared by most of the writers of the New Testament. It is, in fact, a theological view that developed rather late in the early Christian movement: it is not to be found, for example, in the Gospels of Matthew, Mark, or Luke—let alone in the teachings of the historical man Jesus. For me it is an interesting and important theological development, but not one that I find convincing.

I also have trouble with McGill's perspective because it seems to provide an arbitrary, rather than a necessary, understanding of the Christian God. One could just as plausibly argue, theologically, that since Christ took on the suffering of the world, the world no longer needs to suffer. That is, after all, what theologians have argued about sin and damnation: Jesus bore our sin and experienced the condemnation of God precisely so *we* wouldn't have to do so. Why isn't the same true for suffering? Didn't he suffer so that we don't need to?

Moreover, if the Christian God is the one who suffers, then who is the one who created and sustains this world? Isn't it the same God? By saying that God suffers with his creation, we seem to have sacrificed the view that God is sovereign over his creation. In other words, once again, God is not really GOD. And we are still left with the problem of suffering: why is it here?

In this book I've looked at a range of the biblical answers, and most of them, in my opinion, are simply not satisfying intellectually or morally. (It is important to recall that these are *different* explanations for why there is suffering; some of these explanations contradict others.) Is it because God is punishing people for their sins? That's what the prophets of the Hebrew Bible maintain. But I refuse to think that birth defects, massive starvation, flu epidemics, Alzheimer's disease, and genocides are given by God to make people repent, or to teach them a lesson.

Other writers—and the prophets themselves—want to maintain that some suffering is caused because people have the free will to hurt, maim, torture, and kill others. And that's certainly true. Racism and sexism are rampant, there continue to be wars, there are still genocides—not to mention the mean-spirited and malevolent people some of us have to put up with all the time, in our neighborhoods, our workplaces, our government, and so on. But why would God allow human-caused evil in some instances and not others? Why doesn't he *do* something about it? If he was powerful enough to raise up the Babylonian armies to destroy Jerusalem, and then to raise up the Persians to destroy the Babylonians— where was he in Vietnam? or Rwanda? If he could do miracles for his people throughout the Bible, where is he today when your son is killed in a car accident, or your husband gets multiple sclerosis, or civil war is unleashed in Iraq, or the Iranians decide to pursue their nuclear ambitions?

Some of the biblical authors believed that suffering was ultimately redemptive; and it is true that there can often be a silver lining in the hardships we encounter. But I just don't see anything redemptive when Ethiopian babies die of malnutrition, or when thousands of people die today (and yesterday, and the day before) of malaria, or when your entire family is brutalized by a drug-crazed gang that breaks into your home in the middle of the night.

Some authors thought of suffering as a test of faith. But I refuse to believe that God murdered (or allowed the Satan to murder) Job's ten children in order to see whether Job would curse him. If someone killed *your* ten children, wouldn't you have the right to curse him? And to think that God could make it up to Job by giving him an additional ten children is obscene.

Some authors thought that the suffering in the world is caused by forces opposed to God, forces that oppress his people when they try to obey him. This view at least takes seriously the fact that evil exists and that it is all-pervasive. But it is ultimately rooted in mythological views of this world (a three-storied universe; demons as malevolent little devils that try to invade human bodies and do nasty things to them) that do not jibe with what we know about the world today. It is also rooted in a blind faith that eventually everything wrong will be made right—a nice thought, and one that I wish were true. But it is, at the end of the day, blind faith; and it can lead all too easily to social apathy: since problems won't be solved until the end, there is no point in our working to solve them now.

Some authors—such as the one who wrote the powerful poetic dialogues of Job—maintained that suffering is a mystery. I resonate with this view, but I do not think highly of its corollary—that we have no right to ask about the answer to the mystery, since we are, after all, mere peons and God is the ALMIGHTY, and we have no grounds for calling him to task for what he has done. If God made us (assuming the theistic view for a moment), then presumably our sense of right and wrong comes from him. If that's the case, there is no other true sense of right and wrong but his. If he does something wrong, then he is culpable by the very standards of judgment that he has given us as sentient human beings. And murdering babies, starving masses, and allowing—or causing—genocides are wrong.

I have to admit that at the end of the day, I do have a biblical view of suffering. As it turns out, it is the view put forth in the book of Ecclesiastes. There is a lot that we can't know about this world. A lot of this world doesn't make sense. Sometimes there is no justice. Things don't go as planned or as they should. A lot of bad things happen. But life also brings good things. The solution to life is to enjoy it while we can, because it is fleeting. This world, and everything in it, is temporary, transient, and soon to be over. We won't live forever—in fact, we won't live long. And so we should enjoy life to the fullest, as much as we can, as long as we can. That's what the author of Ecclesiastes thinks, and I agree.

In my opinion, this life is all there is. My students have difficulty believing me when I tell them that that's a view taught in the Bible—but it is. It is explicitly the teaching of Ecclesiastes, and it is a view shared by other great thinkers, such as the author of the poetic dialogues of Job. So maybe I'm a biblical thinker after all. In any event, the idea that this life is all there is should not be an occasion for despair and despondency, but just the contrary. It should be a source of joy and dreams—joy of living for the moment and dreams of trying to make the world a better place, both for ourselves and for others in it.

This means working to alleviate suffering and bringing hope to a world devoid of hope. The reality is that we can do more in dealing with the problems people experience in our world. To live life to the fullest means, among other things, doing more. There does not have to be world poverty. The wealth could be redistributed—and still there would be enough for plenty of us to be stinking rich. Even on a microlevel, we could redistribute some of our wealth (I'm not calling for a Marxist revolution). There don't have to be people sleeping on the streets in my city of Durham. Children really don't need to die of malaria; families don't need to be destroyed by waterborne diseases; villages don't need to die of massive starvation. Old people do not need to go for weeks on end without a single visitor. Children don't have to face the prospect of going to school without a healthy breakfast. A living wage for everyone doesn't have to be just an idealistic vision for a group of wide-eyed liberals. The nation doesn't have to spend billions of dollars on wars it cannot win to empower regimes that cannot survive.

We do not have to sit idly by while governments (even in strategically unimportant lands) practice genocide on their people. A lot of people have read about the Holocaust and said "never again." Just as they said "never again" during the mass murders in the killing fields of Cambodia. Just as they said "never again" during the slaughters in Bosnia. Just as they said "never again" during the massacres in Rwanda. Just as they are now saying "never again" during the rape and pillaging and rampant murders in Darfur. It doesn't have to be this way. This is not a liberal plea or a conservative one: it is a human plea.

People do not *have* to be bigots, or racists. Our laws and customs don't have to discriminate on the basis of gender or sexual orientation.

By all means, and most emphatically, I think we should work hard to make the world—the one we live in—the most pleasing place it can be *for ourselves*. We should love and be loved. We should cultivate our friendships, enjoy our intimate relationships, cherish our family lives. We should make money and spend money. The more the better. We should enjoy good food and drink. We should eat out and order unhealthy desserts, and we should cook steaks on the grill and drink Bordeaux. We should walk around the block, work in the garden, watch basketball, and drink beer. We should travel and read books and go to museums and look at art and listen to music. We should drive nice cars and have nice homes. We should make love, have babies, and raise families. We should do what we can to love life—it's a gift and it will not be with us for long.

But we should also work hard to make our world the most pleasing place it can be *for others*—whether this means visiting a friend in the hospital, giving more to a local charity or an international relief effort, volunteering at the local soup kitchen, voting for politicians more concerned with the suffering in the world than with their own political futures, or expressing our opposition to the violent oppression of innocent people. What we have in the here and now is all that there is. We need to live life to its fullest and help others as well to enjoy the fruits of the land.

In the end, we may not have ultimate solutions to life's problems. We may not know the why's and wherefore's. But just because we don't have an answer to suffering does not mean that we cannot have a response to it. Our response should be to work to alleviate suffering wherever possible and to live life as well as we can.

# Notes

## Chapter One: Suffering and a Crisis of Faith

1. A new translation by Wiesel's wife, Marion Wiesel, is now available: *Night* (New York: Hill & Wang, 2006).
2. Harold S. Kushner, *When Bad Things Happen to Good People* (New York: Schocken Books, 1981).
3. Archibald MacLeish, *J.B.: A Play in Verse* (Boston: Houghton Mifflin, 1957).
4. G. W. Leibniz, *Theodicy: Essays on the Goodness of God and the Freedom of Man and the Origin of Evil* (Chicago: Open Court, 1985).
5. David Hume, *Dialogues Concerning Natural Religion,* edited by Martin Bell (London: Penguin, 1991), 108–09. The sentiments are those expressed by Hume's fictitious character Philo.
6. Voltaire, *Candide: or Optimism,* translated by Theo Cuffe (New York: Penguin, 2005).
7. See, e.g., the discussions and bibliographies of Dale Martin, *Sex and the Single Savior: Gender and Sexuality in Biblical Interpretation* (Louisville: Westminster John Knox Press, 2006), and Jeffrey Siker, *Homosexuality in the Church: Both Sides of the Debate* (Louisville: Westminster John Knox Press, 1994).
8. I don't need to list examples of this kind of book: they are available in the hundreds. Simply visit any Christian bookstore!
9. Again, examples of this kind of book are legion. Many of them have titles like "The Problem of Evil" or "God and Evil" or "God and the Problem of Evil." For hard-hitting and critical evaluations of modern philosophers' attempts to deal with theodicy, see especially Kenneth Surin, *Theology and the Problem of Evil* (Oxford: Blackwell, 1986), and Terrence W. Tilley, *The Evils of Theodicy* (Eugene, OR: Wipf & Stock, 2000).

## Chapter Two: Sinners in the Hands of an Angry God:
## The Classical View of Suffering

1. Raul Hilberg, ed., *Documents of Destruction: Germany and Jewry, 1933–1945* (Chicago: Quadrangle, 1971), 68.

2. Hilberg, *Documents of Destruction*, 79.

3. Primo Levi, with Leonardo de Benedetti, *Auschwitz Report*, translated by Judith Woolf (London: Verso, 2006).

4. Levi, *Auschwitz Report*, 62–63.

5. Rudolph Höss, *Death Dealer: The Memoirs of the SS Kommandant at Auschwitz* (New York: Da Capo, 1992).

6. Höss, *Death Dealer*, 36.

7. Höss, *Death Dealer*, 37.

8. Miklos Nyiszli, *Auschwitz: A Doctor's Eyewitness Account*, translated by Tibère Kremer and Richard Seaver (New York: Arcade, 1993), 87–88.

9. *The Trial of the Major War Criminals Before the International Military Tribunal* (Nuremberg: International Military Tribunal, 1947), vol. 8, 319–20.

10. Hilberg, *Documents of Destruction*, 208.

11. Irving Greenberg, "Cloud of Smoke, Pillar of Fire: Judaism, Christianity, and Modernity After the Holocaust," in *Auschwitz: Beginning of a New Era? Reflections on the Holocaust*, edited by Eva Fleischner (New York: Cathedral of St. John the Divine, 1974), 13.

12. For a highly accessible account, which nonetheless is built on substantial historical scholarship, see Richard Friedman, *Who Wrote the Bible?* (San Francisco: HarperSanFrancisco, 1997).

13. There is a massive scholarship on the history of ancient Israel and the historical reliability of the Hebrew Bible's narratives. Some of the most widely used studies, written from various perspectives, are: Gösta W. Ahlström, *The History of Ancient Palestine* (Minneapolis: Fortress, 1993); Philip R. Davies, *In Search of "Ancient Israel"* (Sheffield, England: Sheffield Academic Press, 1992); William Dever, *Who Were the Early Israelites and Where Did They Come From?* (Grand Rapids, MI: Eerdmans, 2003); and J. Maxwell Miller and John H. Hayes, *A History of Ancient Israel and Judah*, 2d ed. (Louisville: Westminster John Knox, 2006).

14. For general discussions of the Hebrew Bible, see these two excellent introductions: John Collins, *Introduction to the Hebrew Bible* (Minneapolis: Fortress, 2004); and Michael D. Coogan, *The Old Testament: A Historical and Literary Introduction to the Hebrew Scriptures* (New York: Oxford Univ. Press, 2006).

15. For a general, accessible introduction to the writing prophets of the Hebrew Bible, see David L. Petersen, *The Prophetic Literature: An Introduction* (Louisville: Westminster John Knox, 2002).

16. For brief discussions of Amos, see Collins, *Hebrew Bible,* 286–95, and Coogan, *Old Testament,* 311–18.

17. Here, again, we do not need to understand Amos as a crystal-ball gazer. Lots of people near the end of 2001 were saying that Saddam Hussein's days were numbered—years before his execution. Amos, possibly in a similar way, saw that Israel's days were numbered. Some scholars, however, have suggested that the specific "prophecies" of destruction were actually written later and placed back on Amos's lips in anticipation of what was to take place.

18. See preceding note. It is not easy to tell if these predictions were made in advance of the events themselves or were written as retrospective prophecies.

19. The phrase "for three transgressions ... and for four" simply indicates an indefinite number of transgressions.

20. See Miller and Hayes, *History of Ancient Israel,* 286–89.

21. For a useful discussion of Hosea, see John Day, "Hosea," in *The Oxford Bible Commentary,* edited by J. Barton and J. Muddiman (Oxford: Oxford Univ. Press, 2001), 571–78. See also Collins, *Hebrew Bible,* 296–304, and Coogan, *Old Testament,* 318–25.

22. See Collins, *Hebrew Bible,* 307–21, 334–47, and Coogan, *Old Testament,* 331–39, 366–76.

23. One key difference is in Isaiah, however. Rather than harking back to the covenant that God made with Israel at the exodus event, Isaiah focuses on the covenant that God made with David—that David would always have a descendant on the throne and that Jerusalem would be inviolable.

24. On Jeremiah, see Collins, *Hebrew Bible,* 334–47, and Coogan, *Old Testament,* 366–76.

25. As with Amos, some scholars have seen this as a "prophecy" made in retrospect, after the events themselves had transpired.

## Chapter Three: More Sin and More Wrath:
## The Dominance of the Classical View of Suffering

1. For an introduction to the Wisdom literature, see Richard J. Clifford, *The Wisdom Literature* (Nashville: Abingdon, 1998), and James Crenshaw, *Old Testament Wisdom: An Introduction* (Louisville: Westminster John Knox, 1998). On Proverbs, see Collins, *Hebrew Bible,* 487–502, and Coogan, *Old Testament,* 468–75.

2. For a good discussion of the Deuteronomistic History, see Steven McKenzie, "The Deuteronomistic History," in *Anchor Bible Dictionary,* edited by David Noel Freedman (New York: Doubleday, 1992), 2:160–68.

3. See the discussion in Dever, *Who Were the Ancient Israelites?*

4. See the useful discussion of Gary Anderson, "Sacrifice and Sacrificial Offerings," in *Anchor Bible Dictionary,* 5:870–86.

5. See Anderson, "Sacrifice."
6. See Collins, *Hebrew Bible,* 380–89, and Coogan, *Old Testament,* 408–25.
7. See the works cited in note 13 in chapter 2.
8. Some scholars see the "servant" as an individual (not as the nation, or part of the nation, of Israel), a kind of representative of the people as a whole. If this view was shared by ancient readers as well, it would naturally have led to the Christians' understanding that the individual was none other than their messiah, Jesus. See the following note.
9. For other interpretations of the "suffering servant," see any good commentary on 2 Isaiah, such as Richard J. Clifford, *Fair Spoken and Persuading: An Interpretation of Second Isaiah* (New York: Paulist, 1984), or Christopher Seitz, "The Book of Isaiah 40–66," in *The New Interpreter's Bible,* edited by Leander Keck (Nashville: Abingdon, 2001), 6:307–551.

### Chapter Four: The Consequences of Sin

1. Josephus, *Jewish Wars,* bk. 6, ch. 4.
2. See note 9 in chapter 3.
3. See note 9 in chapter 1.

### Chapter Five: The Mystery of the Greater Good: Redemptive Suffering

1. See Bart D. Ehrman, *The New Testament: A Historical Introduction to the Early Christian Writings,* 3d ed. (New York: Oxford Univ. Press, 2004), ch. 9.
2. See Ehrman, *New Testament,* 288–91.
3. See John Collins, *The Scepter and the Star: The Messiahs of the Dead Sea Scrolls and Other Ancient Literature* (New York: Doubleday, 1995).
4. Thus 2 Corinthians 11:22–29; see the discussion in chapter 4.

### Chapter Six: Does Suffering Make Sense? The Books of Job and Ecclesiastes

1. As you might imagine, the literature on Job is vast. For an introduction to some of the most important critical issues, see the discussions and bibliographies in Collins, *Hebrew Bible,* 505–17; Coogan, *Old Testament,* 479–89; and James Crenshaw, "Job, Book of," in *Anchor Bible Dictionary,* 3:858–68.
2. See the works cited in chapter 6, note 1.
3. See the works cited in chapter 6, note 1.
4. This, of course, would have been impossible, as my reader Greg Goering has pointed out to me, since Ecclesiastes was written later.
5. See the discussions of Ecclesiastes in Collins, *Hebrew Bible,* 518–27; Coogan, *Old Testament,* 490–95; and James Crenshaw, "Ecclesiastes, Book of," in *Anchor Bible Dictionary,* 2:271–80.

**Chapter Seven: God Has the Last Word: Jewish-Christian Apocalypticism**

1. There is an abundant literature on apocalypticism (and the literary genre "apocalypse"). See the discussions and bibliographies in Adela Yarbro Collins, "Apocalypses and Apocalypticism," in *Anchor Bible Dictionary,* 1:279–92, and in John Collins, *The Apocalyptic Imagination: An Introduction to the Matrix of Christianity* (New York: Crossroad, 1984).

2. For an introduction to the Maccabean period, see Shaye Cohen, *From the Maccabees to the Mishnah* (Philadelphia: Westminster, 1987).

3. See John Collins, "Daniel, Book of," in *Anchor Bible Dictionary,* 2:29–37; Collins, *Hebrew Bible,* 553–71; and Coogan, *Old Testament,* 536–43.

4. For other interpretations, including the view that the "one like a son of man" is an angelic figure who receives the kingdom on behalf of God's chosen people, see the studies cited in the previous note.

5. For this understanding of Jesus as an apocalypticist, see the following books (which represent a tiny fraction of the scholarly literature on the historical Jesus but agree with the majority view that Jesus was an apocalypticist): Dale Allison, *Jesus of Nazareth: Millenarian Prophet* (Minneapolis: Fortress, 1998); Bart D. Ehrman, *Jesus: Apocalyptic Prophet of the New Millennium* (New York: Oxford Univ. Press, 1999); Paula Frederiksen, *Jesus of Nazareth, King of the Jews: A Jewish Life and the Emergence of Christianity* (New York: Knopf, 1999); John Meier, *A Marginal Jew: Rethinking the Historical Jesus* (New York: Doubleday, 1991– ; three volumes have so far appeared); E. P. Sanders, *The Historical Figure of Jesus* (London: Penguin, 1993).

6. In the Gospel narratives, Jesus uses the phrase "Son of Man" to refer to himself. In my book *Jesus: Apocalyptic Prophet of the New Millennium,* I give the arguments that have convinced many scholars—myself included—that the historical Jesus did not use the term as a self-reference, but instead anticipated that someone *else,* a divine figure from heaven, would come in judgment on the earth as the Son of Man.

**Chapter Eight: More Apocalyptic Views: God's Ultimate Triumph over Evil**

1. A brilliant exposition of this view, by one of the great Pauline scholars at the end of the twentieth century, is in J. Christiaan Beker, *Paul the Apostle: The Triumph of God in Life and Thought* (Philadelphia: Fortress, 1980).

2. For a brief discussion of Paul's life, see Ehrman, *New Testament,* ch. 19 (and the bibliography cited there); for a fuller, but still introductory treatment, see E. P. Sanders, *Paul* (New York: Oxford Univ. Press, 1991).

3. There is an extensive literature on the Pharisees. See especially E. P. Sanders, *Judaism: Practice and Belief, 63 BCE–66 CE* (Philadelphia: Trinity Press International, 1992).

4. See my fuller discussion in Ehrman, *New Testament,* ch. 21.

5. See Ehrman, *New Testament,* ch. 20.

6. On the book of Revelation, see Ehrman, *New Testament,* ch. 29. For a lengthier treatment, see Adela Yarbro Collins, "Revelation, Book of," in *Anchor Bible Dictionary,* 5:694–708. A fuller treatment can be found in Adela Yarbro Collins's *Crisis and Catharsis: The Power of the Apocalypse* (Philadelphia: Westminster, 1984).

7. On the various ways of interpreting the book of Revelation, see Bruce M. Metzger, *Breaking the Code: Understanding the Book of Revelation* (Nashville: Abingdon, 1993).

8. This has been recognized by scholars since the second Christian century. Modern scholars have pointed out that the view of the end times is radically different in the Gospel of John and in Revelation—the former has none of the apocalyptic emphases of the latter but understands "eternal life" to be a present (not a future) reality. Apart from theological differences, there are also obvious differences in the writing styles of the two books (in Greek). The Gospel of John was written by someone fluent in Greek; the book of Revelation is not well written and appears to have been composed by someone for whom Greek was not a first language.

## Chapter Nine: Suffering: The Conclusion

1. I am using the translation of Richard Pevear and Larissa Volokhonsky. Fyodor Dostoevsky, *The Brothers Karamazov* (New York: Farrar, Straus & Giroux, 1990).

2. Harold S. Kushner, *When Bad Things Happen to Good People* (New York: Schocken Books, 1981).

3. Arthur McGill, *Suffering: A Test of a Theological Method* (Philadelphia: Westminster, 1982). I am indebted to Fuzzy Siker for this reference.

# Index

# Scripture Index

## NEW TESTAMENT